Immigrants and Welfare

Immigrants and Welfare

The Impact of Welfare Reform on America's Newcomers

Michael E. Fix

Editor

Russell Sage Foundation • New York
Migration Policy Institute • Washington, D.C.

The Russell Sage Foundation

The Russell Sage Foundation, one of the oldest of America's general purpose foundations, was established in 1907 by Mrs. Margaret Olivia Sage for "the improvement of social and living conditions in the United States." The Foundation seeks to fulfill this mandate by fostering the development and dissemination of knowledge about the country's political, social, and economic problems. While the Foundation endeavors to assure the accuracy and objectivity of each book it publishes, the conclusions and interpretations in Russell Sage Foundation publications are those of the authors and not of the Foundation, its Trustees, or its staff. Publication by Russell Sage, therefore, does not imply Foundation endorsement.

BOARD OF TRUSTEES
Mary C. Waters, Chair

Kenneth D. Brody	Kathleen Hall Jamieson	Shelley E. Taylor
W. Bowman Cutter, III	Melvin J. Konner	Richard H. Thaler
Christopher Edley Jr.	Alan B. Krueger	Eric Wanner
John A. Ferejohn	Cora B. Marrett	
Larry V. Hedges	Nancy Rosenblum	

Library of Congress Cataloging-in-Publication Data

Immigrants and welfare : the impact of welfare reform on America's newcomers / Michael E. Fix, editor.
   p. cm.
   Includes bibliographical references and index.
   ISBN 978-0-87154-314-1 (alk. paper)
     1. Immigrants—Government policy—United States. 2. Immigrants—Services for—United States. 3. Public welfare—United States. I. Fix, Michael.
   JV6483.I5646 2010
   362.8—dc22   2009024914

Copyright © 2009 by Russell Sage Foundation. All rights reserved. Printed in the United States of America. No part of this publication may be reproduced, stored in a retrieval system, or transmitted in any form or by any means, electronic, mechanical, photocopying, recording, or otherwise, without the prior written permission of the publisher.

Reproduction by the United States Government in whole or in part is permitted for any purpose.

The paper used in this publication meets the minimum requirements of American National Standard for Information Sciences–Permanence of Paper for Printed Library Materials. ANSI Z39.48-1992.

Text design by Suzanne Nichols.

RUSSELL SAGE FOUNDATION
112 East 64th Street, New York, New York 10065
10 9 8 7 6 5 4 3 2 1

Contents

Acknowledgments		vii
About the Authors		ix

Chapter 1	Immigrants and Welfare: Overview *Michael E. Fix, Randy Capps, and Neeraj Kaushal*	1
PART I	**POLITICAL AND LEGAL CONTEXT**	**37**
Chapter 2	Limiting Welfare Benefits for Noncitizens: Emergence of Compromises *Ron Haskins*	39
Chapter 3	Welfare Reform after a Decade: Integration, Exclusion, and Immigration Federalism *Michael J. Wishnie*	69
PART II	**TRENDS IN BENEFIT USE AND REFORM'S IMPACTS**	**91**
Chapter 4	Immigrant Welfare Receipt: Implications for Immigrant Settlement and Integration *Jennifer Van Hook and Frank D. Bean*	93
Chapter 5	Trends in Immigrants' Use of Public Assistance after Welfare Reform *Randy Capps, Michael E. Fix, and Everett Henderson*	123

Chapter 6	Changes in Immigrants' Use of Medicaid and Food Stamps: The Role of Eligibility and Other Factors *Leighton Ku*	153
Chapter 7	Welfare-Leaving and Child Health and Behavior in Immigrant and Native Families *Ariel Kalil and Danielle A. Crosby*	193
	Index	229

Acknowledgments

I gratefully acknowledge the support for the conference and this volume provided by the Russell Sage Foundation, the Annie E. Casey Foundation, and the Foundation for Child Development. I would like to thank three discussants for their penetrating commentary on the papers presented at the conference: Alexander Aleinikoff, Olivia Golden, and Robert Suro; their comments can be seen online at: https://www.russellsage.org/publications/books/090728.183972. I would also like to thank the moderators of the conference sessions: Mark Greenburg, Marta Tienda, and Margie McHugh. Finally, I would like to thank the editors at the Migration Policy Institute who worked on this volume, Meg Weaver and Kirin Kalia.

Michael E. Fix

About the Authors

MICHAEL E. FIX is senior vice president and director of studies at the Migration Policy Institute (MPI) and codirector of MPI's National Center on Immigrant Integration Policy.

FRANK D. BEAN is Chancellor's Professor of Sociology and Economics and director of the Center for Research on Immigration, Population, and Public Policy at the University of California, Irvine.

RANDY CAPPS is senior policy analyst at the Migration Policy Institute.

DANIELLE A. CROSBY is assistant professor of human development and family studies at the University of North Carolina at Greensboro.

RON HASKINS is senior fellow in the economic studies program and codirector of the Center on Children and Families at the Brookings Institution and senior consultant at the Annie E. Casey Foundation in Baltimore.

EVERETT HENDERSON is statistical analyst at the Institute of Museum and Library Services and was formerly at the Urban Institute.

ARIEL KALIL is professor at the Harris School of Public Policy Studies and director of the Center for Human Potential and Public Policy at the University of Chicago.

NEERAJ KAUSHAL is associate professor at Columbia University School of Social Work and faculty research fellow at the National Bureau of Economic Research.

LEIGHTON KU is professor of health policy and director of the Center for Health Policy Research in the School of Public Health and Health Services at George Washington University.

JENNIFER VAN HOOK is associate professor of sociology and demography at the Pennsylvania State University.

MICHAEL J. WISHNIE is clinical professor of law at Yale Law School and nonresident fellow of the Migration Policy Institute.

—— Chapter 1 ——

Immigrants and Welfare: Overview

Michael E. Fix, Randy Capps, and Neeraj Kaushal

On August 22, 1996, President Bill Clinton signed the landmark Personal Responsibility and Work Opportunity Reconciliation Act (PRWORA) that with much fanfare eliminated welfare as an entitlement, imposed time limits on public assistance, mandated that welfare beneficiaries work, and substantially increased state authority in administering welfare programs (Public Law 104-193).

But the 1996 law introduced another important but far less broadly noted policy change: it restricted legal immigrants' access to cash-transfer programs such as welfare as well as to other social safety net programs such as food stamps and health insurance. It gave states new powers to deny benefits to noncitizen immigrants, and it codified comprehensively for the first time the eligibility of legal immigrants, unauthorized immigrants, and refugees for federal and state public benefits.

These restrictions were driven by a widely held belief that immigrants were drawn to the United States and the states in which they settled by welfare's magnetic force. The provisions were intended to promote immigrant self-sufficiency and serve the immigration policy goal of improving the "quality" of the immigrants admitted. Not insignificantly, the provisions restricting noncitizens' eligibility for benefits were expected to generate 44 percent of the $54 billion in welfare reform's projected savings during its first six years of implementation (Congressional Budget Office 1996).

It could be argued that the law superimposed welfare reform's larger goals—promoting work and marriage and reducing welfare use—on a population generally characterized by comparatively low welfare use, high work levels, and a significantly greater likelihood of living in intact families than the native-born poor. By restricting eligibility for noncitizens and thereby making citizenship a pathway to benefits, it changed both the incentives to naturalize and the value of citizenship. A companion law, the Illegal Immigration Reform and Immigrant Responsibility Act (IIRIRA), also passed in September 1996. The IIRIRA required that sponsors' incomes be included in benefit-eligibility calculations, allowing states to hold sponsors liable for the value of any benefits that sponsored immigrants received (Public Law 104-207). Further, by granting states new authority to discriminate against or support noncitizens, the law foreshadowed the devolution of both immigrant-integration and immigration-enforcement policies to state and local governments. This trend accelerated following the defeat of comprehensive immigration reform legislation in 2006 and 2007.

A central focus of this volume, then, is welfare reform's immigrant provisions, their origins and purposes, what we know about their impacts, and their implications for policy. These chapters explore major trends in immigrants' use of public benefits, the controversies to which these trends have given rise, the myths that have sometimes dominated public discourse, and some of the policy alternatives to curbing benefits that have been proposed in the past and that might find voice in the future. The chapters were initially presented as papers at a conference held in December 2006, PRWORA's tenth anniversary year, at the Migration Policy Institute. The conference and this volume have been supported by the Russell Sage Foundation, with additional support from the Annie E. Casey Foundation and the Foundation for Child Development.

These chapters address a number of frequently contested issues that shaped the debates surrounding welfare reform's passage in 1996 and that continue to shape social welfare and immigration debates today. The central theme that unifies the book and informs these questions is the impact of welfare reform on the integration of immigrants and their children, both as the laws' framers intended and as unfolded after the law was implemented:

Do public benefits serve as magnets that attract immigrants to the United States or to particular states within the country?

Do benefits promote dependency within the immigrant population? Do they provide a disincentive to work?

Do immigrants have a greater propensity to use benefits than the native-born poor?

Do benefits promote a form of negative acculturation that rises with the length of time immigrants remain in the United States? Does use of benefits slow integration?

Are the policy imperatives that drove welfare reform—the need to promote work and marriage within the poverty population—as pertinent to immigrants as to natives?

We also discuss some of the issues that have emerged in the wake of the law:

Have state substitution programs and federal restorations of eligibility for some groups of noncitizens effectively returned noncitizen eligibility policies to the status quo before the law passed?

Has the law had, and does it continue to have, unintended effects on populations that were theoretically protected, specifically refugees and citizen children with noncitizen parents? Did reform have a chilling effect on benefits use by eligible immigrants and their family members, and do those effects persist?

Are the restrictions on noncitizens' eligibility for benefits driving a surge in naturalization, and thereby a decline in the quality of the naturalizing population?

Can welfare reform be linked to patterns of hardship among immigrants?

Has the intent of Congress been met regarding the roles that sponsors should play in supporting immigrants?

The trends in law, policy, poverty, and benefits use presented here are of much more than historical interest. Although welfare reform and the dramatic changes it enacted in citizenship, benefits, federalism, and immigrant-integration policy may now be over a decade old, many of the law's most far-reaching restrictions stand as originally enacted, barring many legal immigrants from safety-net services during a severe economic downturn.

Further, it could be argued that the law's restrictions on legal immigrants' access to the social safety net reflect a broader neglect of immigrant-integration policy at the federal level, despite the nation's comparatively generous admission policies.[1] That is, although the United States annually admits more immigrants on a citizenship track than any other country in the world, its integration policies—especially those at the federal level—remain ad hoc and underfunded. One result is that the burden of financing immigrant integration has been shifted to an increasingly restive set of state and local governments. Restrictions on federally funded benefits for immigrants that shift safety net costs to the state and local level are one such burden.

The impacts of the mismatch between generous immigration rules and poorly defined integration policies are of growing significance given the rapid rise in the nation's immigrant population, which effectively doubled between 1990 and 2006. The significance is likely to increase when the economy recovers and the nation begins to experience shortages of native-born workers as the baby boomers retire.

STRUCTURE OF THE VOLUME

The book is organized with the intent of giving the reader some insight into the complex changes in social policy and federalism that welfare reform presented for immigrants. Part I probes the politics behind the welfare reform law, its legal underpinnings, and its implications for immigrant integration policies at the federal and state levels. In chapter 2, Ron Haskins examines the law's legislative goals, viewing them through the lens of the Republican congressional majority that shaped the law. In chapter 3, Michael Wishnie explores some of the constitutional challenges the law raises and discusses the mostly limited successes of subsequent legal challenges to its immigrant-eligibility restrictions.

Part II focuses on empirical research on trends in immigrants' use of benefits before and after welfare reform, as well as on the law's initial impacts on immigrants and their families. The chapters address the key issues raised earlier in the discussion of the literature: welfare as a magnet for immigration, immigrants' propensity to use welfare, negative acculturation, changes in immigrants' use of benefits following welfare reform, and impacts on children in immigrant families. In chapter 4, Jenny Van Hook and Frank Bean use the Survey of Income and Program Participation (SIPP) to compare the trajectories of Mexican women receiving welfare in more and less generous states before PRWORA was enacted. In chapter 5, Randy Capps, Michael Fix, and Everett Henderson use U.S. Current Population Survey (CPS) data to examine changes in poverty and federal benefits use among low-income legal immigrant families before and following reform. In chapter 6, Leighton Ku focuses on changes in low-income noncitizens' use of food stamps, Medicaid, and State Child Health Insurance Program (SCHIP) benefits. Ku explores not only changes related to shifts in eligibility but also other factors that influence benefits use. Finally, in chapter 7, Ariel Kalil and Danielle Crosby use longitudinal data from the Chicago area to compare health and other outcomes of young Latino families leaving welfare with those who retained benefits—offering an initial glimpse at the law's impacts on children in immigrant families.

THE PERSONAL RESPONSIBILITY AND WORK OPPORTUNITY RECONCILIATION ACT OF 1996

The 1996 welfare reform law had a number of broad aims. According to Alan Weil and Kenneth Finegold, it sought to "increase state flexibility; end parental dependence on government benefits by promoting job preparation, work and marriage; discourage pregnancies outside of marriage; and encourage the formation and maintenance of two parent families" (Weil and Finegold 2002, xiv).

The logic of at least some of these goals did not apply convincingly to low-income immigrants, given that they were more likely to live in intact families and to hold jobs than their native counterparts.[2] Although evidence emerged in the 1980s and early 1990s of expanding noncitizen use of some benefits, it was concentrated within two vulnerable populations—refugees and the elderly—many of whom would not be expected to work (Fix and Passel 1994).

PRWORA's immigrant restrictions also incorporated other goals not common to the native-born populations affected by the law. One was to alter immigrant flows to the United States by increasing the quality of new immigrants and reducing the pull of the welfare magnet (Borjas and Hilton 1996). A second was to shift responsibility for the support of immigrants away from the state and onto newcomers' sponsors. A third was to realize a large, new stream of cost savings.

For immigrants, PRWORA imposed more than just eligibility restrictions for public benefit programs—primarily cash welfare, food stamps, and public health insurance. Rather, the law's immigrant provisions represented a comprehensive legislative scheme that narrowed the access of legal immigrants—including refugees—to federal benefits. In this respect, the law departed from the program-by-program creation of immigrant eligibility rules at the federal level that had been typical in the past and that has reemerged since the law was passed.

Immigrant Eligibility Restrictions

Before welfare reform, legal immigrants who had not yet become U.S. citizens were eligible for public benefits on generally the same terms as citizens. Following reform, eligibility for federal means-tested public benefits turned to a much greater degree on citizenship than it had in the past. In particular, the law placed new restrictions on Temporary Assistance for Needy Families (TANF), Supplemental Security Income (SSI), Medicaid, the State Child Health Insurance Program, and the Food Stamps Program (FSP). Unauthorized immigrants were unaffected by PRWORA: they remained ineligible for most means-tested benefits.

Federal Means-Tested Public Benefit Programs

Temporary Assistance for Needy Families, a fixed block grant distributed to the states as part of the 1996 welfare reform, replaced the entitlement program Aid to Families with Dependent Children (AFDC). TANF provides cash assistance to needy families, primarily single-parent families but in some cases two-parent families as well, while emphasizing work and self-sufficiency. Participants cannot receive federal assistance for more than five years during their lifetimes. Some states elect to shorten this assistance period; others use state funds to lengthen it. States set eligibility thresholds, which range from 17 percent to 163 percent of the federal poverty level in federal fiscal year (FY) 2003 (Administration for Children and Families 2006).[3] TANF's average monthly caseload was approximately 1.6 million families in FY 2008 (see Administration for Children and Families 2009).

Supplemental Security Income (SSI) was established in 1972 to ensure that the aged, blind, and disabled are able to live above the poverty line. SSI is a means-tested federally administered program, but states have the option to supplement SSI benefits. In 2003, forty-five states did so. SSI targets adults age sixty-five and older as well as children and adults who are blind or disabled, as long as they meet income and resource requirements. The amount of SSI received from the federal government is based on the federal benefit rate (FBR) minus income. In 2008, the FBR was $637 per month for individuals and $956 per month for couples (Social Security Administration 2008). The FBR is adjusted for inflation at the beginning of the year and generally is equivalent to 74 percent of the poverty level for individuals and 82 percent for couples. Individuals and couples in states with supplemental programs may receive higher benefits (Davies and Favreault 2003). In 2007, SSI assisted an estimated 7.1 million people with federal funding and an additional 300,000 with state supplementary funding (see Social Security Administration 2008, table 7.A1).

The Food Stamp Program was established by federal law in 1964 to help low-income families purchase nutritious food. FSP is not limited to a specific group of people, such as the elderly, disabled, families with children, or the unemployed, but instead is available to most families with incomes below 135 percent of the federal poverty level. In October 2008, the federal government changed the name of the program from FSP to Supplemental Nutrition Assistance Program (SNAP). In December 2008, the U.S.

8 Immigrants and Welfare

> *Continued*
>
> Department of Agriculture estimated that the program assisted 31.8 million people (2009).
>
> Medicaid was established in 1965 as a joint federal-state program to provide health benefits for low-income children, parents, pregnant women, the elderly, and disabled individuals. Medicaid requires that emergency services are provided for all immigrants regardless of status or eligibility, but regular Medicaid coverage is unavailable to unauthorized and some legal immigrants. Eligibility for Medicaid, including SCHIP expansion programs, can range from 100 to 300 percent of the federal poverty line depending on the state and the age of the child (Henry J. Kaiser Family Foundation 2009). In 2007, approximately 44 million people were Medicaid beneficiaries (Henry J. Kaiser Family Foundation 2007).
>
> The State Children's Health Insurance Program was created in 1997 to provide insurance coverage for low- to moderate-income children, that is, those in families with incomes just above states' Medicaid eligibility threshold. Some states have SCHIPs that are expansions of their Medicaid programs for children, and others have stand-alone programs. Eligibility for stand-alone SCHIP programs ranges from 150 to 350 percent of the federal poverty line depending on the state (Henry J. Kaiser Family Foundation 2009). In FY 2008, approximately 7.4 million children were enrolled in SCHIP (Center for Medicare and Medicaid Services 2009b).

PRWORA's comprehensive redefinition of immigrant eligibility for benefits created three bright lines. The first divided naturalized citizens from noncitizens. Naturalized citizens continued to be eligible for TANF, SSI, food stamps, Medicaid, SCHIP, and other means-tested benefits on the same terms as U.S.-born citizens (see immigrant eligibility categories).

The second line separated qualified from unqualified aliens. Qualified aliens include those holding a range of immigration statuses, the most common being LPRs and refugees. Some groups of qualified aliens, whom we refer to as legal immigrants throughout this volume, retained eligibility for means-tested benefits; others became ineligible for certain periods of time or under certain conditions.[4] PRWORA created complex rules surrounding the eligibility of qualified immigrants, rules that varied depending on the program and created a great deal of confusion in immigrant communities.

Immigrant Eligibility Categories

Naturalized citizens are legal immigrants who have lived in the United States at least five years (three years if married to a U.S. citizen) and have passed the citizenship test. PRWORA retained naturalized citizens' eligibility for all federal programs on the same basis as U.S.-born citizens.

Qualified aliens include legal permanent residents, refugees, and some other smaller categories of legal noncitizens. PRWORA restricted the eligibility of some groups of qualified aliens for some benefits, but others remained eligible.

Legal permanent residents (LPRs) are immigrants admitted for permanent residency, and thus on a track to citizenship, usually based on petitions from sponsors. Most LPR sponsors are close family members, such as spouses or parents, who are citizens or LPRs living in the United States. Other LPRs are sponsored by employers. A small proportion are admitted without sponsors, including refugees and winners of the diversity lottery.

Preenactment immigrants are those LPRs and other qualified aliens who entered the United States before August 22, 1996, when PRWORA was signed into law. Preenactment immigrants are generally eligible for all means-tested federal benefits.

A ten-year work history in the United States, at least forty quarters, was required of LPRs and some other qualified aliens, even if they were preenactment immigrants, before they could receive food stamps. Aliens could count their spouse's and their parent's work history (when they were under age eighteen) toward the requirement. Subsequent legislation changed the food stamp eligibility from a ten-year work requirement to a five-year bar for adults.

Postenactment immigrants are qualified aliens entering the United States after August 22, 1996. A five-year bar established under PRWORA made

> *Continued*
>
> most postenactment legal immigrants ineligible for TANF, SSI, Medicaid, and SCHIP for five years after their arrival in the United States. Subsequent legislation dropped the bars for legal immigrant children for food stamps, Medicaid, and SCHIP, but left them in effect for legal immigrant adults.
>
> *Refugees, asylees, and Cuban-Haitian entrants* are immigrants admitted for permanent residency on the basis of persecution or a well-founded fear of persecution. Technically, refugees are admitted directly from other countries, whereas asylees and entrants are granted refugee status after arriving in the United States. But all three groups are eligible for federal resettlement assistance and their eligibility for means-tested benefits was reduced less than other legal immigrants by PRWORA. We refer to all of these groups as refugees throughout the volume. Refugees become LPRs after one year in the United States, but retain eligibility for benefits based on their admission as refugees for their first five to seven years. The ten-year work requirement for food stamps and five-year bars on TANF, SSI, Medicaid, and SCHIP eligibility were not applied to refugees.
>
> Active-duty military, veterans, and their spouses retain eligibility for all means-tested programs. The bars on eligibility did not apply to this group.
>
> Unqualified aliens include unauthorized immigrants, some groups of temporary legal migrants, and applicants for permanent legal status already residing in the country. Unauthorized immigrants are those who have entered the country illegally (often across the border with Mexico), overstayed their visas, or otherwise violated the terms of their admission. Unqualified temporary migrants include students and immigrants with temporary work permits, among others. Unqualified aliens are ineligible for means-tested federal programs but are eligible for some benefits, such as emergency Medicaid, immunizations, diagnosis and treatment of communicable diseases, nutritional supplements for infants and young children, and the school lunch and breakfast programs.

Unqualified immigrants are entirely ineligible for means-tested benefits. The largest group, the 11 to 12 million immigrants in the United States without legal authorization, were ineligible for most federal programs before 1996 and remain so today. Smaller groups include temporary migrants such as students, workers, and longer-term immigrants in the process of applying for permanent legal status. Some programs for which unauthorized and other unqualified immigrants are eligible include emergency Medicaid, immunizations, diagnosis and treatment of communicable diseases, nutritional supplements for infants and young children, and the school lunch and breakfast programs (Fix and Passel 2002; Broder 2005). But these programs were not the central focus of welfare reform and are not discussed in this volume.

A third line was drawn between qualified *preenactment* and qualified *postenactment* immigrants. Preenactment immigrants—those who entered the United States before August 22, 1996—retained eligibility for means-tested benefits except food stamps. PRWORA made most legal immigrants ineligible for food stamps regardless of when they entered the country unless they could show they had worked in the United States for at least ten years. This severe restriction was revised twice in subsequent legislation. But preenactment immigrants remained eligible for the other means-tested programs—including TANF, SSI, Medicaid, and later, when it was created, SCHIP—mostly at federal government expense.

Postenactment immigrants—those entering the United States after August 22, 1996—were barred from TANF, SSI, Medicaid, SCHIP, and other means-tested programs for their first five years. Policy analysts have referred to this provision as a five-year bar, and the bar remains in force for legal immigrant adults more than ten years after PRWORA was enacted. The five-year bar on food stamps, Medicaid, and SCHIP eligibility has been removed for legal immigrant children, though it is still in place for these children in TANF and SSI.

To make matters even more complex, some groups of qualified immigrants were exempted from the ten-year work requirement for food stamps and the five-year bar for the other programs. The largest protected group is refugees and asylees, who are also eligible for federal resettlement assistance. Refugees and asylees are eligible for means-tested benefits for their first five to seven years in the United States, in contrast to other qualified aliens, who are barred during their first five years. Active-duty military, veterans, and their spouses are also eligible without any restrictions, as are some groups of immigrants who have been trafficked or experienced domestic abuse.

On balance, these many distinctions have meant that tougher restrictions are imposed on the rapidly growing population of postenactment immigrants. As of 2006, the roughly 4 million postenactment LPRs living in the United States represented 40 percent of the LPR population.

Limited Devolution of Noncitizen Eligibility Rules

Within the complex rules for noncitizen eligibility set up by PRWORA, Congress allowed states to make two sets of important choices. The first choice was restrictive. Congress allowed states to restrict eligibility for qualified immigrants who entered the United States before PRWORA was enacted. Only two states opted to restrict eligibility for preenactment immigrants: Alabama for TANF and Wyoming for Medicaid (Zimmermann and Tumlin 1999).

The second choice was expansive and more inclusionary. Congress allowed states to extend means-tested benefits to postenactment immigrants, including those within the five-year bar. Many of the larger, more traditional immigration states—such as California, Massachusetts, New Jersey, and New York—extended TANF, Medicaid, SCHIP, and food stamps to postenactment immigrants. A handful of other states with smaller immigrant populations did so as well (Zimmermann and Tumlin 1999). There was a catch, however: states could only extend these benefits to postenactment immigrants with their own funding. As a result, the programs became expensive and states may be forced to rescind them. California has the largest programs and recently considered ending them because of its budget crisis. The budget plan it enacted in February 2009, however, retained eligibility for legal immigrants (California Immigrant Policy Center 2009), but the state's fiscal crisis has worsened since that time.

Sponsorship

In September 1996, a month after passing welfare reform, Congress passed the Illegal Immigration Reform and Immigrant Responsibility Act (IIRIRA). This law required, for the first time, that legal immigrants' sponsors have incomes higher than 125 percent of the federal poverty threshold.[5] The law also required that sponsors sign a legally enforceable affidavit of support, pledging to support the immigrants until they naturalize or work forty quarters. Sponsors remain liable for reimbursing most public benefits immigrants use during this period. Although similar requirements had been in place before IIRIRA, courts had found them legally unenforceable. Sponsors' new income requirements and potentially open-ended support obligations could be viewed as a backdoor reform of the legal immigration system intended to keep out the poorest and most welfare-prone immigrants, reinforcing welfare reform's immigration-control thrust.

In sum, these two 1996 reform laws, PRWORA and IIRIRA,

- introduced a comprehensive reform of the social safety net for legal immigrants—a reform that went well beyond cash assistance to a large range of federally financed work support programs;
- reduced noncitizens' access to benefits, thereby increasing their incentives to naturalize;
- generated a complex set of eligibility rules for different programs, creating confusion about eligibility in immigrant communities;
- expanded states' power to determine legal immigrants' eligibility for public benefits;
- redefined the requirements for and obligations of sponsorship; and
- reinforced the ineligibility of unauthorized immigrants and temporary migrants for public benefits.

Changes in Legal Immigrants' Eligibility

Some commentators have argued that though welfare reform's immigrant restrictions initially represented a major shift in public policy, subsequent actions by Congress and the states have largely returned the nation to the earlier status quo, that is, to the more generous rules and higher use rates that prevailed before 1996 (Borjas 2001; Camarota 2003). A review of legislative changes since PRWORA supports this claim for children but not for adults.

With the Balanced Budget Act of 1997 (Public Law 105-33), Congress restored SSI, and with it Medicaid, benefits to all elderly and disabled immigrants receiving SSI at the time welfare reform was enacted, to all LPRs then in the United States who become disabled in the future, and to refugees during their first seven (versus five) years following entry.[6] Later that year, with the Agriculture, Research Extension and Education Reform Act of 1998 (Public Law 105-185), Congress restored food stamp eligibility to LPR children and to elderly and disabled LPRs in the United States at the time of PRWORA's signing, and to those in the country for at least five years.

In 2002, President George W. Bush signed the Farm Security and Rural Investment Act (Public Law 107-17), which restored food stamp eligibility to disabled LPRs and to all LPR adults with five years of legal residence. Food stamps were also restored to all LPR children regardless of how long they had lived in the United States. This restoration crossed the line represented by the five-year bar on postenactment immigrants' eligibility.

In February 2009, newly elected President Barack Obama signed the Children's Health Insurance Program Reauthorization Act (Public Law 111-3, section 214). The law lifted the five-year bar on states' authority to use federal Medicaid and SCHIP funds to cover all legal immigrant children and pregnant women. However, states must change their own policies, in some cases through legislation, before they can draw down these funds. States, such as California and New York, that have been funding Medicaid and SCHIP for five-year bar children using only their own funding have incentives to change their policies to draw down the federal match. States not currently covering these children do not have such an incentive, and might opt not to change their policy because they would have to provide state matching funds during a difficult fiscal climate.

In sum, postenactment immigrants' access to public benefits has expanded since PRWORA was enacted, but the eligibility rules have not returned to the previous status quo. The replacement programs enacted by some states at their own expense have further muted the impact of PRWORA, but these programs are in jeopardy in the current economic and fiscal crisis.

PRWORA and Unauthorized Immigrants

Welfare reform did not significantly change the already limited eligibility of unauthorized immigrants for federal public benefits. That said, there are numerous indirect connections between PRWORA, the charged debate over unauthorized immigrants, and the proposed regularization of their status under differing immigration reform proposals. First, as Michael Wishnie points out in this volume, the devolution of immigrant eligibility rules to the states can be seen as foreshadowing the proliferation of state and local legislation that began to emerge in the middle of the current decade. Many of these laws sought to restrict a wide range of rights of the unauthorized: the right to work, housing, drivers' licenses, public benefits, and services.

Second, abiding if largely misplaced concerns over unauthorized immigrants' use of federal and other public benefits have driven new identification and verification requirements at the state and local levels and within the federal Medicaid program (Rodriguez 2008). For example, the 2006 Deficit Reduction Act mandates that all Medicaid applicants prove they are citizens or otherwise legally present.[7] The rules appear to have had their biggest impact not on the unauthorized immigrants who were purportedly the focus of the rules, but on the native poor who could not prove they were citizens and whose applications were delayed or who lost eligibility for Medicaid altogether.

Finally, it could be that the political prospects of legislation that provides the unauthorized with a path to citizenship, as proposed in past Congresses, may be enhanced by existing restrictions on the eligibility of recent legal immigrants for benefits because the restrictions hold down the overall costs of a legalization program. Indeed, under proposals advanced in 2006, legalizing immigrants would not have been eligible for means-tested federal programs until 2020, at which point their economic integration would likely have limited their need for assistance (U.S. Congress 2006).

OBSERVATIONS ON THE LITERATURE

Before delving into the substance of this volume, it is important to review the substantial literature on immigrants' use of public benefits before and after the passage of welfare reform. The political debate over welfare reform's immigrant provisions reflected parallel academic debates that involved differing methodologies and often competing outcomes. Here we sketch a few particularly charged debates in the literature and note some of the methodological approaches taken to such contested issues as estimating immigrants' use of benefits, their propensity toward benefits relative to natives, and their intergenerational transmission patterns. Literature on trends in immigrants' benefit use since welfare reform, and the impacts of the law's benefit restrictions, is also reviewed.

One widely debated issue has been the degree to which public benefits function as a magnet, influencing international and interstate flows of migrants. In a highly influential paper, George Borjas used 1980 and 1990 census data to show that immigrants were more likely than natives to settle in states with generous welfare policies (1999). He used this evidence to support what he termed the welfare-magnets hypothesis, which held that immigrants were attracted to the United States because of its relatively generous welfare programs. Madeline Zavodny used Immigration and Naturalization Services (INS) data on LPRs to examine associations between state welfare generosity and legal immigrants' initial settlement patterns (1999). She rejected Borjas's hypothesis that immigrants' location choices were associated with relative state welfare generosity.

After PRWORA was enacted, state rules concerning legal immigrants' benefit eligibility varied widely. This variation created a natural experiment that allowed analysts to test whether legal immigrants were attracted to states with relatively generous welfare policies. Neeraj Kaushal used INS data and found no evidence during the post-PRWORA period that newly arrived immigrants preferred to settle in states that reinstated benefits for immigrants, such as California and New York, versus states that did not, such as Texas and Florida (2005).

Another long-standing concern has been the purportedly greater propensity of immigrants to use means-tested benefits. Earlier research analyzed cross-sectional data from the 1976 Survey of Income and Education and concluded that immigrants were less likely to depend on welfare, broadly defined to include payments from the Aid to Families with Dependent Children program, SSI, and public assistance (Blau 1984; Simon 1984). Some argued that the probability that an immigrant family would become dependent on welfare, however, changed over time as the composition of the immigrant population changed. George Borjas, with Stephen Trejo and on his own, used U.S. Census Bureau data and found that later waves of immigrants were more likely to receive welfare than natives, and use of means-tested programs among immigrants of a particular entry cohort increased with the duration of their stay in the United States (Borjas and Trejo 1991; Borjas 1995).

Other researchers noted that benefits use was concentrated within two highly vulnerable subpopulations. One includes elderly, recently arrived immigrants whose ineligibility for Social Security led them to turn to SSI for support and access to health insurance. The second includes refugees, who come to the United States fleeing persecution and thus can be seen as involuntary migrants. Refugees often suffer mental and physical disabilities, and receive comparatively generous benefits under the Refugee Resettlement Program (Fix and Passel 1994).

A third concern is that longer-term U.S. immigrants and those who came as children will depend more on welfare than more recent immigrants, and that this dependency will result in less work effort. The negative-acculturation theory holds that as immigrants learn more about American society, they adopt behaviors that negatively influence their health and well-being, such as higher rates of smoking, drinking, drug use, and delinquent behavior (Portes and Zhou 1993; Rumbaut 1994). This theory posits higher welfare use among longer-term and second-generation immigrants, especially in high-poverty neighborhoods where welfare dependency is relatively high and workforce participation relatively low (Borjas 1998; Borjas and Hilton 1996). The concern with immigrants, as with the general population, is that the availability of welfare benefits will lead to long-term dependency. Thus concerns about negative acculturation of immigrants tie into larger concerns about the moral hazards of welfare expressed by many of those in favor of the broader goals of welfare reform.

In the wake of PRWORA's enactment, a substantial body of research on how benefits use affects the behavior and well-being of immigrants has been undertaken. These studies explore welfare reform's impact on immigrants' use of means-tested programs, their employment and earnings, their health insurance, their food insecurity and health, and their citizenship (Loftstrom and Bean 2002; Borjas 2001, 2003, 2004; Davies and Greenwood 2004; Haider et al. 2004; Joyce et al. 2001; Fix and Passel 1999, 2002; Kaestner and Kaushal 2005, 2007; Kaushal and Kaestner 2005, 2007; Van Hook 2003).

Most of this literature reports sharp declines in the use of social welfare programs after PRWORA was enacted, with the declines more pronounced among immigrants than natives (Zimmermann and Fix 1998; Borjas 2001; Fix and Passel 1999, 2002; Lofstrom and Bean 2002; Haider et al. 2004; Kaestner and Kaushal 2007).[8] Researchers attribute the declines to three primary factors: the economic expansion of the 1990s, federal- and state-level changes in immigrant eligibility and access to means-tested programs, and PRWORA's chilling effect, which created an atmosphere of fear and confusion among immigrants, discouraging them from applying for benefits even when they were eligible (Fix and Passel 1999; Lofstrom and Bean 2002; Kaestner and Kaushal 2005, 2007). The degree to which each of these factors affected immigrant use of means-tested programs continues to be an issue of debate.

In one of the first papers on this issue, Michael Fix and Jeffrey Passel attributed the sharp decline in immigrant use of means-tested programs to the chilling effect of welfare reform (1999). Surveys by the National Health Law Program and the National Immigration Law Center indicated that fear of deportation from the

United States discouraged immigrants from obtaining publicly subsidized health care even when they were entitled to it (Schlosberg and Wiley 1998). The Kaiser Commission on Medicaid and the Uninsured found that, after reform, many immigrants did not seek public health insurance because they feared it would affect their immigration status or jeopardize their opportunity to become a citizen (Feld and Power 2000). Along similar lines, Kaushal and Robert Kaestner found that PRWORA affected the public coverage of immigrants who had been in the United States for more than five years as adversely as it affected their less-than-five-years counterparts, even though the latter were subject to more stringent provisions in a number of states (2005).

Analysts and policymakers also became concerned that the chilling effects of PRWORA would be felt by mixed-status families—those with one or more citizen children and one or more noncitizen parents. In these families, the children are eligible for benefits on the same terms as other U.S. citizens; the parents, however, may be ineligible on the basis of noncitizen eligibility restrictions. This group of families has been demographically significant for some time: in 2000, one in ten children in the United States lived in mixed-status families (Fix and Passel 2002). Research has shown that the low-income citizen children in these families had significantly lower TANF and food stamp use than their counterparts in citizen families, and benefits use among mixed-status families declined substantially after PRWORA (Fix and Passel 2002).

As discussed earlier, there has been some expansion of eligibility to legal immigrants affected by PRWORA, especially children. At the federal and state levels, PRWORA was followed by expansions in immigrant eligibility for some programs and populations (such as food stamps, SSI and, recently, Medicaid-SCHIP for some groups of legal immigrants), expanded outreach to immigrant communities for some programs (for SCHIP and food stamps, for example), and program administrative changes that made it easier for immigrants to apply (such as by allowing applications by mail, phone, or over the Internet). A small literature traces immigrant responses to these reforms, finding they likely improved access and use (Holcomb et al. 2003; Capps et al. 2004; Buchmueller, Lo Sasso, and Wong 2008).

COMPETING METHODOLOGIES

Conclusions about the propensity of immigrants to use welfare, its magnetic effect, trends in use before and after reform, and the impact of welfare reform on immigrants and their children all vary depending on a wide range of study choices. In other words, the methodological choices taken in the literature and in the chapters in this volume are important and strongly affect the findings. One such choice is the analyst's approach to disaggregating results by legal status. That is, results are often driven by whether results are reported for all immigrants or all noncitizens as a group, or by whether analysts disaggregate results by legal status categories, such as naturalized citizens, refugees, legal permanent residents, temporary legal visitors, and unauthorized immigrants. As we have noted, welfare reform altered eligibility for some of these groups (legal immigrants and refugees) but not others (unauthorized immigrants and naturalized citizens).

A related issue is whether children in unauthorized immigrant families are included in estimates of benefits use along with those in legal immigrant families. For example, in chapter 6 of this volume, Ku finds higher rates of no insurance among low-income immigrant families with children than Capps, Fix, and Henderson do in chapter 5. This discrepancy owes at least in part to the fact that Ku includes children of unauthorized immigrants in his analysis and Capps, Fix, and Henderson exclude them.

A second critical choice is the unit of analysis selected: whether benefits use is estimated for the household, family, or individual. Household-level analyses tend to generate higher use rates than individual-level analyses because any household that has at least one individual using a benefit is defined as a household using that benefit. Eligibility, however, is in fact determined for different units depending on the program: families for TANF; households for food stamps; and individuals for SSI, Medicaid, and SCHIP. Thus the unit of analysis that corresponds most closely to real-world eligibility decisions varies widely by program, complicating cross-program comparisons.

A related issue is selecting the study and comparison groups, that is, whether analysts should focus more narrowly on lower-income families and individuals. Studies that compare benefits use among all citizen families versus all immigrant families will find that immigrants' use exceeds that of natives. Part of the explanation is that immigrant families have much lower incomes, which make them more likely to be eligible. Chapters 5 and 6 limit their samples to low-income families, who correspond most closely to families that would meet income eligibility thresholds for means-tested programs.

A third defining choice is the scope of benefits included: whether use is limited to the federal means-tested public benefits defined by PRWORA—the largest of which are TANF, SSI, food stamps, Medicaid, and SCHIP—or whether benefits are conceptualized more broadly to include those not restricted by welfare reform, such as free and reduced-price school lunches. More expansive definitions of benefits yield higher use levels. Throughout this volume we focus more narrowly on the four largest means-tested benefit programs because they were the target of the welfare reform law.

PRINCIPAL FINDINGS

The main findings of the volume focus on several key questions that surround the congressional intent behind the welfare reform law's immigrant eligibility provisions, the implications of the law for equal protection of immigrants under the U.S. Constitution, the validity of welfare reform's goal of reducing the propensity of immigrants to use welfare and hence welfare's magnetic effects, the effects of the immigrant eligibility rules on legal immigrants' access to and use of benefits, and the impacts of the restrictions on the health and well-being of immigrant families and children. Throughout the book, the main theme is the impact of the welfare reform law—both intended and realized—on the integration of immigrants and their children.

Concerns and Values

In chapter 2, Ron Haskins of the Brookings Institution reexamines the congressional intent behind PRWORA and the sources for the law's immigrant restrictions. These included concerns about rapidly rising use of SSI by noncitizens—mostly the elderly—during the early 1990s, worries of growing welfare dependence among immigrants alongside the moral hazard that welfare represents, and the substantial savings that cuts in immigrants' benefits use could generate for the federal government. Haskins argues the restrictions also derived from a strong value-based judgment that even in the absence of means-tested public benefits, legal immigrants enjoy a great bargain in coming to the United States: mostly open access to the labor market, full rights for their mostly U.S.-born citizen children, and access to job-training programs and to the Earned Income Tax Credit for lawfully present working parents with children. He argues further that a strong historical precedent exists for withholding benefits from newcomers for a probationary period, and that the law posed a further fundamental values question: "Do U.S. taxpayers have an obligation to support noncitizens who immigrate to the United States from the moment they arrive in the United States, or does the obligation begin only when the immigrants become citizens?"

At the same time, Haskins points out several abiding concerns that welfare reform's critics have also noted. One is the asymmetry the law introduced between the obligations of immigrants and the benefits they receive. A second is the cost shift that replacement programs in health and welfare represent between the federal government and the states. A third is the worry that loss of health benefits could endanger the development of immigrant children—an especially vulnerable population and one the nation's economy will increasingly need.

State Discrimination

As we suggest, the law represented a significant departure not just in federalism but also in the definitions of membership in U.S. society and equal protection under U.S. laws. In chapter 3, Michael Wishnie places welfare reform's legal-immigrant-eligibility restrictions within the context of developments in constitutional law, federalism, and state and local activism over controlling illegal immigration, and the constant tension in U.S. society between integration and exclusion. After reviewing the surprisingly scant case law challenging welfare reform's immigrant provisions, Wishnie addresses the central constitutional question the law raises: Does a state's choice to deny lawful permanent residents welfare benefits that it provides to citizens violate the equal protection clause of the Fourteenth Amendment when Congress has authorized, but not required, such discrimination? He concludes that more than a decade after the law's enactment, the question has not been resolved and remains largely unanswered by the courts. There have been comparatively few legal challenges, and the limited judicial results to date point in quite differing and somewhat inconclusive directions.

Wishnie contends that the issue has been largely uncontested in part because surprisingly few states accepted Congress's invitation to restrict eligibility for preenactment legal immigrants. As a result, the "race to the bottom" in terms of restrictions on long-term LPR eligibility that many close observers predicted did not materialize. At the same time, advocacy organizations may have resisted challenging the law in fear that they might draw attention to the benefits that some states were extending to recent LPRs made ineligible for federal assistance by PRWORA. Further, since 2000, the political and legal struggle over the powers of the federal government versus the states to control immigration and shape integration policy has shifted from legal to unauthorized immigrants. This struggle has taken the form of state laws mandating verification of immigrants' authorization to work and agreements between the federal government and state and local law enforcement agencies to enforce immigration laws. The entry of states and even some local governments into immigration enforcement policy may have been foreshadowed by the new powers to discriminate against legal immigrants extended them under welfare reform.

Welfare and Immigration

Do immigrants have a higher propensity to use welfare, and does welfare represent a magnet for further immigration? Does welfare lead to negative acculturation? As Haskins points out in chapter 2, welfare reform was premised on a view that use of public benefits constituted a moral hazard not just for natives but also for immigrants. But was that policy model supported—even at the time the law was enacted? How strong were claims that immigrants have a greater propensity to use benefits, grow dependent on them, and that they drive patterns of negative assimilation such as reduced work?

In chapter 4, Jennifer Van Hook of Pennsylvania State University and Frank Bean of the University of California, Irvine, use longitudinal data on the welfare (AFDC) use of immigrant women drawn from Survey of Income Program Participation (SIPP) data for 1990 to 1996—a period that predates welfare reform. To test the welfare magnet theory, the authors focus on how patterns of benefits use and work varied across states with more-or-less generous welfare programs before PRWORA was enacted.

They find that when compared with natives, Hispanic immigrants rely less on welfare in states with more generous welfare programs. They find that before welfare reform, welfare receipt was concentrated among recently arrived rather than longer-term immigrants. Why do immigrants in more generous states fare better than those in less generous ones? The authors suggest that the circumstances that lead immigrants to welfare are different and more temporary than those that lead natives: immigrants are less familiar with the labor market and have less-developed networks outside their own families.

Van Hook and Bean also explore the evidence for and against the negative acculturation hypothesis, by examining AFCD receipt rates and spells (that is, duration of benefit receipt) of immigrants before welfare reform, using the SIPP. They find that AFDC benefits were used less and for a shorter time among longer-term immigrants and those who arrived as children. They find little evidence of long-term welfare dependency among prereform immigrants, and argue to the contrary that AFDC mostly functioned as a form of short-term resettlement assistance.

Van Hook and Bean conclude that the restrictions enacted in 1996 were based on the flawed assumption that the etiology of welfare receipt among immigrants is the same as it is for natives and these restrictions could delay the progress of immigrants, who generally need some initial assistance to help them integrate. The findings in Van Hook and Bean's chapter call into question assumptions about the propensity of immigrants to use benefits, the validity of the welfare-magnet construct, the moral hazards of welfare receipt among immigrants, and, ultimately, the continuing merits of imposing higher bars on legal immigrant use of means-tested benefit programs.

Public Benefit Use Patterns

How has welfare reform affected immigrants' use of public benefits? How have use patterns varied between the U.S.-born population and legal immigrants? In chapter 5, Randy Capps and Michael Fix of the Migration Policy Institute and Everett Henderson, formerly of the Urban Institute, analyze the use of TANF, SSI, food stamps, Medicaid, and SCHIP by low-income families with children during 1994 and 2004. Low-income families headed by U.S.-born citizens are compared with those headed by legal permanent residents, who were the main target of the law. Comparisons are also made with refugee and naturalized-citizen families whose eligibility for benefits did not change significantly.

Contrary to the received wisdom, Capps, Fix, and Henderson find that even before welfare reform, low-income legal immigrant families' use of TANF and food stamps was lower than that of low-income native families. Second, TANF and food stamp use by LPR families declined markedly after PRWORA, and TANF use continued to decline as late as 2004. Third, the rates of TANF and food stamp use by LPR families remained well below natives' rates through 2004. In light of these findings, it is hard to argue that immigrants have had a greater propensity than natives to use cash welfare or food stamps either before or after welfare reform.

The chapter's findings on Medicaid tell a different story. LPR families used Medicaid more than native families did in 1994, and this use increased over the study period, continuing at a relatively high rate through 2004. But these results can be viewed as the product of several policy successes: the introduction of the SCHIP program, extensive outreach to immigrant families, and broader institutional reforms that expanded access to health care. One important factor contributing to rising Medicaid and SCHIP coverage rates has likely been the emergence of state-funded health insurance programs that cover recently arrived LPRs; these programs are much more common for Medicaid-SCHIP than for TANF or food stamps (Zimmermann and Tumlin 1999). Nonetheless, despite increases in their Medicaid coverage, low-income LPR and refugee children were almost twice as likely as native-born children to lack health insurance—owing in large part to substantial losses of private insurance, a broad trend felt disproportionately— though not only—by children in immigrant families.

The authors also compare the benefit use of refugee and native-born families. Perhaps the most surprising results can be found among refugees, a population largely protected in welfare reform that receives targeted federal resettlement benefits. Unlike other immigrant populations, refugees are generally eligible for public assistance immediately after they arrive in the United States. Although welfare use among refugees has historically been quite high, by 2004, it had fallen across all programs to levels that were either lower or the same as natives, depending on the program.

Capps, Fix, and Henderson draw a third set of comparisons between native-born citizen families and families headed by naturalized citizens. In theory, PRWORA created incentives for immigrants to naturalize in order to obtain eligibility for public benefits. If this theory were correct, we would expect naturalized immigrants' use of benefits to rise substantially after PRWORA's enactment. Instead, the authors find that low-income naturalized families' benefits use rates for all programs fall below rates for native families—even though the two groups' eligibility does not differ under PRWORA. In short, modest increases in poverty among naturalized citizens did not lead to significant increases in benefits use, and they remained less likely to use public benefits than comparable natives almost ten years after welfare reform.

In chapter 6, Leighton Ku of George Washington University explores changes in noncitizens' use of the two most commonly used means-tested, work-support benefits: food stamps and Medicaid. Ku examines trends in the health insurance coverage of low-income noncitizen children and parents, finding that public coverage through Medicaid and SCHIP dropped for noncitizens overall between 1995 and 2005 and that the proportion of noncitizen children and parents without health insurance rose over the same period. Because the data Ku uses define noncitizens to include both legal immigrants and the unauthorized, some of the trends he observed may be the result of the growing share of unauthorized immigrants in the noncitizen population. In chapter 5, Capps, Fix, and Henderson focus separately on LPRs and refugees—the two main categories of legal noncitizens. Declining employer and other private health insurance coverage is a trend common to both the LPRs discussed in chapter 5 and the larger population of all noncitizens analyzed in chapter 6.

Impact of Reform

Were welfare reform's impacts confined to the target population of legal immigrants? To what extent did they spill over to protected populations such as citizen children? In his analysis of food stamp eligibility and participation, Ku finds that despite the Farm Bill's restoration of benefits to some noncitizens, their 2004 eligibility rate (that is, the proportion of noncitizens who actually qualified for food stamps) was about one-third below the 1994 eligibility rate. Overall, noncitizen immigrants' food stamp use fell by about 60 percent between 1994 and 2004. He attributes about half of the decrease to eligibility changes and the other half to factors such as economic growth, chilling effects, and declining eligibility for TANF and other programs that serve as gateways to food stamps. Although the eligibility rules did not change for citizen children with noncitizen parents, their participation fell by about one-third—owing entirely to other access issues, such as language barriers and noncitizen parents' fears about FSP participation. Ku finds a rise between 2000 and 2004 in food stamp participation among eligible noncitizen populations, not just as a result of benefit restorations but also program simplification and expanded outreach.

Early Effects on Children

What appear to be the early effects of welfare reform on children with immigrant parents who left the welfare system? One real worry about welfare reform's immigrant restriction—voiced by Ron Haskins—is that the law's mandate and implementation would lead to poorer health outcomes among the children of immigrants who lost benefits when they or their parents were cut off. Finding these effects and tying them to welfare reform directly is difficult empirically. In chapter 7, Ariel Kalil of the University of Chicago and Danielle Crosby of the University of North Carolina at Greensboro take an important first step in examining the impact of welfare reform on immigrant families using child well-being as their lens. The authors compare the differing health outcomes for children of Latino-immigrant and of Latino-native parents who left welfare after PRWORA was passed. Using a unique longitudinal data set developed by the Project on Human Development in Chicago Neighborhoods (PHDCN), Kalil and Crosby examine changes in the health outcomes of children in Chicago from 1995 to 1998.

They find that the Latino preschool-age children of immigrants in families that left TANF "fared significantly worse in terms of their health" than children with native-born Latino parents who left welfare. Postwelfare economic circumstances of immigrant versus native households cannot explain the differential in health outcomes because the Latino immigrant families studied were not appreciably worse off financially than their native counterparts. Kalil and Crosby's findings also suggest that Latino children of immigrants whose parents left TANF fared worse than children of immigrants whose parents remained eligible for and continued participating in the program. Although the chapter's findings are not definitive, they offer a cautionary signal on the impacts of restricting access to health and other public benefits for children in immigrant families, especially younger children who are at a critical stage in their development. The findings again call into question the degree to which immigrant restrictions are promoting the integration of immigrant families and children into the U.S. economy and society.

CONCLUSION

The papers collected in this volume make clear that the goals of the framers of welfare reform's immigrant provisions were partially met. Consistent with the expectations of the framers, cash welfare and food stamp use among low-income legal immigrants fell sharply over the decade following reform. The declines were partly the product of PRWORA's restrictions on program eligibility but also partly the product of other access barriers, as well as a strong economy that improved economic conditions for native and immigrant families alike. At least initially, declines coincided with a drop in poverty among all legal-immigrant populations through 2000. Food stamp use rebounded somewhat, however, after federal restorations, and participation in federal health insurance programs for low-income families rose.

However, some of the data present worrying trends. Young children of immigrant Latino welfare leavers in Chicago had poorer health outcomes than welfare stayers. Food stamp participation fell among citizen children with noncitizen parents nationally. Low health-care coverage persisted among low-income children in refugee and other legal-immigrant families, and about half of low-income noncitizen parents and noncitizen children are uninsured—more than twice the rates for comparable native-born populations.

Further, the results reported in this volume provide little support for some of the most frequently voiced worries about the nature and consequences of immigrants' use of benefits: a propensity toward dependency, a magnetic attraction of immigrants toward states with generous eligibility rules, and negative acculturation toward welfare and away from work. Put simply, the authors do not find that welfare represents or represented the kind of moral hazard that so concerned policymakers when welfare reform was enacted.

Viewed through a federalism lens, PRWORA's enactment has sparked a patchwork of immigrant-integration policies that differ widely across the states—with policy divisions widening even more when it comes to unauthorized immigrants. These trends leave us with a more uneven national landscape in regard to immigrants and integration than we have seen since the federal government enacted national immigration laws for the first time.

The benefits use and other trends described in this volume, in turn, raise the question whether these fragmented policies are good vehicles for carrying us forward in the twenty-first century. To what extent will the devolution of policies regarding immigrants' benefits eligibility, membership, and basic rights to the states affect the pace of immigrants' settlement decisions and the relative pace of their integration? Welfare reform did not set off a race to the bottom in terms of legal immigrants' eligibility for public benefits. However, PRWORA's progeny—state and local restrictive ordinances and enforcement activities aimed at unauthorized immigrants—may have wide-ranging consequences for immigrant integration in the future.

Here the significance of recent research findings regarding the importance of the climate of reception becomes clear (Van Hook, Brown, and Bean 2006). If, as they suggest, more-generous rather than less-generous benefit policies promote higher employment levels and better economic integration, then states with such policies, including California, Illinois, Maine, Massachusetts, and New York, may find economic and social rewards down the road, as immigrants integrate and become productive, taxpaying citizens. Van Hook, Brown, and Bean's findings may also mean that the proxy policy of substituting benefits restrictions for comprehensive legislation to restrict or alter immigration flows may, in the end, be counterproductive.

In light of these findings and assertions, perhaps we should follow the policy model suggested by Hiroshi Motomura (2006) and promote integration by extending full benefit access to legal immigrants at the time of their arrival (or adjustment) in return for their pledge to eventually become citizens. In short, we would make them better citizens by treating them like citizens sooner.

NOTES

1. Further evidence of the weak support for immigrant integration can be seen in declining federal spending on English language acquisition programs at the elementary and secondary level and for adult English language learners (see Gelatt and Fix 2007).
2. In 1996, at the time the law was enacted, 65 percent of low-income immigrant families with children were two-parent families versus only 40 percent of native families. Eighty percent of working-age men in low-income immigrant families were in the labor force versus 70 percent for men in native families.
3. The threshold for the poverty level in 2009 was $18,310 for a family of three, and higher for larger families but lower for smaller families (see Center for Medicare and Medicaid Services 2009a).

4. Qualified aliens retained eligibility without conditions for a broad range of other federal programs such as Social Security, Pell Grants for higher education, and the Earned Income Tax Credit, which we do not analyze here.
5. The poverty thresholds are defined, in part, on the basis of family size. For assessing the sponsorship criteria, the threshold is based on the numbers of adults and children in the combined families of the sponsored immigrant and the sponsor, thus increasing the amount of income required of the sponsor.
6. In December 2006, the Justice Department was sued by disabled refugees who had been in the United States for more than seven years and were threatened with the loss of their SSI and Medicaid benefits. The loss of benefits owed to the failure of the Department of Homeland Security to process the plaintiffs' naturalization or legal permanent resident applications in a timely manner. Kaplan v. Chertoff, Civil Action No. 06-5305 (E.D. PA) was settled with the government agreeing to rapidly process the citizenship applications. Hence no change in the time limits was made. In August 2008, the U.S. Senate joined the House in passing legislation that provides an additional two years of eligibility to "humanitarian immigrants" approaching the seven-year time limit (see Wiley 2008).
7. The Deficit Reduction Act of 2006 (Public Law 109-171) requires states to obtain "satisfactory documentary evidence of an applicant's or recipient's citizenship and identity in order to receive Federal financial participation."
8. George Borjas found that outside of California, the decline in immigrant use of Medicaid and SSI was negligible and that of cash welfare and food stamps was relatively modest after PRWORA's passage (2001). These patterns led Borjas to attribute the decline in immigrant use of public assistance to the chilling effect of Proposition 187 enacted in California in November 1994, which restricted benefits for unauthorized but not legal immigrants, rather than PRWORA. Other studies have generally found more substantial declines in immigrants' benefits use outside of California since PRWORA was enacted.

REFERENCES

Administration for Children and Families. 2006. *Seventh Annual TANF Report to Congress*. Washington: U.S. Department of Health and Human Services.
———. 2009. "TANF: Total Number of Families, Fiscal and Calendar

Year 2008, as of January 21, 2009." Washington: U.S. Department of Health and Human Services. Available at: http://www.acf.hhs.gov/programs/ofa/data-reports/caseload/2008/2008_family_tan.htm (accessed April 2009).

Blau, Francine D. 1984. "The Use of Transfer Payments by Immigrants." *Industrial and Labor Relations Review* 37(2): 222–39.

Borjas, George J. 1995. "Immigration and Welfare: 1970–1990." NBER working paper no. 4872. Cambridge Mass. National Bureau of Economic Research.

———. 1998. "Immigration and Welfare: A Review of the Evidence." In *The Debate in the United States over Immigration*, edited by Peter J. Duignan and Lewis H. Gann. Stanford, Calif.: Hoover Institution Press.

———. 1999. "Immigration and Welfare Magnets." *Journal of Labor Economics* 17(4): 607–37.

———. 2001. "Welfare Reform and Immigration." In *The New World of Welfare*, edited by Rebecca M. Blank and Ron Haskins. Washington, D.C.: Brookings Institution Press.

———. 2003. "Welfare Reform, Labor Supply and Health Insurance in the Immigrant Population." *Journal of Health Economics* 22(6): 933–58.

———. 2004. "Food Insecurity and Public Assistance." *Journal of Public Economics* 88(7–8): 1421–443.

Borjas, George J., and Lynette Hilton. 1996. "Immigration and the Welfare State: Immigrant Participation in Means-Tested Entitlement Programs." *Quarterly Journal of Economics* 111(2): 575–604.

Borjas, George J., and Stephen J. Trejo. 1991. "Immigrant Participation in the Welfare System." *Industrial and Labor Relations Review* 44(2): 195–211.

Broder, Tanya. 2005. "Immigrant Eligibility for Public Benefits." In *Immigration & Nationality Handbook*. Washington, D.C.: The American Immigration Lawyers Association.

Buchmueller, Thomas C., Anthony T. Lo Sasso, and Kathleen N. Wong. 2008. "How Did SCHIP Affect the Insurance Coverage of Immigrant Children?" *The B.E. Journal of Economic Analysis and Policy* 8(2): Article 3. Available at: http://works.bepress.com/thomas_buchmueller (accessed April 2009).

California Immigrant Policy Center. 2009. "Immigrant Programs Preserved under California's New Budget Plan." CIPC Budget Update, March 1, 2009. Sacramento: California Immigrant Policy Center. Available at: http://www.caimmigrant.org/source/CIPC_Budget_Update030109.pdf (accessed April 2009).

Camarota, Steven A. 2003. *Back Where We Started: An Examination of*

Trends in Welfare Use Since Welfare Reform. Washington, D.C.: Center for Immigration Studies.

Capps, Randolph, Robin Koralek, Katherine Lotspeich, Michael E. Fix, Pamela Holcomb, and Jane Reardon Anderson. 2004. *Assessing Implementation of the 2002 Farm Bill's Legal Immigrant Food Stamp Restrictions.* Washington, D.C.: The Urban Institute.

Center for Medicare and Medicaid Services. 2009a. "2009 Poverty Guidelines." Washington: U.S. Department of Health and Human Services. Available at: http://www.cms.hhs.gov/MedicaidEligibility/Downloads/POV09Combo.pdf (accessed April 2009).

———. 2009b. "SCHIP Ever Enrolled in Year." Washington, D.C.: U.S. Department of Health and Human Services. Available at: http://www.cms.hhs.gov/NationalSCHIPPolicy/downloads/SCHIPEverEnrolledYearGraph.pdf (accessed April 2009).

Congressional Budget Office. 1996. *Federal Budgetary Implications of the Personal Responsibility and Work Opportunity Reconciliation Act of 1996.* Washington: Congressional Budget Office.

Davies, Paul S., and Melissa M. Favreault. 2003. *Interactions Between Social Security Reform and the Supplemental Security Income Program for the Aged.* Washington, D.C.: The Urban Institute.

Davies, Paul S., and Michael J. Greenwood. 2004. "Welfare Reform and Immigrant Participation in the Supplemental Security Income Program." Michigan Retirement Research Center working paper no. 2004–087. Ann Arbor: University of Michigan.

Feld, Peter, and Britt Power. 2000. *Immigrants' Access to Healthcare after Welfare Reform: Findings from Focus Groups in Four Cities.* Washington, D.C.: The Henry J. Kaiser Family Foundation.

Fix, Michael E., and Jeffrey S. Passel. 1994. *Immigration and Immigrants: Setting the Record Straight.* Washington, D.C.: The Urban Institute.

———. 1999. *Trends in Noncitizens' and Citizens' Use of Public Benefits Following Welfare Reform: 1994–1997.* Washington, D.C.: The Urban Institute.

———. 2002. "The Scope and Impact of Welfare Reform's Immigrant Provisions." *Assessing the New Federalism* discussion paper no. 02–03. Washington, D.C.: The Urban Institute.

Gelatt, Julia, and Michael E. Fix. 2007. "Federal Spending on Immigrant Families' Integration." In *Securing the Future: US Immigrant Integration Policy,* edited by Michael E. Fix. Washington, D.C.: Migration Policy Institute.

Haider, Steven J., Robert F. Schoeni, Yuhua Bao, and Caroline Danielson. 2004. "Immigrants, Welfare Reform, and the Economy." *Journal of Policy Analysis and Management* 23(4): 745–64.

Henry J. Kaiser Family Foundation. 2007. "Total Supplemental Security Income (SSI) Beneficiaries, 2007." Available at: http://statehealthfacts.kff.org/comparemaptable.jsp?ind=253&cat=4&sub=63&yr=62&typ=1&o=a&sort=n (accessed April 2009).

———. 2009. "Income Eligibility Levels for Children's Regular Medicaid and Children's SCHIP-funded Medicaid Expansions by Annual Incomes and as a Percent of Federal Poverty Level (FPL), 2009." Available at: http://www.statehealthfacts.org/comparemaptable.jsp?ind=203&cat=4 (accessed April 2009).

Holcomb, Pamela A., Karen C. Tumlin, Robin Koralek, Randolph Capps, and Anita Zuberi. 2003. *The Application Process for TANF, Food Stamps, Medicaid and SCHIP: Issues for Agencies and Applicants, Including Immigrants and Limited English Speakers*. Washington, D.C.: The Urban Institute / U.S. Department of Health and Human Services.

Joyce, Ted, Tamar Bauer, Howard Minkoff, and Robert Kaestner. 2001. "Welfare Reform and the Perinatal Health and Health Care Use of Latino Women in California, New York City, and Texas." *American Journal of Public Health* 91(11): 1857–864.

Kaestner, Robert, and Neeraj Kaushal. 2005. "Immigrant and Native Responses to Welfare Reform." *Journal of Population Economics* 18(1): 69–92.

———. 2007. "Welfare Reform and Immigrants: Does the Five Year Ban Matter?" In *Research in Labor Economics*, vol. 27: *Immigration Policy*. Bingley, U.K.: Emerald Group Publishing.

Kaushal, Neeraj. 2005. "New Immigrants' Location Choices: Magnets without Welfare." *Journal of Labor Economics* 23(1): 59–80.

Kaushal, Neeraj, and Robert Kaestner. 2005. "Welfare Reform and Health Insurance of Immigrants." *Health Services Research* 40(3): 697–722.

———. 2007. "Welfare Reform and the Health of Immigrant Children." *Journal of Immigrant and Minority Health* 9(2): 61–74.

Lofstrom, Magnus, and Frank D. Bean. 2002. "Assessing Immigrant Policy Options: Labor Market Conditions and Post-Reform Declines in Welfare Receipt among Immigrants." *Demography* 39(4): 617–37.

Motomura, Hiroshi. 2006. *Americans in Waiting: The Lost Story of Immigration and Citizenship in the United States*. New York: Oxford University Press.

Portes, Alejandro, and Min Zhou. 1993. "The New Second Generation: Segmented Assimilation and Its Variants." *The Annals of the American Academy of Political and Social Science* 530(1): 74–96.

Rodriguez, Cristina M. 2008. "The Significance of the Local in Immigration Regulation." *Michigan Law Review* 106(4): 567–642.
Rumbaut, Rubén G. 1994. "The Crucible Within: Ethnic Identity, Self-Esteem, and Segmented Assimilation among the Children of Immigrants." *International Migration Review* 28(4): 748–94.
Schlosberg, Claudia, and Dinah Wiley. 1998. *The Impact of INS Public Charge Determinants on Immigrant Access to Health Care.* Washington, D.C.: National Health Law Program.
Simon, Julian. 1984. "Public Expenditures on Immigrants in the United States, Past and Present." *Population and Development Review* 22(1): 99–109, 202, 204.
Social Security Administration. 2008. *Annual Report of the Supplemental Security Income Program.* Washington: U.S. Government Printing Office. Available at: http://www.ssa.gov/policy/docs/statcomps/supplement/2008/7a.pdf (accessed April 2009).
U.S. Congress. House. Committee on Ways and Means. 2006. *Hearing on the Impacts of Border Security and Immigration on Ways and Means Programs.* "Immigrants' Costs and Contributions: The Effects of Reform." Testimony of Michael E. Fix. 109th Cong., 2d sess., July 26, 2006.
U.S. Department of Agriculture. Food and Nutrition Service. 2009. "Supplemental Nutrition Assistance Program Participation, as of February 27, 2009." Washington: U.S. Government Printing Office. Available at: http://www.fns.usda.gov/pd/34SNAPmonthly.htm (accessed April 2009).
Van Hook, Jennifer. 2003. "Welfare Reform Chilling Effects on Noncitizens: Changes in Noncitizen Recipiency or Shifts in Citizenship Status?" *Social Science Quarterly* 84(3): 613–31.
Van Hook, Jennifer, Susan K. Brown, and Frank D. Bean. 2006. "For Love or Money? Welfare Reform and Immigrant Naturalization." *Social Forces* 85(4): 643–66.
Weil, Alan, and Kenneth Finegold, eds. 2002. "Introduction." In *Welfare Reform: The Next Act.* Washington, D.C.: The Urban Institute.
Wiley, Dinah. 2008. "Senate Passes Supplemental Security Income (SSI) Extension for Refugees and Other Humanitarian Immigrants." Press Release, August 6. Washington, D.C.: National Immigration Law Center. Available at: http://www.nilc.org/immspbs/ssi/ssi009.htm#senate (accessed November 2008).
Zavodny, Madeline. 1999. "Determinants of Recent Immigrants' Locational Choices." *International Migration Review* 33(4): 1014–30.
Zimmermann, Wendy, and Michael E. Fix. 1998. *Declining Immigrant*

Applications for Medi-Cal and Welfare Benefits in Los Angeles County. Washington, D.C.: The Urban Institute.

Zimmermann, Wendy, and Karen Tumlin. 1999. "Patchwork Policies: State Assistance for Immigrants under Welfare Reform." *Assessing the New Federalism* occasional paper no. 24. Washington, D.C.: The Urban Institute.

Part I

Political and Legal Context

—— Chapter 2 ——

Limiting Welfare Benefits for Noncitizens: Emergence of Compromises

Ron Haskins

THE 1996 WELFARE reform law—the Personal Responsibility and Work Opportunity Reconciliation Act—changed almost every aspect of noncitizen eligibility for welfare benefits, especially by limiting their access to benefits. My goal in this chapter is to review the reform policies and their origins, to consider the arguments for and against the reforms, and to examine their impacts on receipt of welfare by noncitizens as well as several associated issues. By way of full disclosure, I worked with other congressional staffers from the Ways and Means and Judiciary Committees in the House to draft the original and most subsequent versions of the reforms, and I believed then, as I do now, that they are fully justified by American tradition, the principals of immigration policy, and practical considerations.

RESTRICTING WELFARE FOR NONCITIZENS

In determining welfare eligibility for noncitizens, two broad criteria are taken into account. The most general screen is the concept of the *qualified* versus the *not qualified* alien. Qualified aliens are noncitizens who have been permitted to live permanently in the United States. They include lawful permanent residents (LPRs), refugees, asylees, Cuban and Haitian entrants, and a few others. Qualified immigrants may be eligible for federal and state means-tested benefit programs that aim to help families with limited income and resources, especially after they have lived in the United States for five years.[1] Not qualified aliens (mostly unauthorized aliens and temporary immigrants), by contrast, are ineligible for all except emergency benefits, a policy that was largely in place even before the 1996 reforms.[2]

The second criterion is date of entry into the United States. In the 1996 legislation, qualified immigrants who entered after August 22, 1996, were barred from Supplemental Security Income (SSI) and food stamps until they became citizens and from Temporary Assistance for Needy Families (TANF) and Medicaid for five years after entry. Qualified immigrants who entered before August 22, 1996, have wider eligibility for these benefits in part because states have elected to pay for some benefits and in part because federal legislation enacted since 1996 maintained eligibility for some benefits for those already in the United States when the welfare reform law passed. As a result, most immigrants who entered before 1996 remain eligible for TANF, Medicaid, food stamps, and SSI.

In addition to these two broad criteria, several others condition noncitizens' eligibility for welfare benefits. All children of immigrant parents born in the United States are citizens under the Constitution and are therefore eligible for benefits on the same basis as native citizens. Refugees and asylees are eligible for all welfare benefits during the first seven years they live in the United States, after which their eligibility is greatly reduced (unless they naturalize).[3] Noncitizens who have worked for ten years and armed forces personnel and their dependents are eligible for all benefits. Emergency benefits, especially emergency health care, immunizations for communicable diseases, and services for the victims of child maltreatment, are provided to all noncitizens, both qualified and not qualified.

An important exception to the various restrictions on means-tested benefits stems from the fact that Congress wanted noncitizens to participate in programs that could help them improve their education and their job skills or that provide them with an incentive to work. Thus, the 1996 reforms have two themes, not just one, as often claimed by opponents. The first theme, vigorously opposed by many if not most Democrats both in 1996 and currently, is strict restrictions on welfare benefits for those who enter the United States after 1996. In contrast to these restrictions, the second theme is support for working noncitizens trying to improve themselves. As a result, and despite the general bar on welfare receipt, noncitizens are eligible for the Earned Income Tax Credit (EITC), a wage supplement of up to $4,716 per year if they have two or more children, up to $2,853 if they have one child, and up to $428 (all figures for 2008) if they have no children. In addition, noncitizen children are eligible for Head Start, child care, Title I of the No Child Left Behind Act of 2002 (NCLB), and other education programs. Adults are eligible for adult education, benefits from the Workforce Investment Act, and similar programs. Finally, because the programs associated with Social Security are based on insurance principles rather than welfare, including regular contributions by potential beneficiaries, qualified noncitizens are eligible for unemployment insurance, Social Security benefits, disability insurance, and Medicare on the same basis as citizens.

Critics of the 1996 law were right about one major point. The law as enacted would have abruptly terminated the benefits of those who had been on welfare for many years, especially the elderly and disabled on SSI, most of whom the American public does not expect to work, and who might have become destitute. Some would have been thrown literally onto the street. A retroactive policy like this is unreasonable because the elderly, the disabled, and others do not have time to anticipate and adjust.[4] The same policy is fair if applied to new entrants because they know the rules from the beginning and can prepare to live by them. Indeed, if they don't like the rules, they can stay in their country of origin or emigrate to another country.

Unfairness is not the only flaw in the 1996 policy of abruptly terminating the benefits of those habituated to welfare. The policy was also politically unwise. Americans do not like to see destitute elderly people on the streets. The major reason Republicans adopted a policy this tough was that they were making strenuous efforts to end the nation's budget deficit and the policy yielded savings on the order of $13 billion per year. For his part, President Clinton, who was also trying to balance the federal books, sharply disagreed with the policy (see Haskins 2006, chapter 10). In signing the bill into law at a Rose Garden ceremony in August 1996, Clinton stated that his administration would in the following year do everything possible to restore some of the cuts (Clinton 1996). On a bipartisan basis, and with considerable cooperation between President Clinton and Republicans on the Ways and Means Committee, SSI and Medicaid were restored to those already in the country when welfare reform passed, including those who subsequently qualified for SSI because of a disabling condition or old age. The provisions were included in the Balanced Budget Act of 1997 (Public Law 105-33), despite the fact that they cost more than $9 billion over five years (U.S. Congress 1997, 1170)—just in time to avoid those elderly noncitizens winding up on the streets. But the preservation of these benefits in no way weakened the most important welfare prohibition of the 1996 policy; namely, the denial of most benefits to most qualified newly arriving noncitizens, other than refugees and asylees, for five years after entry.

Nor was the 1997 preservation of SSI for those already in the United States the last action taken to chip away at the 1996 prohibitions. Legislation enacted in 1998 restored food stamp eligibility for children, the elderly, and the disabled who lived in the United States before 1996. This legislation liberalized eligibility without piercing the five-year bar on those who entered after 1996. But in 2002, acting on a proposal from President Bush that caused behind-the-scenes consternation among many Republicans, Congress enacted a provision that extended food stamps to qualified immigrants after they had been in the United States for five years and to children and the disabled regardless of when they had arrived. Republican critics were especially disappointed because, by penetrating the five-year bar for the first time, the expansion may have put the 1996 policies on a slippery slope that all but invited subsequent erosion of the reforms.

The Republicans who wrote the original 1996 legislation were aware that immigrants were subject to the same unfortunate, often random, events that disrupt the well-being of citizens, including illness, job loss, accidents, divorce, and so on. But because the welfare programs that help citizens deal with these unfortunate events would not be available to noncitizens, a major provision of the Illegal Immigration Reform and Immigrant Responsibility Act, a companion to the 1996 welfare reform law, requires that most legal immigrants have sponsors and that the sponsors have incomes over 125 percent of the federal poverty line. This provision requires the income of sponsors to be deemed as available to the immigrant when calculating eligibility for welfare benefits, thereby often disqualifying the immigrant from benefits even after the five-year bar has expired. The sponsor is also held liable for the costs of any welfare benefit the immigrant uses and can be sued by both the government and the sponsored immigrant if the financial commitment is not met. The purpose of these requirements is to have a mechanism that provides noncitizens with some insurance against unfortunate events but does not impose the costs on taxpayers.

ARE THE WELFARE PROHIBITIONS JUSTIFIED?

These restrictions on welfare for noncitizens were controversial in 1996 even in the context of the sweeping reforms of SSI, AFDC (Aid to Families with Dependent Children), the Food Stamp Act, and other programs that were part of the same legislation. As is often the case in policy debates, one's position on whether noncitizens should be eligible for welfare benefits hinges in large part on values. A number of other important considerations also come into play in deciding whether noncitizens should be eligible for welfare, as we will see, but in the end, values are the most basic. In this case, the value at issue is whether noncitizens deserve to qualify for welfare by virtue of their presence in the United States or whether they must first become citizens before qualifying for welfare. The answer to this question depends in large part on the answer to an underlying question: do U.S. taxpayers have an obligation to support noncitizen immigrants from the moment they arrive or only when they become citizens?

The history of U.S. welfare policy for noncitizens appears to be on the side of those who believe that immigrants should not immediately qualify for welfare benefits. As pointed out by the nonpartisan Congressional Research Service in an official publication of the House Ways and Means Committee, opposition to welfare for noncitizens dates from colonial times (U.S. Congress 2004, appendix J). As early as 1645, the Massachusetts Bay colony prohibited the entry of paupers. Other colonies, such as New York, had similar provisions that barred entry to people likely to become dependent on others. Then, in 1882, in the first major legislative action Congress took to deal with immigration, a provision was included that barred entry to "any person unable to take care of himself or herself without becoming a public charge" (J-10). Despite this provision, when Congress began enacting means-tested programs in profusion during and after the 1960s, the programs usually did not contain specific provisions on limiting benefits of noncitizens. Federal policy was thus ambiguous: immigration law contained provisions that instructed immigration officials to restrict entry of those likely to become public charges and even gave immigration officials the authority to deport those who became or were likely to become dependent. But the laws that established welfare programs were usually silent on the issue, thereby allowing noncitizens to qualify for most benefits.

Despite this ambiguity, evidence is extensive that Congress and the states wanted to limit eligibility of noncitizens for welfare benefits. First, because federal law on means-tested programs did not bar noncitizens from participation, states enacted restrictions in their own statutes. This attempt failed to limit noncitizens from participating, however, because in 1971 the U.S. Supreme Count handed down the sweeping Graham v. Richardson, 403 US 365 (1971), decision that held that the equal protection clause of the Fourteenth Amendment prevented states from discriminating against noncitizens. Only the federal government could enact laws regulating immigration, said the court, thereby setting aside all state laws limiting welfare for noncitizens. Second, in attempting to enforce the congressional provision on public charges, the Immigration and Naturalization Service (INS), now the U.S. Citizenship and Immigration Services (USCIS), adopted procedures aimed at determining whether immigrants could rely on their own funds, on a job they had already secured or seemed likely to secure, or on largesse from individuals or organizations that would sponsor them. With regard to sponsorship, the INS developed a procedure by which individuals and organizations could declare support for an immigrant by signing an affidavit of support. This attempt to limit public welfare for noncitizens was also knocked down by the courts. In a series of cases culminating in State v. Binder in Michigan, 235 Mich. 73 (1959), courts held that affidavits of support were not binding because they had no basis in federal statute.

Given these mostly ineffective attempts to restrict noncitizen access to means-tested programs, in 1972 Congress included provisions in the legislation establishing the SSI program to legally restrict alien eligibility for benefits. Congress first required that only noncitizens legally admitted to the United States would be eligible. Subsequently, it includes provisions in the SSI, AFDC, and food stamps statutes requiring sponsor-to-alien deeming of income for three years after entry. In 1993, Congress expanded the deeming provision to five years in the SSI program, though these limitations on benefits had little effect on the rapid expansion of noncitizen participation in SSI.

Based on this legislative history, including laws enacted by colonial, state, and federal legislative bodies over three and a half centuries, the 1996 provisions barring noncitizen eligibility for most means-tested benefits for at least five years following entry can be seen as consistent with past attempts to limit alien welfare benefits. The 1996 legislation was therefore conservative in the most basic sense that Republicans were attempting to enforce a traditional policy rooted in the colonial period.

Another argument against welfare eligibility for noncitizens was the substantial cost to taxpayers of providing the benefits. Cost was part of a constellation of issues on welfare use by noncitizens, both real and imagined, that stirred up a certain level of animosity among Republicans, some pundits, and perhaps the American public. Thus the reasonable objection that giving welfare to noncitizens imposed costs on taxpayers blended with objections that evidence did not necessarily support. A good example of the latter is the frequently heard claim that the United States was a welfare magnet that attracted lazy foreigners who came here to live on welfare.

By 1995, on the eve of the welfare debate, noncitizens were more likely to participate in welfare programs than natives. In an extensive review of the Census Bureau's Survey of Income and

Program Participation, George Borjas of Harvard University showed that by the early 1990s, fully 21 percent of noncitizen households received benefits from at least one welfare program versus only 14 percent of native households. Borjas even concluded that "there might be ethnic networks that transmit information about the availability of particular benefits to new immigrants" (Borjas and Hilton 1996, 575). During the 1995 to 1996 debate that led to the 1996 reform law, both the Congressional Budget Office (CBO) and the Congressional Research Service provided Congress with abundant information documenting noncitizen participation in welfare programs and estimating the budget impact of their participation (see, for example, U.S. Congress 1996, appendix J). By contrast, the claim that noncitizens came to the United States to get on welfare seemed to rest primarily on anecdotes.

As often happens, powerful anecdotal information all but drowned out the data. After all, cases of systematic fraud by noncitizens in the SSI program were well documented. In 1994, for example, the Committee on Ways and Means conducted a hearing on SSI fraud involving middlemen from Southeast Asia. The hearing was worthy of the CIA as one witness, using the alias John, wearing a hood and sitting behind a partition so the audience at the hearing could not see him, testified about his involvement as an undercover agent in the middlemen gangs operating their various scams. San Martin, the chief investigator of the Bureau of Medi-Cal Fraud in the California Department of Justice, explained several schemes that he and his investigators had uncovered, including one in which middlemen were coaching noncitizens in how to feign the symptoms for psychological disabilities that would convince certain doctors, some of whom were subsequently shown to be involved in the scam, that they were disabled under the SSI definition (U.S. Congress 1994b). The revelation of fraud was simply the icing on the cake as the dramatic expansion of noncitizen participation in SSI had a major impact on Republican thinking about the need for restrictions on welfare benefits for noncitizens. Although even a brief look at work rates among noncitizens would show that the vast majority held jobs, their extensive use of welfare provoked an almost inevitable reaction of legislative attempts to limit benefits (see Meissner, Abraham, and Hamilton 2006, 14).

As to the 1996 Republican proposals on cutting welfare for noncitizens, the policy was based first on the principle of following historical precedent, and this was reinforced by the money that could be saved by cutting noncitizen benefits. In this regard, a brief bit of history is instructive. In the spring of 1993, more than eighteen months before the congressional elections of 1994 that gave Republicans control of the House and Senate and opened the way to the 1996 reforms, the House Republican leadership appointed a task force charged with the responsibility of writing a welfare reform bill that would unite House Republicans (see Haskins 2006, chapter 3). I had the good fortune to conduct much of the staff work for the task force. Among other guidelines, we were determined to write a bill that would spend more on welfare-to-work programs, especially for child care and job search, but be revenue neutral or actually save money. To help with the task of finding spending cuts to offset the new spending, I kept a list of possible cuts and how much they would save over five years.

Fortuitously, a few days after the first meeting of the Republican welfare reform task force, a group of House Republicans invited Doug Besharov of the American Enterprise Institute to talk with them about welfare reform. During that meeting, which was chaired by Chris Shays of Connecticut, one of the most moderate Republicans in the House, the issue of welfare for noncitizens came up. As a senior staffer on welfare for the Ways and Means Committee, which had jurisdiction over a host of welfare programs, I was annoyed as the discussion proceeded because I knew very little about the basic facts of welfare for noncitizens, other than that many noncitizens received welfare benefits. Two facts emerged from that brief 1993 discussion. Nearly every Republican in the room was against giving welfare to noncitizens, and no one had any idea of how many noncitizens were receiving welfare nor how much it cost the government to pay for the benefits.

Following the meeting, I undertook a survey of the statutes on welfare for noncitizens, in which I received competent and nonpartisan assistance from analysts at the Congressional Research Service. I also began talking with analysts at the Congressional Budget Office about how much it cost to provide welfare benefits to noncitizens, and—implicitly—how much could be saved if the benefits were modified or terminated.[5] Within a week or so, I wrote Shays a memo, which was widely distributed to Republicans, summarizing the basic facts of welfare use by noncitizens.

When the issue of welfare benefits came up at the next meeting of the welfare reform task force, everyone was astounded that noncitizens could apparently participate in most welfare programs on the same basis as citizens and that the estimated cost of paying for the benefits, which we guessed, based on discussions with CBO, could be as much as $2 or $3 billion per year. There was virtually no controversy about ending some or all of the benefits, and the staff began immediately drafting provisions to achieve this end. Over the next three years, the provisions were modified and perfected, especially when Ways and Means staffers worked with their Judiciary Committee counterparts to write the final legislative text in 1995 and 1996, but controversy among Republicans over the basic policy of cutting some or all welfare benefits of noncitizens was scant. Indeed, from the spring of 1993 until the final bill was signed in August 1996 the only major dispute among Republicans was over whether noncitizens already receiving benefits should be grandfathered for a time so that they could adapt to losing their benefits.

Members of the task force, as well as Republicans in general, were especially irate about the participation of noncitizens in the SSI program. Figure 2.1 presents SSI enrollment data for noncitizens in the years preceding passage of the welfare reform law.[6] The steep increase in enrollment—an explosion in welfare use that saw more than six times as many noncitizens getting SSI in 2004 as in 1992—was enough to rile almost any Republican and in all likelihood most American citizens. As we have seen, based on testimony from hearings conducted by the Ways and Means Committee in 1994 before Republicans took control of Congress, it came to be widely believed that legal immigrants were bringing their parents to the United States and then, after the mandatory waiting period of three years (changed to five years in 1993), putting them on SSI. Even worse were the numerous documented cases of fraud involving noncitizens (U.S. Congress 1994a). Many Democrats refused to defend the rapid increase in SSI enrollment, with several suggesting that Congress focus its attention on the

FIGURE 2.1 **Noncitizens Receiving Supplemental Security Income**

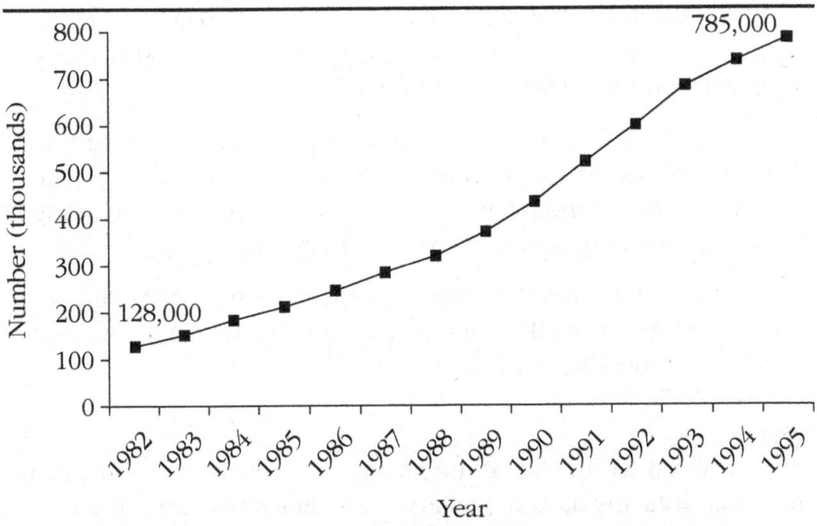

[Figure: Line graph showing number of noncitizens (in thousands) receiving SSI from 1982 to 1995. Values rise from 128,000 in 1982 to 785,000 in 1995. Y-axis: Number (thousands), 0–800. X-axis: Year.]

Source: Author's adaptation based on U.S. Congress (2004).

SSI program rather than all welfare programs for noncitizens. Here was a case of abuse and fraud in one program tainting a much broader array of programs and those who used them.

Another justification for supporting welfare restrictions on noncitizens is the basic fairness of the bargain America presents to those who come here for opportunity. Consider what American policy offers to adult immigrants when they appear on our shores:

> Come to the United States, enjoy great individual freedom, and participate in the world's greatest economy, an economy that generates almost as many jobs as there are workers willing to work.

> In the bargain, your children will have the legal right to attend the public schools free of charge and, if they are born in the United States, to qualify for all public programs including cash welfare, child nutrition, health care, and subsidies for postsecondary education on the same basis as other citizens.

Moreover, you yourself will be qualified for many education and training programs and will even qualify for a wage subsidy through the tax code that could provide you with an income supplement of up to nearly $5,000 (in 2008) every year if you have two or more children.

Further, after five years, you can apply for citizenship and, in a total of six or seven years after arrival, become a citizen with all the attendant rights and responsibilities—including the right to have access to welfare benefits.

In return, you are expected to obey the law, pay Social Security taxes as well as income taxes if you make enough money, and avoid welfare.[7]

Sound fair?

In addition to these arguments against welfare for noncitizens, most Republicans have a bias against welfare because, in addition to providing a cash strand in the nation's rather moderate safety net, it reduces the incentive to work (Danziger, Haveman, and Plotnick 1981). We return to this argument shortly.

Although the case against welfare eligibility for most noncitizens is reasonable, those who argue that noncitizens should be eligible for welfare benefits also have impressive arguments, three of which are especially notable. First, they argue that a truly open society would welcome noncitizens on the same basis as citizens. As long as noncitizens pay taxes and obey the law, they should be treated like citizens, including the right to receive welfare benefits. To withhold welfare is an act of discrimination against noncitizens, making it less likely that they will regard their new homeland as fair and impartial to new entrants while they are trying to become Americans. Second, in the case of noncitizens who fall on hard times and need assistance, federal government refusal to provide benefits will result in great pressure on state and local governments to provide them. This outcome would be especially unfair because, under the Constitution, the federal government has exclusive control of admission of noncitizens to the United States and states and localities must allow noncitizens to live within their jurisdiction. As a result, if noncitizens become destitute, states and localities have no choice except to pick up the tab for welfare benefits. In short, the federal government admits noncitizens but then does not provide adequate accommodations for their well-being. Following the federal lead by more or less ignoring those in destitution would be especially difficult for states when the destitute are young, old, or disabled and also would be difficult in states, such as New York and California, that have a tradition of providing generous welfare benefits.

This consideration of destitution raises a third and especially compelling argument to justify welfare for noncitizens. The first two arguments rest on the well-being of the noncitizens themselves. The well-being of their children, however, broadens the argument considerably. It is a truism of social policy that children are the future. For those who don't like broad abstractions, here is a translation of what it means for children to be the future: the solvency of Social Security and Medicare depend completely on the earnings of the next generation. It follows that there are good reasons for ensuring that children receive the support and nurturance requisite to healthy development because they are the ones who will be supporting the Social Security edifice in the future. From this perspective, whether the children are immigrants themselves, the children of immigrants, or the children of natives is largely irrelevant. After all, Social Security and Medicare are pay-as-you-go programs in which current tax payments are used to pay current benefits.[8] So the productivity of today's children becomes the basis for Social Security solvency for today's adults when they retire. Hence, current workers who are concerned about the financing of their retirement should care about the development of the children who will pay their retirement benefits. Given that one out of five American children is now foreign-born or born to parents who are foreign-born—a figure that seems certain to grow—their development is vital to the solvency of the Social Security programs and therefore the future of the nation (Capps et al. 2004).

This social argument also comes in a negative version. The claim is often made that children reared in poverty, especially when it afflicts them early in life and over a period of years, show developmental deficits that lead to poor health, school failure, special education placement, school dropout, and even delinquency (Mayer 1997; Duncan, Brooks-Gunn, and Klebanov 1994;

Duncan, Ziol-Guest, and Kalil 2007). Thus, to ignore the development of noncitizen children could lead to increased expenditures for remedial education, police, incarceration, health care, and so forth (Currie 2005; Nelson 2000; Shonkoff and Phillips 2000). Similarly, future contributions to economic growth and tax revenues by noncitizens children could be lower because they have stunted development leading to lower productivity.

Clearly, both those for and against providing welfare to noncitizens have solid arguments supporting their position. Some of the arguments, such as whether noncitizen children suffer because they do not receive welfare, must be examined in the light of empirical evidence, a project I undertake briefly in the following section. Even so, noncitizens received welfare for many years primarily because Democrats believed people were better off when they could rely on having their needs met through welfare if they could not meet them through their own efforts. But, in 1996, Republicans had the votes to pass legislation and used their leverage to reverse at least part of the Democratic policy of giving entitlement welfare benefits to both citizens and noncitizens without demanding much in return. An important question now is whether the restrictions are effective in reducing welfare use by noncitizens, an issue to which we now turn our attention.

CHANGES IN PARTICIPATION IN FOUR MAJOR WELFARE PROGRAMS, 1994 THROUGH 2004

The data in figure 2.2 are drawn from chapter 5 of this volume and trace changes in participation rates for low-income noncitizen and citizen families in TANF, food stamps, and Medicaid between 1994 and 2004.[9] The data point for each program and each year is the percentage of families with one or more children and incomes under 200 percent of the federal poverty level (about $40,000 for a family of four in 2006) receiving the benefit. Trends in the TANF program are precisely what the authors of the 1996 reforms intended. Between 1994 and 2004, participation plummeted from 19 percent to 5 percent of low-income noncitizen families, a reduction of nearly 75 percent.[10] Similarly, participation

FIGURE 2.2 Low-Income Citizen and Noncitizen Families with Children in Public Benefit Programs

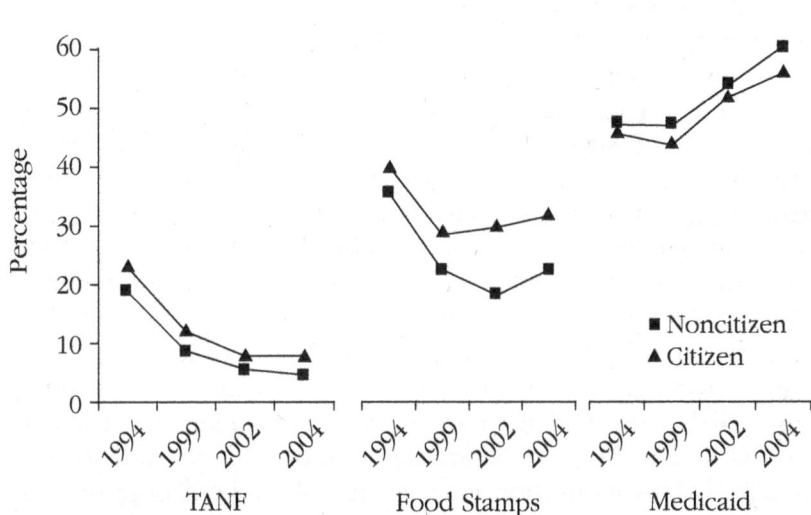

Source: Fix (2006).

in food stamps dropped from 35 percent to as low as 18 percent, a fall of 50 percent, before rising slightly to 22 percent between 2002 and 2004. It is notable that enrollment of noncitizens in both TANF and food stamps was lower than that of natives both before and after welfare reform.

Noncitizen participation in Medicaid does not fit the pattern of substantial decline seen in the other two programs. Indeed, following a modest decline for two years after 1996, Medicaid enrollment of noncitizens increased between 1999 and 2002 and again between 2002 and 2004. Over the entire period, Medicaid enrollment by noncitizens was up by more than 30 percent, from 46 percent to 59 percent. A remarkably high percentage of low-income noncitizen families with children—nearly 60 percent—is enrolled in Medicaid. This percentage is nearly three times as high as the percentage enrolled in food stamps and twelve times as high as that enrolled in TANF. Moreover, unlike any of the other welfare programs, a higher percentage of noncitizen families than citizen families are enrolled in Medicaid.

Medicaid thus stands out as the welfare program in which

noncitizens participate most frequently, at a higher rate than natives, and with increasing frequency over time. None of these characteristics were intended by the authors of the 1996 reforms. Several factors seem likely to be playing a role. First, most states elected to exercise the option of continuing the coverage of those who were on Medicaid when the 1996 reforms were enacted. Second, fifteen states elected to provide Medicaid to noncitizen children and nine states elected to provide it to adults who reached the end of the five-year ban (U.S. Congress 2004, J-16–17; Leighton Ku, personal communication, 2007). Third, the 1997 restoration of SSI benefits was accompanied by a restoration of Medicaid for SSI noncitizen recipients as well, thereby contributing a few hundred thousand more noncitizen beneficiaries.[11]

Moreover, given the importance of Medicaid to maintaining personal health—and for parents, for maintaining the health of their children—noncitizens are highly motivated to participate in Medicaid. This motivation is especially likely both because low-income families have more health problems than their wealthier counterparts (Reardon-Anderson, Capps, and Fix 2002) and because all families are anxious about health and being able to receive care when they—or their children—need it. Regardless of the reason, the high level of health coverage for noncitizens was not intended by the Republicans who wrote the 1996 legislation. On the other hand, during the time they controlled the majority in Congress and the presidency, Republicans did not make any serious attempts to curtail the participation of noncitizens in Medicaid, even after 2000, when it became clear that noncitizen enrollment in Medicaid was high and growing.

Noncitizen participation in SSI differs substantially from that of noncitizens in the other welfare programs examined earlier because families with children are only a small fraction of the noncitizens who enroll in SSI. As shown, at the peak of their enrollment in 1994, 19 percent of low-income noncitizen families with children were enrolled in TANF and 35 percent in food stamps. By contrast, only 5 percent were enrolled in SSI. The explanation for this difference is that SSI serves two broad categories of the poor, the elderly and the disabled. Although the disabled can be of any age, recipients must be sixty-five or older to qualify as elderly. It follows that focusing attention on a sample of families

FIGURE 2.3 Noncitizens Receiving Supplemental Security Income

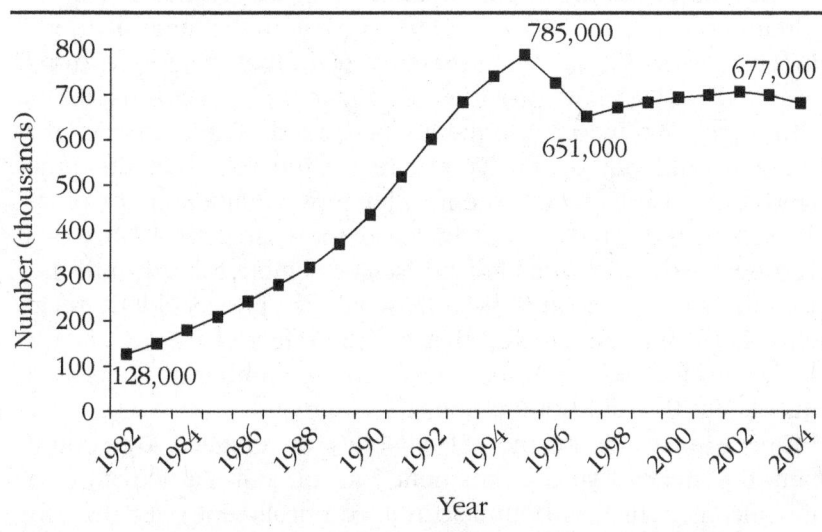

Source: Author's compilation based on U.S. Congress (2004); Social Security Administration (2005), table 17.

with children excludes most of the elderly and thereby the demographic group most likely to enroll in SSI. If, instead of examining SSI enrollment among a sample of families with children from the Census Bureau's Current Population Survey, we examine SSI enrollment based on administrative data from the Social Security Administration, it is clear that there has been a moderate decline in noncitizen participation in SSI (see figure 2.3). After the huge increases in the years before the 1996 reforms, there was a substantial drop in noncitizen SSI participation in both 1996 and 1997. At the end of 1997, participation in SSI had declined from 785,000 to 651,000, about 17 percent. Although less than the decline in the other caseloads, a more modest drop is to be expected because of the 1997 legislation that allowed noncitizens already receiving SSI to stay on the rolls. After 1999, SSI enrollment by noncitizens increased slightly for five years before falling again in 2003 and 2004. By 2004, the percentage of noncitizens enrolled in SSI had fallen from about 6.6 to about 3.2.[12]

These trends are hard to explain. Part of the reason for the continuing high levels of noncitizen enrollment in SSI may be a combination of factors that were not anticipated in 1996. The most important, of course, was the 1997 provision that grandfathered noncitizens on SSI, allowing them to retain their eligibility. In addition, the 1997 law provided coverage to noncitizens in the country in 1996 who subsequently became disabled, a policy that clearly would put upward pressure on the rolls. On the other hand, the SSI rolls would seem to have two major sources of decline: first, the rapid rate of increase shown before 1996 would stop because noncitizens are no longer eligible for SSI until they become citizens; second, the rolls would decline as elderly recipients die. It was anticipated that the net effect of the two factors would produce a continuing decline in the number of noncitizens on SSI. But that did not happen. Why not?

One reason may be the SSI eligibility of refugees. By contrast with the general and permanent bar on SSI participation by noncitizens, which is bound to reduce enrollment over the long run, refugees are specifically allowed to enroll in welfare programs for their first seven years in the country. That Asian noncitizens, many of whom are refugees, are much more likely to be enrolled in SSI than noncitizens from South America and Central America, few of whom are refugees, suggests that refugees are in fact helping keep SSI enrollment high. On the other hand, figure 2.4 shows that in every welfare program including SSI, the percentage of refugee families has declined since 1994, albeit in an uneven pattern. Indeed, the pattern of welfare receipt among refugees in most respects mirrors that of other noncitizens with regard to the percentage of families participating in each of the four programs, the comparative levels of enrollment in each program (highest in Medicaid, lowest in TANF and SSI, intermediate in food stamps), and the pattern of change after 1994. Especially the last outcome is surprising in view of the fact that, unlike other noncitizens, refugees retained their eligibility for all welfare programs during their first seven years in the country. Perhaps the decline in welfare use by refugees reflects a general movement among noncitizens following the 1996 reforms to use as little welfare as possible. There may also be confusion among refugees about their continued welfare eligibility, especially given that many other noncitizens are ineligible for benefits.

This brief overview shows that the provisions of the 1996 law

FIGURE 2.4 Low-Income Noncitizen and Refugee Families with Children in Public Benefit Programs

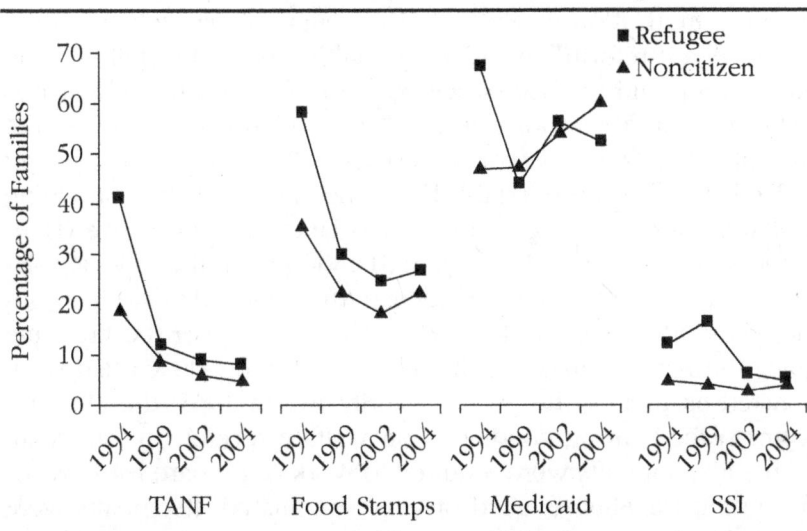

Source: Fix (2006).

designed to reduce participation in welfare programs by noncitizens have been partially effective. The TANF program has the lowest rate, at 5 percent, but a very low one for citizens as well, at 8 percent. The actual increase in Medicaid participation, and the continued high enrollment in SSI—the program that was most on the minds of Republicans when they crafted the provisions—were not anticipated by the authors. Thus, from the perspective of those who wrote and strongly supported the 1996 provisions, these outcomes must be disappointing. On the other hand, advocates of welfare for noncitizens must be pleased. A conservative cynic might conclude that welfare is a lot like kudzu—you can trim it, but it just keeps coming back.

WELFARE, WORK INCENTIVE, AND WELL-BEING

Many advocates, scholars, and elected officials believe that eligibility for welfare provides individuals, especially children, with an important safety net that reduces destitution. Others, however, believe that welfare interferes with self-sufficiency, especially with the motivation to work. As the congressional debate on the 1996 welfare reform law shows, Republicans tend to fall into the latter group and to base policy goals on the assumption that it is better to help able-bodied adults leave welfare or avoid it in the first place in favor of work (Haskins 2006, chapters 4, 8). And indeed, the literature establishing unequivocally that providing welfare does reduce hours of work is large and impressive (Danzinger, Haveman, and Plotnick 1981). Moreover, the 1996 legislation itself provides solid evidence that restricting welfare increases work effort (Haskins 2006, chapter 15). For the first time since the nation's major cash welfare program (AFDC) had been enacted as part of the Social Security Act in 1935, the 1996 reforms placed strong conditions on welfare receipt. In particular, nearly all recipients were required to work or prepare for work or have their benefits reduced or even terminated. Recipients were also subjected to a five-year time limit on receipt of cash welfare.

In contrast to these welfare restrictions, in the years leading up to passage of welfare reform, the federal government had expanded or created a host of programs that provided support to low-income working families. Either before passage or as part of the law, childcare funds were dramatically expanded, the value of the EITC was expanded greatly to the point that it could be worth as much as $4,000 (in 1995, and nearly $5,000 in 2008) to working families with two or more children, Medicaid had been expanded and a new child health insurance program created so that nearly all children in families with incomes less than 200 percent of poverty were covered by health insurance, and other programs had been modified so they would provide more effective support for working families (see U.S. Congress 2004, section 15, 83–89). Most analysts now agree that the combination of restrictions on welfare and the generosity of the work support system, as well as a strong economy that was producing many jobs, resulted in perhaps 2 million poor mothers leaving the welfare rolls and taking jobs after the 1996 law was enacted.[13] In other words, sticks and carrots proved to be the best way to increase work effort.

In a similar vein, Republicans who wrote the 1996 noncitizen provisions made the point that welfare creates a kind of moral hazard in that it can lure immigrants into welfare dependency. Especially in the case of adults who come to America specifically to pursue economic opportunity, welfare can actually be an impediment to self-reliance and economic advancement.

Although welfare does reduce the work effort of many, some who lose welfare become destitute. If they are parents, their children also become destitute. Based on evidence from the response of welfare mothers to the 1996 reforms, it is clear that most respond appropriately, go to work, and improve their financial status. However, some, for a variety of reasons, fail to work steadily. Like every other policy, replacing welfare with work yields both benefits and costs. On the evidence of welfare reform, Americans are willing to accept a certain level of destitution among adults—hence our tolerance for seeing homeless people on the streets—and so far the 1996 reforms have been very popular, despite the apparent fact that some mothers have not responded well and appear to be worse off, as are their children (Haskins 2006; Blank 2007; Loprest 2003; Wood and Rangarajan 2003; Zedlewski et al. 2003).

How have noncitizens responded to the loss of welfare benefits? As with welfare reform, this question takes on added importance because many noncitizen families have children. It is one thing for adults to live in poverty, but when children are destitute, the ante rises. Thus, especially because about 20 percent of all children in America live in immigrant families, decisions about welfare for noncitizens—including those made in 1996—should be open to reexamination in light of evidence on both work effort and destitution and other outcomes, especially among children (see Fix, Passel, and Sucher 2003).

The question is whether the cuts in welfare for noncitizens led to the increases in poverty predicted by Democrats, child advocates, and many editorial page writers, or whether the effects were mostly positive like those produced by other provisions in the 1996 welfare reform law.[14] The evidence to make a firm judgment on this issue is modest, but such evidence as there is suggests that the results have been neutral or slightly positive. Recall that Census Bureau data on welfare receipt show a decline in participation in welfare programs other than Medicaid after the 1996 reforms. Despite this decline, Census Bureau statistics on poverty

FIGURE 2.5 Poverty Rates among Foreign-Born and Native-Born

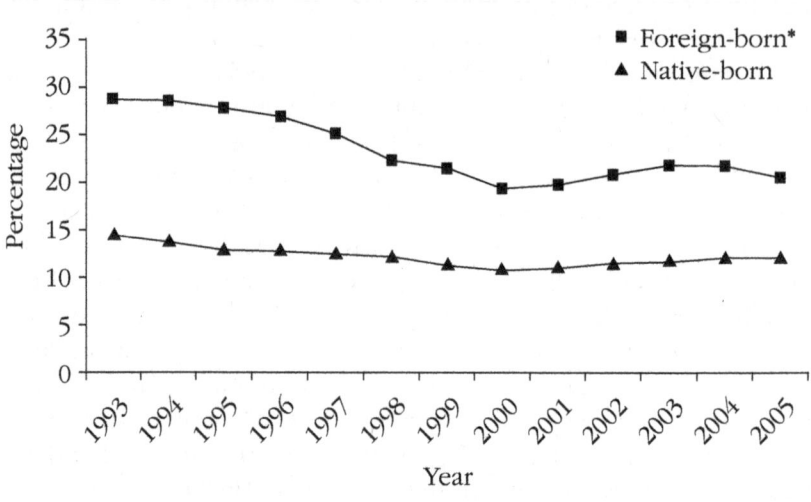

Source: Author's compilation based on U.S. Bureau of the Census (2006), table 23.
*Does not include naturalized citizens.

show that poverty among the foreign-born has declined since 1996 (see figure 2.5). Before welfare reform, the rate of poverty among the foreign-born was about twice that of the native-born. After reform, in the midst of a hot economy generating numerous jobs, including low-income jobs for which poorly educated noncitizens could qualify, poverty for both the foreign-born and natives declined every year until the recession of 2001. However, poverty among nonnatives declined even faster than poverty among natives, falling from 28 to 23 percent and from 15 to 12 percent, respectively. In 2000, when poverty for both groups reached its lowest level before the recession of 2001, the gap between nonnatives and natives had closed by nearly 45 percent.

Poverty among noncitizen children compared with that among native children showed the same pattern (see figure 2.6). Among children, poverty declined even more steeply than among all noncitizens, by 40 percent between 1995 and 2001 before increasing slightly after 2001. Over this period, then, the poverty rates of

FIGURE 2.6 Poverty Rates among Noncitizen and Native-Born Children

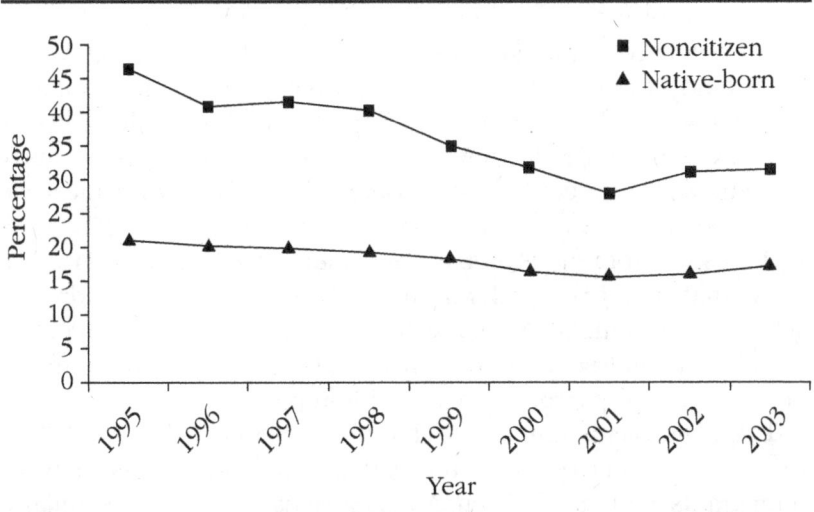

Source: Authors' compilation based on U.S. Bureau of the Census (various years), table 1.11.

noncitizen children declined rapidly and the poverty gap between native and noncitizen children closed by nearly 55 percent. These data provide no evidence that noncitizens are worse off as a result of losing welfare benefits. Indeed, they suggest that most noncitizens parents are perfectly capable of providing for themselves and their children without welfare. It may be that noncitizen poverty would have dropped even more if noncitizens still had access to welfare. In addition, destitution may have occurred near the bottom of the income distribution and be missed by blunt measures like the poverty index. The poverty index tells how many families are below the poverty line, but tells nothing about how far below the line they are.[15]

NONCITIZEN CHILDREN: A SPECIAL CASE

Although their poverty rate did not increase following welfare reform, evidence that noncitizen children are worse off on a wide range of measures than native children is abundant. We have just seen that their poverty rate, though declining, is still considerably above that of native children. In a series of publications based on a representative national sample of families, Jane Reardon-Anderson, Randy Capps, and Michael Fix have shown that, compared with native children, noncitizen children are less healthy, live in families with lower incomes, have less-educated parents, have parents with limited English proficiency, have higher levels of food insecurity, and live in more crowded housing (2002). Similarly, results from the National Assessment of Educational Progress show that immigrant children are well behind native children in school achievement. At grade four, for example, 62 percent of noncitizen children are in the lowest category of reading performance, versus 36 percent of native children.[16]

These problems immigrant children experience are hardly surprising. In recent decades, the gap in education levels between immigrants and native-born Americans has grown substantially. George Borjas has analyzed U.S. Census Bureau data on the relative education levels of immigrants from 1960 to 2000. Although immigrants and natives were quite similar in 1960, by 2000 large gaps had emerged. Almost 30 percent of immigrants did not have a high school degree in 2000, for example, versus only about 7 percent of natives. Further, the immigrant share of all workers without a high school degree rose from about 6 percent in 1960 to nearly 40 percent by 2000. This huge difference explains much of both the excess poverty among immigrants and the nearly 20 percent lower average wages they earn (Borjas 2005).

In short, the United States is now receiving immigrants—both legal and illegal—with far less education than natives.[17] As shown, many immigrant children also seem to be struggling in school. The essential law of educational achievement, established by the Coleman Report in 1996 and reinforced many times since, is that family background is the greatest single determinant (Coleman et al. 1966; Jencks et al. 1972; Mosteller and Moynihan 1972; Rothstein 2004). If the United States admits immigrants with low education and job skills, it is inevitable that they and their families, on average, will live on modest incomes and that their children will perform below average in school and grow up to fill jobs that require less skill and pay lower wages than those taken by more educated children. There is little evidence that these problems will be solved by giving more welfare to noncitizen children and their families. The real solutions, like those for disadvantaged native children, are likely to involve direct interventions, both during the preschool and school-age years. Preventive health care may also play a role. Although our health and education interventions are at best modestly successful, these investments are much more likely to bear fruit than equivalent investments in welfare programs (Currie 2005; Duncan and Ludwig 2007).

SUMMARY

Both on the grounds of precedent and fairness to American taxpayers, ending the welfare benefits of most newly arrived noncitizens is reasonable policy. A decade into its implementation, it is clear that the 1996 reforms have saved billions of dollars for taxpayers, although more welfare benefits are being given to noncitizens—especially by the Medicaid program—than the authors of the original legislation intended. Nor is there good evidence that the reforms have caused undue hardship, or even higher poverty levels, among noncitizens. In fact, the data show remarkable declines in poverty among noncitizen adults and children. On the other hand, given that noncitizen children are disproportionately poor, have more health problems, and do worse in school than native children, the future productivity of the American economy and the solvency of the Social Security system could both be improved if additional investments were made in their health and education.

NOTES

1. The term *means-tested* refers to programs that provide aid conditional on an individual or family having income below some specified criteria—for example, the poverty level.
2. Children who are illegally in the United States are also eligible for public education.

3. The basic logic of immigration is turned on its head by refugees and asylees (asylees are refugees who have managed to leave their own county, immigrate to the United States, and apply for refugee status when already in the United States). Immigrants move to a new country by choice because they are seeking opportunity; refugees and asylees do so not by choice, but because they are being persecuted in some way. Refugees and asylees often leave without any of their material or financial possessions. They are eligible for welfare benefits for seven years because they are allowed to apply for citizenship after living in the United States for five years (three years if they marry a U.S. citizen) and are then given an additional two years to have their paperwork handled by the U.S. Department of Citizenship and Immigration Services. By definition, asylees and refugees are legal residents of the United States.
4. By *retroactive*, I mean that the policy of ending welfare benefits applied to people who were already on welfare as well as those who entered the United States after 1996.
5. After Republicans gained control of Congress, I had the opportunity to edit the widely respected Ways and Means *Green Book*, a huge compendium of federal social programs and statistics related to employment, poverty, wealth, health, and similar issues. One outcome of our work on welfare benefits for noncitizens was that we asked the Congressional Research Service to write an overview of the history of welfare for noncitizens that included data on immigration, citizenship, welfare receipt, and related topics. The result was a thirty-page appendix to the *Green Book* that stands as one of the most succinct and readable treatments of the issue (see U.S. Congress 2004, appendix J).
6. As SSI enrollment by noncitizens was increasing, so was the number of noncitizens. Although the number of noncitizens in the United States for all the years between 1982 and 1995 is not available from the Census Bureau, available numbers suggest that the rates of noncitizens on SSI to noncitizens living in the United States more than doubled in the decade between 1980 and 1990.
7. Mexican and many other South American and African immigrants with a high school diploma can expect to make seven times as much in the United States as in their home countries; college graduates can expect about a nine-fold increase in salaries (see Rosenzweig 2006, table 4).
8. Since the Social Security reforms of 1983, Social Security has been on a firmer financial footing. The system is now in the black, but beginning again in 2017 its benefits will exceed its income from

taxes, and by 2041 its trust account will go bankrupt. Medicare is in even worse shape and is expected to be bankrupt by 2018 (see OASDI 2008).

9. I thank Michael Fix and Randy Capps for providing me with the data displayed in figures 2.2 and 2.4. See the Urban Institute analysis of Current Population Survey, March Annual Social and Economic Supplement, various years; augmented by the Urban Institute's analysis of legal status of noncitizens, including refugees, asylees, and lawful permanent residents.

10. By comparison, the decline in the TANF rolls for citizens over the same period was about 65 percent.

11. The State Child Health Insurance Program (SCHIP) was enacted by Congress and President Clinton in 1997 and has greatly expanded the number of children covered by health insurance. Further, many states and localities mounted programs to promote Medicaid availability.

12. These estimates are based on my estimates of the number of noncitizens in the United States in 1995 (15.2 million) and in 2004 (21.1 million) using data from the Census Bureau and the Pew Hispanic Center.

13. The welfare rolls declined by around 3 million families between 1994 and 2005. Research shows that between 50 and 60 percent of the adults in these families had jobs at any given moment after leaving welfare and up to 70 percent had worked at some time after leaving welfare (see Haskins 2006, chapter 15).

14. Representative Robert Matsui, a senior member of the Ways and Means Committee in the House, said the bill was "plain and simply" an "attack on legal immigrants" (see "Some Look at the Welfare Plan with Hope, but Others Are Fearful," *New York Times*, August 4, 1996, A26). To Raul Yzaguirre, the head of the National Council of La Raza, perhaps the nation's leading Hispanic organization, the welfare bill was "mean-spirited," and a "disaster for the nation" that would "kick 1 million kids out into poverty" (see Tom Hayes, "Welfare Bill 'A Disaster,' La Raza President Says," *Desert News* [Salt Lake City], August 9, 1996, 3).

15. The decline in welfare use and the simultaneous decline in poverty rates are not necessarily causally related. Still, that these two trends took place simultaneously certainly demonstrates that it is possible to reduce poverty without increasing welfare payments.

16. See the National Assessment of Educational Progress Data Explorer, http://nces.ed.gov/nationsreportcard/nde/ (accessed December 5, 2006).

17. The educational level of immigrants is diverse; both the number of immigrants with college degrees or advanced degrees and the number who are school dropouts has increased over the last three decades (see Haskins 2008, 81–89).

REFERENCES

Blank, Rebecca M. 2007. "Improving the Safety Net for Single Mothers Who Face Serious Barriers to Work." *Future of Children* 17(2): 183–97.

Borjas, George J., and Lynette Hilton. 1996. "Immigration and the Welfare State: Immigrant Participation in Means-Tested Entitlement Programs." *Quarterly Journal of Economics* 111(2): 575–604.

———. 2005. "Immigration Policy and Human Capital." Unpublished paper. Harvard University, Cambridge, Massachusetts.

Capps, Randolph, Michael E. Fix, Jason Ost, Jane Reardon-Anderson, and Jeffrey Passel. 2004. *The Health and Well-Being of Young Children of Immigrants*. Washington, D.C.: The Urban Institute.

Clinton, William J. 1996. "Statement on Signing the Personal Responsibility and Work Opportunity Reconciliation Act of 1996." *Public Papers of the President, William J. Clinton, 1996*, vol. 2. Washington: Government Printing Office.

Coleman, James, Ernest Q. Campbell, Carol J. Hobson, James McPartland, Alexander M. Mood, Frederic D. Weinfeld, and Robert L. York. 1966. *Equality of Educational Opportunity*. Washington: Government Printing Office.

Currie, Janet M. 2005. "Health Disparities and Gaps in School Readiness." *Future of Children* 15(1): 117–38.

Danziger, Sheldon, Robert Haveman, and Robert Plotnick. 1981. "How Income Transfers Affect Work, Savings, and the Income Distribution: A Critical Review." *Journal of Economic Literature* 19(3): 975–1028.

Duncan, Greg J., Jeanne Brooks-Gunn, and Pamela K. Klebanov. 1994. "Economic Deprivation and Early-Childhood Development." *Child Development* 65(2): 296–318.

Duncan, Greg J., and Jens Ludwig. 2007. "Reducing Poverty through Preschool Interventions." *Future of Children* 17(2): 143–60.

Duncan, Greg J., Kathleen Ziol-Guest, and Ariel Kalil. 2007. "Early Childhood Poverty and Adult Attainment, Behavior, and Health." Paper prepared for the Conference on Long-Run Impact of Early Life Events at the National Poverty Center, University of Michigan. Ann Arbor (December 13).

Fix, Michael. 2006. "Trends in Immigrant Benefit and Use Following

Welfare Reform." Presentation to the Association of Public Policy and Management Association Annual Meeting. Madison, Wisc. (November 3).

Fix, Michael E., Jeffrey S. Passel, and Kenneth Sucher. 2003. *Immigrant Families and Workers, Trends in Naturalization.* Washington, D.C.: The Urban Institute.

Haskins, Ron. 2006. *Work over Welfare: The Inside Story of the 1996 Welfare Reform Law.* Washington, D.C.: Brookings Institution Press.

———. 2008. "Immigration: Wages, Education, and Mobility." In *Getting Ahead or Losing Ground: Economic Mobility in America,* edited by Julia Isaacs, Isabel Sawhill, and Ron Haskins. Washington, D.C.: Brookings and Pew Charitable Trusts.

Jencks, Christopher, Marshall Smith, Henry Acland, Mary Jo Bane, David Cohen, Herbert Gintis, Barbara Heyns, and Stephan Michelson. 1972. *Inequality: A Reassessment of the Effect of Family and Schooling in America.* New York: Basic Books.

Loprest, Pamela. 2003. "Disconnected Welfare Leavers Face Serious Risks." *Snapshots of America's Families,* no. 7. Washington, D.C.: The Urban Institute.

Mayer, Susan E. 1997. *What Money Can't Buy: Family and Children's Life Changes.* Cambridge, Mass.: Harvard University Press.

Meissner, Doris, Spencer Abraham, and Lee H. Hamilton. 2006. *Immigration and America's Future: A New Chapter.* Washington, D.C.: Migration Policy Institute.

Mosteller, Frederick, and Daniel P. Moynihan, eds. 1972. *On Equality of Educational Opportunity.* New York: Random House.

Nelson, Charles A. 2000. "Neural Plasticity and Human Development: The Role of Early Experience in Sculpting Memory Systems." *Developmental Science* 3(2): 115–36.

Old Age, Survivors, and Disabilities Insurance Board of Trustees (OASDI). 2008. *2008 Annual Report of the Board of Trustees of the Federal Old-Age and Survivors Insurance and Disability Insurance Trust Funds.* Washington: U.S. Government Printing Office.

Reardon-Anderson, Jane, Randolph Capps, and Michael E. Fix. 2002. *The Health and Well-being of Children in Immigrant Families.* Series B, no. B-52. Washington, D.C.: The Urban Institute.

Rosenzweig, Mark. 2006. "Global Difference and International Student Flows." In *Brookings Trade Forum.* Washington, D.C.: Brookings Institution Press.

Rothstein, Richard. 2004. *Class and Schools: Using Social, Economic, and Educational Reform to Close the Black-White Achievement Gap.* New York: Teachers College Press.

Shonkoff, Jack, and Deborah Phillips. 2000. *From Neurons to Neighbor-*

hoods: *The Science of Early Childhood Development*. Washington, D.C.: National Academies Press.

Social Security Administration. 2005. *SSI Annual Statistical Report*. Washington: Government Printing Office.

U.S. Bureau of the Census. Various years. *Current Population Survey, Annual Social and Economic Supplement*. Washington: U.S. Department of Commerce.

———. 2006. *Current Population Survey, Annual Social and Economic Supplement*. Washington, D.C.: U.S. Department of Commerce.

U.S. Congress. House. Committee on Ways and Means. 1994a. *Report on Reforms to Address Supplemental Security Income Fraud and Abuse Involving Middlemen*. 103d Cong., 2d sess., May 12, 1994.

———. 1994b. *Supplemental Security Income Fraud Involving Middlemen*. 103d Cong., 2d sess., February 24, 1994.

———. 1996. *1996 Green Book*. H. Rept. 104–14. 104th Cong., 2d sess., 1996.

———. 1997. *Report of the Committee on the Budget, House of Representatives, to Accompany H.R. 2015*. H. Rept. 105–149. 105th Cong., 1st sess., 1997.

———. 2004. *2004 Green Book*. H. Rept. 108–6. 108th Cong., 2d sess., 2004.

Wood, Robert G., and Anu Rangarajan. 2003. "What's Happening to TANF Leavers Who Are Not Employed?" Issue brief 6. Princeton, N.J.: Mathematica Policy Research.

Zedlewski, Sheila R., Sandi Nelson, Kathryn Edin, Heather K. Koball, Kate Pomper, and Tracy Roberts. 2003. *Families Coping without Earnings or Government Cash Assistance*. Washington, D.C.: The Urban Institute.

—— Chapter 3 ——

Welfare Reform after a Decade: Integration, Exclusion, and Immigration Federalism

Michael J. Wishnie

THE ALIENAGE RESTRICTIONS of the Personal Responsibility and Work Opportunity Reconciliation Act of 1996 (PRWORA) raised one principal constitutional question: does a state's choice to deny lawful permanent residents (LPRs) the same welfare benefits it provides to citizens, where Congress has authorized but not required such discrimination, violate the equal protection clause of the Fourteenth Amendment? Ten years after enactment of PRWORA, the question remains largely unanswered by the courts. This is because, to the relief of millions of indigent immigrant families, and to the surprise of many prognosticators, few states have accepted the federal invitation to discriminate against LPRs. Even in some instances where they have, local welfare and immigrant rights advocates have chosen not to organize affirmative challenges to the alienage classifications, lest their efforts draw public attention to those other benefits that continue to be available to LPRs and thereby jeopardize continued access. As a result, the case law addressing the constitutionality of federally authorized, state-imposed alienage classifications is scant.

Most states did not accept PRWORA's invitation to discriminate against LPRs for a variety of reasons. For one, in the immediate aftermath of PRWORA's enactment, states did not want to forgo the federal matching funds available for cooperative federal-state programs such as Temporary Assistance for Needy Families (TANF) and Medicaid. State coffers were also generally flush. Additionally, local immigrant and welfare rights movements were effective in preserving many state benefits programs. Moreover, local political impulses to target immigrants for disfavored treatment (whether borne of raw nativism, economic anxiety, or something else) and to protect state budgets from perceived exploitation by noncitizens have come in the last five years to focus much more powerfully on the undocumented population than on legal immigrants such as LPRs, even though it was primarily legal immigrants who were rendered ineligible for benefits by PRWORA.[1] These exclusionary sentiments have found expression in state and local proposals and ordinances: to fine employers and landlords who hire or rent to the undocumented; to amend procurement and licensing laws to forbid firms that employ the undocumented from doing business with state or local governments, or even to retain corporate status; and to deny in-state tuition to undocumented students at public postsecondary institutions. They also surface in the discriminatory enforcement of housing codes and trespass, loitering, and public nuisance laws; in police agreements to enforce federal immigration laws; in English-only policies; and in other exclusionary measures.

This struggle has of course been joined, nationally and locally, by those who have resisted exclusionary measures and urged instead the integration of immigrants into civic life, including undocumented immigrants. These integrationist sentiments, in turn, are evident in state and local confidentiality and "don't ask, don't tell" policies. They show up in police policies barring immigration enforcement, and are evident in the preservation of in-state tuition benefits, regardless of immigration status. They appear in the insistence on state labor and employment rights for covered workers regardless of immigration status, in bilingual government service initiatives, in day-laborer shape-up sites, in the elimination of immigration status requirements in licensing laws, and in the issuance of municipal identification cards to residents who wish a government identity document.

In other words, although PRWORA appeared to usher in an era of state political debate, and eventually court battles, over LPR access to public benefits, in fact PRWORA now seems merely to have foreshadowed the exclusion-versus-integration contest, and the shift of that debate from its historic sites—Congress and the federal Executive Branch—to the states and localities. Although the constitutional guarantee of equal protection under law applies to undocumented as well as lawful noncitizens (Plyer v. Doe, 457 US 202 [1982]), and although Congress has not authorized state and local anti-immigrant discrimination other than in PRWORA, it is important to note that the legal terrain differs in some respects as to the constitutionality of these more recent state or local measures directed at undocumented immigrants.

In this chapter, I review briefly the state of play of the chief constitutional question posed by PRWORA—whether federally authorized state-imposed discrimination against LPRs violates the equal protection clause—in light of legislative developments and judicial opinions since 1996. Second, I place the state debate about immigrant access to public benefits in the broader context of the struggles over immigrant integration and exclusion at the state and local level, including some examination of the constitutional issues raised by the scope of state and local immigration regulation of the undocumented.

THE LEGAL LANDSCAPE: PRWORA AT TEN

In 1996, as it debated sweeping welfare legislation, Congress was on the verge of denying TANF and Medicaid benefits to many LPRs and other noncitizens. Such a measure threatened to cause incalculable suffering for millions of indigent families across the country, yet President Bill Clinton had indicated he was unlikely to veto the bill if enacted. In a last-ditch gambit, immigrant and welfare advocates urged their legislative allies to offer a substitute for the mandatory elimination of TANF and Medicaid benefits—a local option, in which states were authorized, but not required, to deny these benefits to permanent residents and other noncitizens. Advocates were not optimistic that, if the local options were enacted, states would forgo the federal invitation to discriminate. Nevertheless, for those seeking to preserve the access of indigent noncitizens to public benefits for which they were otherwise eligible, the local-option strategy was surely preferable to a mandatory federal bar. And the strategy succeeded. Although various provisions of PRWORA mandate that certain noncitizens be ineligible for certain federal,[2] state,[3] or joint federal-state programs such as TANF and Medicaid, the law enacted by Congress and signed by the president left to the states the decision whether most LPRs[4] would be eligible for TANF or Medicaid, as well as for purely state-supported cash or medical assistance programs.

The drama then shifted to the states. Remarkably, the race-to-the-bottom predicted by many,[5] in which one state after another would deny benefits to LPRs lest each become a magnet for indigent immigrants, has not materialized. States budgets were generally in the black in the late 1990s,[6] and efforts by local welfare and immigrant rights advocates succeeded in dissuading most states from embracing the federally authorized option to adopt state alienage classifications. The threat of litigation played a role in some state choices as well. The attorneys general of Pennsylvania and Connecticut each concluded that proposals to deny state medical or cash assistance to LPRs would be unconstitutional, for instance.[7] In Louisiana, an executive branch regulation would have denied legal immigrants access to Medicaid, but under threat of litigation, the state rescinded its rule just before implementation (Wishnie 2001, 515, note 116). The current economic crisis has prompted state and local proposals to restrict public benefits programs (see Erik Eckholm, "States Slashing Social Programs for Vulnerable," *New York Times*, April 11, 2009, A1). It may yet lead some to suggest excluding noncitizens in particular, but to date there has been no such trend.

A few states have excluded LPRs from purely state programs such as state medical assistance or from their Medicaid or TANF programs (see Wishnie 2001, 495, note 9; see also Soskin v. Reinertson, 353 F.3d 1242 [10th Cir. 2004]). Others have enacted immigrant-only eligibility requirements. On the whole, however, far more states have eschewed the federal option to deny benefits to LPRs than have accepted it. Instead, most continue to offer TANF and Medicaid to LPRs on the same terms as to citizens, and states with state benefits programs generally offer those benefits to LPRs as well.[8]

The equal protection problem posed by PRWORA was not wholly avoided, however. The problem arises from two Supreme

Court cases, each unanimous, and decided only five years apart. In Graham v. Richardson, 403 US 365 (1971), the Court invalidated Arizona and Pennsylvania welfare laws that discriminated between citizens and LPRs as violative of equal protection. Observing that LPRs no less than citizens are subject to military conscription and obligated to pay taxes, the Court reasoned that state "classifications based on alienage, like those based on nationality or race, are inherently suspect and subject to close judicial scrutiny. Aliens as a class are a prime example of a 'discrete and insular' minority for whom such heightened judicial solicitude is appropriate" (371–72, notes and citations omitted). Applying strict scrutiny to the state welfare classifications, the Court held the laws not narrowly tailored to advance a compelling government interest and struck them down. In Toll v. Moreno, 458 US 1, 20–21 (1982), Justice Blackmun, the author of the Court's opinion in Graham, elaborated on the Court's reasoning: "Disparate treatment accorded a class of 'similarly circumstanced' persons who historically have been disabled by the prejudice of the majority led the Court to conclude that alienage classifications 'in themselves supply a reason to infer antipathy' . . . and therefore demand close judicial scrutiny."

Yet, five years later, the Supreme Court unanimously upheld a federal alienage classification in the Medicare program that distinguished between citizens and LPRs. In this second case, Mathews v. Diaz, 462 US 67 (1976), the Court concluded that the Medicare rule implicated foreign affairs and the federal immigration power, and therefore triggered judicial doctrines of deference to Congress and the Executive Branch. The Court did not formally immunize federal alienage classifications from all judicial scrutiny; rather, it explained that it would uphold a federal alienage classification in the face of an equal protection challenge unless the classification was "wholly irrational" (83). The Mathews opinion addressed Graham, affirming that Graham remained the law as to state discrimination against LPRs. But Mathews specifically distinguished "the Fourteenth Amendment's limitation on state powers" from "the constitutional provisions applicable to the federal power over immigration and naturalization" (86–87).

Together, the Graham and Mathews opinions reflected the three doctrinal traditions that trace through more than a century of jurisprudence on immigration and state authority. These traditions—the plenary power doctrine (judicial deference to immigration law and policymaking as an aspect of foreign affairs and diplomacy), equal protection doctrines (close scrutiny of state but not federal discrimination against noncitizens), and federalism doctrines (federal preemption of state laws in conflict with federal policies)—are all manifest in the decisions.

Until PRWORA, these twin decisions established the constitutional framework for evaluating federal and state discrimination between LPRs and citizens. Courts generally applied strict scrutiny to state alienage classifications and invalidated them, but subjected similar federal classifications only to rationality review and upheld them.[9] The constitutional question posed by PRWORA, then, was one left open by Graham, Mathews, and their progeny: what level of equal protection scrutiny would courts apply to federally authorized, state-imposed alienage classifications? Would courts treat post-PRWORA state denials of TANF, Medicaid, or state cash or medical assistance as more like the state laws at issue in Graham—state alienage classifications that are presumptively invalid? Or would they treat them more like the federal alienage classifications at issue in Mathews that are presumptively valid?

I have argued that the power to regulate immigration is an exclusively federal power that Congress may not, by statute, devolve to the states. This argument derives from a close examination of the textual and extraconstitutional sources of the unenumerated immigration power, the history of those clauses, and two centuries of Supreme Court jurisprudence (Wishnie 2001). I have concluded that PRWORA's authorization of state alienage classifications cannot secure for states the judicial deference applied in Mathews, which Congress plainly sought to accomplish in PRWORA. Rather, state alienage classifications remain subject to heightened judicial scrutiny even after PRWORA's enactment.[10] Although structural in nature, sounding in themes of preemption and state-federal relations, my argument was motivated by a commitment to antisubordination and equality principles, and a conviction that courts should not interpret PRWORA as authorization for the states to do what the Fourteenth Amendment had previously been held to forbid.

This constitutional question remains largely unresolved in the courts, however. Few states have denied benefits to LPRs, and of those that have, only some have been challenged. Given differences in local program design and the overall paucity of judicial decisions, it is too early to discern particular principles. The highest courts in two states, New York and Maryland, have concluded that the denial of state benefits to LPRs violates the equal protection clause, per Graham, notwithstanding PRWORA's express authorization for such discrimination.[11] The Supreme Judicial Court of Massachusetts concluded in Doe v. Commissioner of Transitional Assistance, 773 N.E.2d 404 (Mass. 2002), that imposition of a six-month residency requirement in an immigrant-only state-substitute cash assistance program does not violate equal protection, because there is no discrimination between LPRs and citizens.[12] One U.S. Court of Appeals has considered the issue, concluding in a 2–1 decision that Colorado's denial of Medicaid to LPRs did not violate the equal protection clause, in light of PRWORA's authorization.[13]

In other words, of three high state courts and one U.S. court of appeals, two upheld post-PRWORA state choices to deny some benefits to some LPRs, and two invalidated similar choices. Nor is there a chronological trend. The first, Aliessa v. Novello, 96 N.Y.2d 418 (N.Y. 2001), and last, Ehrlich v. Perez, 908 A.2d 1220 (Md. 2006), invalidated the state classifications. The second, Doe v. Commissioner of Transitional Assistance, 773 N.E.2d 404 (Mass. 2002), and third, Soskin v. Reinertson, 353 F.3d 1242 (10th Cir. 2004), upheld them.[14] Nor is it evident that programmatic distinctions can explain the different outcomes. Aliessa concerned a state medical assistance program. Doe and Ehrlich involved an immigrant-only state substitute program to replace benefits for some LPRs denied TANF or Medicaid due to mandatory PRWORA provisions. Soskin addressed a cooperative federal-state program, Medicaid.

On the whole, the case law is underdeveloped and the significant constitutional question largely unaddressed. For instance, a number of these cases discuss the separate constitutional command of uniformity in naturalization laws.[15] Yet the federal power to regulate immigration does not derive solely from the naturalization clause; the Supreme Court has located this power also in the foreign affairs and foreign commerce clauses, as well as in extra-constitutional notions of sovereignty. Only Soskin grapples even briefly with the naturalization clause, let alone these other sources (353 F.3d, 1256–57; compare Ehrlich, 908 A.2d, 1244, note 22).[16]

THE BROADER CONTEXT: INTEGRATION, EXCLUSION, AND THE STATE-LOCAL DEBATE

One of the most significant population trends of recent years is the extraordinary dispersion of new immigrants throughout the United States. The establishment of immigrant communities far beyond the traditional receiving states, the growth of the undocumented population, and the failure of Congress to modernize our immigration laws together have challenged state and local officials to adapt police, fire, education, licensing, and many other government functions to the realities of these new immigrant communities. The consequence has been an explosion of state and local regulations directed at immigrants. In this tumultuous debate, voices favoring integration of new immigrants into the fabric of civic life, regardless of the newcomers' immigration status, have frequently clashed with those favoring exclusion and more rigorous enforcement of the present laws. The localized debate, integration versus exclusion, itself is older than the country, dating at least to the Acadian refugee crisis of the 1750s. Yet, against this backdrop, it is even more striking that states have generally not accepted PRWORA's invitation to deny benefits to LPRs, nor pressed the looming constitutional issue.

Exclusionary state and local policies or proposals are numerous, addressing education, employment, licensing, policing, and other issues. A handful of local jurisdictions have adopted sanctions on employers or landlords for hiring or renting to undocumented immigrants, and many others have considered such ordinances. Some of the most notorious, such as those adopted in Hazelton, Pennsylvania, have been preliminarily enjoined in litigation,[17] as have the implementation of several others. The courts have generally invalidated these employer and landlord sanctions laws,[18] hundreds of which have been debated across the country (see National Conference of State Legislatures 2006). At least one federal court has also rejected an attempted federal criminal prosecution of a landlord for renting to undocumented tenants.[19] The principal exception to the trend of judicial invalidation of employer and landlord sanction laws is the recent decision in Chicanos Por La Causa, Inc. v. Napolitano, in which the Ninth Circuit rejected a facial challenge to an Arizona statute providing for the suspension or revocation of the business license of any employer who hired an undocumented immigrant.[20] The Arizona statute, the court concluded, fit within the narrow savings clause that exempts licensing laws from a federal provision otherwise preempting state employer sanctions measures.

Second, approximately seventy-seven cities, counties, or states have executed Memoranda of Understanding (MOU) with the U.S. Bureau of Immigration and Customs Enforcement (ICE) pursuant to INA 287(g), in which state or local police are deputized as immigration agents, authorized to exercise the immigration powers of ICE agents—after undergoing training at the state's expense (U.S. Immigration and Customs Enforcement 2009). Massachusetts partially rescinded its MOU in 2007 (see Katie Zezima, "Massachusetts Rescinds Deal on Policing Immigration," *New York Times*, January 12, 2007, A17). According to ICE, many additional MOU applications are pending (U.S. Congress 2009; see also Kareen Fahim, "Should Immigration Be a Police Issue?" *New York Times*, April 29, 2007).

Third, local police in many jurisdictions have agreed to make immigration arrests based on administrative warrants entered into the FBI's chief criminal history database, the National Crime Information Center (NCIC), which police routinely check on stopping a motorist or pedestrian in the course of ordinary policing duties (see Gladstein et al. 2005). Others have expanded interrogation of criminal detainees regarding their immigration status.[21]

Fourth, a number of local authorities have engaged in discriminatory enforcement of housing codes and public nuisance, loitering, and trespass laws, often but not always in connection with a local controversy about day-laborer shape-up sites.[22]

Finally, some states have sought more actively to participate in joint federal-local immigration enforcement operations. For instance, in New York, North Carolina, and elsewhere, some state or local probation and parole departments have begun to share information with ICE and even to participate in sting operations in which ICE arrests probationers upon their mandatory visits (see, for example, "Immigration Officers Turn to Probation Officers for Help," *Asheville Citizen-Times*, May 21, 2007; "U.S. Moves to Deport 45 Sex Offenders," *New York Times*, November 30, 2006, B4). Another example of widening state or local participation involves police participation in ICE's Operation Return to Sender, a program targeting 575,000 persons subject to a deportation, exclusion, or removal order who remain in the country (U.S. Department of Homeland Security 2007).

On the other hand, many state and local authorities have responded to the establishment of new immigrant communities, growth of the undocumented population, and federal failure to update our immigration laws with local integrationist policies. Many jurisdictions have adopted confidentiality policies that direct public employees not to inquire about immigration status and, if such information is obtained, not to communicate such information with ICE, despite a federal statute that arguably forbids such laws.[23] Some municipalities have implemented police general orders barring civil immigration enforcement,[24] crafted programs to accommodate day laborers (Vesna Jaksic, "Stamford Minister Reaches Out to Assist Day-Laborers," *Stamford Advocate*, August 2, 2005), and passed laws prohibiting participation in federal employment eligibility verification systems.[25] Others have reformed municipal licensing laws to repeal outdated alienage restrictions.[26] In one of the most widespread developments, countless jurisdictions now provide government service materials in multiple languages[27] and interpreters in local administrative hearings.[28] Some have formalized these initiatives in local language access ordinances.[29] And in one innovative local measure, the city of New Haven has begun issuing an Elm City Resident Card, a form of municipal identification, to any city resident, without regard to immigration status (Jennifer Medina, "New Haven Approves Program to Issue Illegal Immigrant IDs," June 5, B6).[30]

At the state level, many labor and employment agencies have interpreted their laws as preserving workplace protections for all covered workers regardless of immigration status, despite arguably contrary Supreme Court authority.[31] Numerous states now offer in-state tuition rates to students at public postsecondary institutions, regardless of the immigration status of the students and a federal statute that some contend forbids such laws.[32]

I do not attempt to analyze the myriad legal issues raised by this explosion of state and local activity addressed to immigration and immigrants, but note that several aspects of the statutes and case law addressing such measures differ from the equal protection framework for assessing state welfare discrimination against LPRs.

First, there is no disputing that PRWORA facially authorizes states to deny TANF, Medicaid, and state benefits to many LPRs. In contrast, statutory preemption arguments have been and will be raised against many state and local measures, both exclusionary and integrationist. Courts have adjudicated lawsuits contending that federal statutes preempt integrationist measures, such as local confidentiality rules,[33] in-state tuition statutes,[34] and state employment laws allowing back pay to undocumented workers.[35] The courts have also begun to rule in lawsuits challenging exclusionary programs, such as local employer sanctions provisions[36] and police enforcement of immigration laws (Wishnie 2004). The availability of statutory preemption arguments in many of these disputes matters a great deal. In general, courts are more reluctant to invalidate government action on constitutional grounds than on the basis of a statute. Legislatures can amend statutes more readily than a constitution, after all, and judges recognize that constitutional rulings are more likely to endure. To the extent that judges are dubious about the lawfulness of a particular local measure, whether integrationist or exclusionary, the possibility of invalidating it on a nonconstitutional basis may invite more judicial injunctions than in the welfare arena, where the principle arguments involve only constitutional equal protection arguments.

Second, these state and local measures generally target the undocumented, rather than LPRs. The Supreme Court has not extended its Graham holding, that state alienage classifications are subject to heightened scrutiny, beyond LPRs.[37] Further, in De Canas v. Bica, 424 US 351 (1976), the Court recognized that states have a degree of leeway in regulating the undocumented population, in the course of exercising a state's traditional police powers. Thus federal equal protection challenges to state or local alienage discrimination aimed at persons other than LPRs may not be as successful as Graham and its progeny. On the other hand, where a state or local alienage classification is merely a proxy for discrimination based on race, ethnicity, or national origin, courts are likely to invalidate the measure. As Plyer v. Doe demonstrates, even undocumented immigrants are protected from invidious local discrimination by the equal protection clause. Moreover, a number of state constitutional provisions afford greater rights against discrimination than the federal equal protection clause (see, for example, Kerrigan v. Commissioner of Public Health, 957 A.2d 407 [Conn. 2008]). Some state or local anti-immigrant measures that do not violate the U.S. Constitution, for instance, because they target the undocumented rather than LPRs, might nevertheless run afoul of more robust state constitutional provisions.

Third, courts may come to recognize a material distinction between state or local immigration policymaking and immigration enforcement. Even De Canas acknowledged that a state or local effort to engage in the "regulation of immigration" would be necessarily preempted by the "unquestionably exclusive" federal immigration power (424 US, 354–55). Some exclusionary measures, such as the Hazelton-type ordinances imposing employer and landlord sanctions, appear expressly designed to regulate entrance and abode—the classic domain of immigration law—within the local jurisdiction. If so, they are more likely to be struck down as constitutionally preempted. This was the sort of analysis a U.S. District Court used in Villas at Parkside Partners v. City of Farmers Branch, 577 F.Supp. 2d 858 (N.D. Tex. 2008), to invalidate the exclusionary ordinance adopted in Farmers Branch, Texas.

In short, subfederal choices regarding noncitizen access to welfare programs today arise in a landscape of widespread state and local policymaking addressed to new immigrant communities. Effective local governance requires attention to the needs and interests of new immigrants, in welfare programs no less than police, education, fire, licensing, and other government services. The legal issues raised by the denial of welfare benefits to lawful permanent residents differ from those presented by, for instance, local penalties on landlords that rent to, or businesses that employ, undocumented immigrants.

CONCLUSION

PRWORA raises a momentous constitutional question, one that implicates plenary power, federalism, and equal protection norms. But the dog has not barked. Few courts have yet addressed whether federally authorized, state-imposed discrimination against LPRs is constitutionally permissible.

At the same time, state and local activity concerning immigrants has been extraordinary. Much of the policymaking has been addressed to issues other than welfare benefits and to populations other than LPRs. Both exclusionary and integrationist local measures have been challenged in court, often on preemption and equal protection grounds familiar from the immigrant welfare debate. It is reasonable to suggest that much of this activity is not in fact motivated by structural concerns about the proper role of the federal government and subfederal jurisdictions in our constitutional architecture. Rather, it is driven by the far older conflict between integrationist and exclusionary sentiments.

Our nation is not likely ever to resolve this conflict. In the absence of a federal immigration system designed for the realities of human migration in the twenty-first century, however, state and local officials will continue to implement statutes and policies addressing the large numbers of noncitizens resident in their communities. The friction generated by these local debates may eventually help spur Congress to enact comprehensive immigration reform. This said, more than ten years after enactment of PRWORA, the judiciary has only just begun to evaluate the equal protection, plenary power, and preemption questions raised by state and local measures regulating immigrants, in welfare and innumerable other contexts.

The author thanks Margot Mendelson and Michael Tan for able research assistance.

NOTES

1. Undocumented immigrants were already ineligible for nearly all federal, state, and federal-state benefits programs, and PRWORA did not significantly alter their continued eligibility for the small number of programs open to them. It did, however, effect dramatic changes in the eligibility of LPRs and other lawful noncitizens for benefits, especially food stamps, Supplemental Security Income (SSI), TANF, and Medicaid.
2. Most important, PRWORA enacted numerous restrictions on noncitizen eligibility for food stamps and Supplemental Security Income. These restrictions have been upheld by the courts without exception. See, for example, City of Chicago v. Shalala, 189 F.3d 598 (7th Cir. 1999); Rodriguez v. United States, 169 F.3d 1342 (11th Cir. 1999); Lewis v. Thompson, 252 F.3d 567 (2d Cir. 2001); Aleman v. Glickman, 217 F.3d 1191 (9th Cir. 2000).
3. See 8 USC. § 1621(a), (d).
4. PRWORA provides that LPRs who enter the United States on or after PRWORA's enactment, even though qualified aliens, are ineligible for TANF or Medicaid for five years (8 USC § 1613(a)). As Hiroshi Motomura has pointed out, the denial of benefits for the five years most LPRs must wait to pursue naturalization is especially punitive to citizens-in-waiting and directly contrary to the notion that U.S. immigration policies should support the integration of at least those on a path to citizenship (2006).
5. "It seems likely that upon the next economic downturn or wave of nativism, more states will seek to accept the broad federal invitation to enact anti-immigrant restrictions in local benefits programs" (Wishnie 2001, 518).
6. In 2000, for instance, all fifty states reported a budget surplus, including thirty-six with a surplus in excess of 5 percent of spending (National Association of State Budget Officers 2000).
7. Official Opinion No. 96-1, Op. Att'y Gen. of Pa. (Dec. 9, 1996) (concluding Pennsylvania denial of cash and medical assistance to legal immigrants is unlawful); Opinion No. 2004-002, Off. of Att'y Gen. of Conn. (Feb. 24, 2004) (same as to Connecticut denial of cash and medical benefits).
8. In addition to the state option, Congress barred many lawful immigrants from eligibility for two major federal programs, food stamps and SSI. 8 USC § 1611(a). Congress's partial restoration of food stamps and SSI eligibility for some legal immigrants since 1996 has ameliorated but not eliminated these restrictions.

9. Compare Bernal v. Fainter, 467 US 216 (1984) (invalidating state prohibition on LPR serving as notary public); Nyquist v. Mauclet, 432 US 1 (1977) (invalidating state prohibition on student financial aid to LPR); Examining Bd. v. Flores de Otero, 426 US 572 (1976) (invalidating state prohibition on civil engineering license for LPR); In re Griffiths, 413 US 717 (1973) (invalidating state prohibition on admission of LPR to bar); Sugarman v. Dougall, 413 US 634 (1973) (invalidating state prohibition on civil service employment for LPR) with Mathews v. Diaz, 426 US 67 (1976) (upholding federal Medicare restriction for LPRs); City of Chicago v. Shalala, 189 F.3d 598 (7th Cir. 1999) (upholding federal restriction on LPR access to benefits); Rodriguez v. United States, 169 F.3d 1342 (11th Cir. 1999) (same). The Supreme Court has recognized only one exception to the rule that states may not discriminate against LPRs, permitting such classifications in certain categories of public employment. Cabell v. Chavez-Salido, 454 US 432 (1982) (deputy probation officers); Ambach v. Norwick, 441 US 68 (1979) (public school teachers); Foley v. Connelie, 435 US 291 (1978) (state troopers).
10. 8 USC § 1601; committee reports.
11. See Aliessa v. Novello, 96 N.Y.2d 418 (N.Y. 2001) (invalidating denial of state medical benefits to LPRs and other legal immigrants); Ehrlich v. Perez, 908 A.2d 1220 (Md. 2006) (invalidating denial of state-substitute medical benefits to LPRs other than children and pregnant women); see also Kurti v. Maricopa County, 33 P. 3d 499 (Ariz. App. 2001) (invalidating denial of certain state and county emergency medical benefits to LPRs); Teytelman v. Wing, 773 N.Y.S. 2d 801 (N.Y. Sup. Ct., 2003) (invalidating denial of state food assistance benefits to some legal immigrants).
12. See also Avila v. Biedess, 78 P.3d 280 (Ariz. App. 2003) (depublished) (upholding denial of state medical benefits to LPRs, where state eligibility criteria paralleled federal alienage classifications); Khrapunskiy v. Doar, 12 N.Y. 3d 478 (N.Y. 2009) (holding aged, blind, or disabled legal immigrants not entitled to state benefits to achieve "additional state payment" level, as substitute for SSI benefits for which they were ineligible).
13. Soskin v. Reinertson, 353 F.3d 1242 (10th Cir. 2004) (upholding Colorado denial of Medicaid benefits to LPRs); compare at 1265–76 (Henry, J., dissenting) (arguing that notwithstanding PRWORA, state choice to deny benefits should be subject to strict scrutiny per Graham and invalidated); Ehrlich, 908 A.2d at 1237 note 12 (rejecting Soskin analysis).

14. There is one noticeable trend: each opinion is longer than its predecessors.
15. US Const. Art. I, § 8 cl. 4. See, for example, Aliessa v. Novello, 96 N.Y.2d at 432–33 (noting that divergent state welfare laws regarding immigrants may violate uniformity mandate of Naturalization Clause); Graham v. Richardson, 403 U.S. at 382 (same); see also Avila v. Biedess, 78 P.3d at 285–88 (depublished) (holding that state adoption of uniform federal alienage classification, such as five-year ineligibility for LPRs arriving after date of PRWORA enactment, satisfies uniformity requirement); Sudomir v. McMahon, 767 F.2d 1456 (9th Cir. 1985) (state law that adopts uniform federal alienage classification subject only to rational basis review).
16. Moreover, the Supreme Court has interpreted the constitutional requirement of uniformity in bankruptcy and tax laws as satisfied by either geographic uniformity or a uniform federal system for incorporation of divergent state laws, see Hanover National Bank v. Moyses, 186 US 181 (1902) (rejecting uniformity challenge to federal bankruptcy statute); Knowlton v. Moore, 178 US 41 (1900) (tax law must be uniform across geographic jurisdictions). With the exception of brief treatment in Soskin, the post-PRWORA welfare opinions invalidating state welfare rules have not analyzed why a checkerboard pattern of state alienage classifications violates the uniform rule of naturalization, nor why a state choice to conform state welfare laws to federal classifications (where other states do not so conform) does satisfy uniformity requirements.
17. Lozano v. City of Hazelton, 496 F.Supp.2d 277 (M.D. Pa. 2007) (permanently enjoining prohibition on employment of unauthorized immigrants as preempted and prohibition on landlord-tenant arrangements involving undocumented immigrants as violative of due process and 42 U.S.C. § 1981), appeal filed, No. 07-3531 (3d Cir. Aug. 23, 2007).
18. Villas at Parkside Partners v. City of Farmers Branch, 577 F.Supp.2d 858 (N.D. Tex. 2008) (granting permanent injunction); Verified Complaint, Riverside Coalition of Business Persons and Landlords v. Township of Riverside, No. (N.J. Super. Ct. Oct. 18, 2006); Garrett v. City of Escondido, 465 F.Supp.2d 1043 (S.D. Ca. 2006) (granting TRO); Reynolds v. City of Valley Park, No. 06-CC-3802 (Mo. Cir. Ct. Sept. 27, 2006) (second TRO issued Sept. 27, 2006), vacated as moot, 254 S.W.2d 264 (Mo. App. E.D. 2008); Robert Stewart, Inc. v. Cherokee County, No. 07-CV-0015 (N.D. Ga. Jan. 4, 2007) (granting TRO); but see Gray v. City of Valley Park, Mo., 567 F.3d 976 (8th Cir. 2009) (dismissing challenge to local employer and landlord

sanctions measure). The challenges typically raise numerous claims, including discrimination in violation of the equal protection clause, 42 USC § 1981, the Fair Housing Act, and state law, violations of state home rule laws, and others.

19. Delrio-Mocci v. Connolly Properties, No. 2:08-cv-02753-WJM-MP (D. N.J. filed Apr. 9, 2009).

20. See Chicanos Por La Causa, Inc. v. Napolitano, 544 F.3d 976 (9th Cir. 2008) (dismissing challenge by business and civil rights organizations to state law suspending or revoking license to do business for employers who hire unauthorized immigrants). In addition, the governor of Arizona issued an executive order directing that under the state's procurement laws, public contractors found knowingly to have employed unauthorized workers may not do business with the state. Exec. Order No. 2005-30, 11 Ariz. Admin. Reg. 4320 (Oct. 28, 2005).

21. See, for example, Roe I v. Prince William County, 522 F.Supp.2d 799 (E.D.Va. 2007) (dismissing for lack of standing challenge to county resolution authorizing police officers to question detainees regarding immigration status).

22. Doe v. Village of Mamaroneck, 462 F.Supp. 2d 520, (S.D.N.Y. 2006) (finding that police harassment campaign designed to remove day laborers from town violated equal protection); Complaint, El Comite de Trabajadores por el Progreso y Bienestar Social v. Freehold Borough, No. 3:03-cv-06180 (D.N.J. Dec. 30, 2003) (class action accusing borough of denying day laborers' rights to solicit employment and subjecting them to discriminatory law and code enforcement); New Hampshire v. Barros-Batistele, No. 05-CR-1474 (N.H. Dist. Ct. Aug. 12, 2005) (holding that criminal trespassing charges against undocumented residents were unconstitutional attempts to regulate immigration); Comite de Jornaleros v. City of Redondo Beach, No. 2:04-cv-09396 (C.D. Cal. Apr. 27, 2006) (barring enforcement of anti-solicitation ordinance); Complaint, Barrera v. Boughton, No. 3:07-cv-01436 (D.Conn. filed Sept. 26, 2007) (civil rights suit challenging local police harassment of day-laborers and ICE participation in campaign); Bill Turque, Herndon Anti-Solicitation Law Challenged, Wash. Post, Jan. 18, 2007, at B1 (reporting state court challenge to anti-solicitation ordinance).

23. See, for example, Office of the Governor of Maine, Exec. Order No. 13 FY 04/05 (Apr. 9, 2004, rev'd Feb. 28, 2005); New York City, NY, Exec. Order No. 41 (Sept. 17, 2003), available at http://www.nyc.gov/html/imm/downloads/pdf/exe_order_41.pdf (amending Executive Order 34; accessed September 11, 2009); Seattle, WA,

Mun. Code § 4.18.015 (2006); Minneapolis, MN, Mun. Code § 19.10-19.50 (2006); Chicago, IL, Exec. Order 2-173-020 (Mar. 2006); Hartford, CT, "Ordinance concerning the City of Hartford's policy of providence of City services as it relates to residents' immigration status" (Aug. 2008). These ordinances are generally tailored to a Second Circuit decision stating that PRWORA and IIRIRA provisions barring certain state or local "anti-snitch" policies may violate the Tenth Amendment if applied to generalized confidentiality policies. City of New York v. United States, 179 F.3d 29 (2d Cir. 1999).

24. Houston, TX, Police Dept. Gen. Order No. 500-5 (June 1992); Hartford, CT (Aug. 2008); New Haven, CT, Police Gen. Order 06-2 (Dec. 14, 2006); Los Angeles, CA, Special Order 40 (Nov. 1979); Major Cities Chiefs, MCC Immigration Committee Recommendations for Enforcement of Immigration Laws by Local Police Agencies (June 2006) (highlighting concerns about state and local law enforcement agencies enforcing federal immigration law); Int'l Assoc. of Chiefs of Police, Enforcing Immigration Law: The Role of State, Tribal and Local Law Enforcement (Dec. 1, 2004) (same).

25. In August 2007, the Illinois legislature amended the Illinois Right to Privacy Act in order to prohibit employers from using employment eligibility verification until the system met specific standards for accuracy and speed, Ill. Public Act 95-138. The law was subsequently invalidated in part on the grounds that it violated the Supremacy Clause. United States v. Illinois, No. 07-3261 (C.D. Ill. Mar. 12, 2009) ("Illinois cannot dictate to Congress the standards that federal programs must meet. This [act] clearly frustrates the Congressional purpose of making the Federal Program available to all employers.")

26. See Intro. 491A, N.Y. City Council, enacted July 11, 2005 (repealing requirement that applicant for street vendor license demonstrate citizenship or work authorization).

27. See, for example, Cal. Gov. Code §§ 7290–99 (requiring state agencies to distribute non-English language written materials through its local offices or facilities that serve substantial number of non-English speaking persons); Fla. Stat. Ch. § 443.151 (requiring that educational and instructional materials produced by state agencies to describe their services and benefits be translated); Md. Code Ann. §§10-1101–10-1104 (mandating that state agencies provide equal access to public services for individuals with limited English proficiency and that certain "vital documents" to be translated into any language spoken by LEP group that constitutes 3 percent of overall population within geographic service area); Mass. Gen. Laws ch.

151A § 62A. (state unemployment compensation law providing that all notices and materials be available in English, Spanish, Chinese, Haitian Creole, Italian, Portuguese, Vietnamese, Laotian, Khmer, Russian, and any other language that is primary language of at least 10,000 or .5 percent of all residents of commonwealth); N.J. Stat. Ann. § 31:9A-7.2 (addressing bilingual services for Spanish-speaking claimants); Tex. Lab. Code § 301.064 (addressing bilingual services for Spanish-speaking claimants).

28. See, for example, Ark. Code Ann. § 25-15-101; D.C. Code Ann. § 31-2702; Ind. Code § 4-21.5-3-16 Minn. Stat. § 15.441; N.Y. Unemp. Law Tit. 12, Ch. 7 § 461.4; Or. Rev. Stat. § 45.275; Tex. Lab. Code § 301.064; Wash. RCW 2.43.030.

29. See, for example, San Francisco, Cal., Admin. Code §§ 89.1-89.14 (requiring city departments to offer bilingual services and materials if substantial or concentrated portion of public utilizing their services does not speak English effectively); N.Y. Admin. Code §§ 8-1001-1010 (affording access to all city services to LEP individuals); Oakland, Cal., Mun. Code § 2.30.030 (same).

30. The city of San Francisco has also enacted a municipal ID program (see Wyatt Buchanan, "S.F. Supervisors Approve ID Card for Residents," *San Francisco Chronicle*, November 14, 2007). Other jurisdictions are contemplating similar measures (see, for example, Jocelyn Wiener, "Coalition Seeks Oakland ID Card," *East Bay Express*, September 17, 2008).

31. See Hoffman Plastic Compounds, Inc. v. NLRB, 535 US 137 (2002) (holding undocumented worker who tendered false documents and who was illegally fired for union organizing activity not eligible for back pay under National Labor Relations Act); but see Balbuena v. IDR Realty LLC, 812 N.Y.S.2d 416 (N.Y. 2006) (undocumented worker injured in construction accident eligible for back pay under state Scaffolding Law, notwithstanding employer argument that remedy preempted by Hoffman Plastic); Madeira v. Affordable Housing Foundation, Inc., 469 F.3d 219 (2d Cir. 2006) (same, after independently analyzing federal preemption question).

32. National Immigration Law Center 2009 (noting that since 2001, ten states have passed in-state tuition laws, namely, Texas, California, Utah, Washington, New York, Oklahoma, Illinois, Kansas, New Mexico, and Nebraska).

33. See 8 USC § 1644; City of New York v. United States, 179 F.3d 29 (2d Cir. 1999) (holding New York City anti-snitch policy preempted by § 1644).

34. Day v. Bond, 500 F.3d 1127 (10th Cir. 2007) (dismissing challenge

to in-state tuition law for lack of standing); Martinez v. Regents of University of California, 83 Cal. Rptr. 3d 518 (Cal. App. Dist. 3 2008) (reversing trial court dismissal of challenge to California in-state tuition provision), petition for review granted, 87 Cal. Rptr. 3d 198 (CA 2008).

35. See 8 USC § 1324a(h)(2) (preempting state or local civil sanction for employment of unauthorized immigrant); Balbuena v. IDR Realty LLC, 812 N.Y.S.2d 416 (NY 2006) (rejecting employer argument that § 1324a(h)(2) preempts award of back pay under state law to undocumented worker injured on construction site).

36. Villas at Parkside Partners v. City of Farmers Branch, 577 F.Supp.2d 858 (N.D. Tex. 2008) (granting permanent injunction); Lozano v. City of Hazelton, 496 F.Supp.2d 277 (M.D.Pa. 2007) (permanently enjoining prohibition on employment of unauthorized immigrants as preempted and prohibition on landlord-tenant arrangements involving undocumented immigrants as violative of due process and 42 U.S.C. § 1981), notice of appeal pending.; but see Chicanos Por La Causa, Inc. v. Napolitano, 544 F.3d 976 (9th Cir. 2008) (dismissing challenge by business and civil rights organizations to state law suspending or revoking license to do business for employers who hire unauthorized immigrants).

37. But see Aliessa v. Novello, 96 N.Y.2d 418 (N.Y. 2001) (holding New York may not deny state benefits to various categories of legal immigrants, not limited to LPRs, consistent with equal protection principles). In Toll v. Moreno, 458 US 1 (1982), the Court invalidated a state law denying financial aid to students in G-4 visa status, but it did so on preemption rather than equal protection grounds. See also Plyler v. Doe, 457 US 202 (1982) (invalidating denial of public education to undocumented children as failing intermediate scrutiny).

REFERENCES

Gladstein, Hannah, Annie Lai, Jennifer Wagner, and Michael Wishnie. 2005. "Blurring the Lines: A Profile of State and Local Police Enforcement of Immigration Law Using the National Crime Information Center Database, 2002–2004." Washington, D.C.: Migration Policy Institute. Available at: http://www.migrationpolicy.org/pubs/MPI_report_Blurring_the_Lines_120805.pdf (accessed September 11, 2009).

Motomura, Hiroshi. 2006. *Americans in Waiting: The Lost Story of Immigration and Citizenship in the United States.* New York: Oxford University Press.

National Association of State Budget Officers. 2000. *The Fiscal Survey of States: December 2000.* Washington, D.C.: National Association of State Budget Officers.

National Conference of State Legislatures. 2006. *2006 State Legislation Related to Immigration: Enacted and Vetoed.* Washington, D.C.: National Conference of State Legislatures.

National Immigration Law Center. 2009. *Basic Facts About In-State Tuition for Undocumented Immigrant Students.* Los Angeles: National Immigration Law Center. Available at: http://www.nilc.org/immlawpolicy/DREAM/instate-tuition-basicfacts-2009-02-23.pdf (accessed September 11, 2009).

U.S. Congress. House. Homeland Security Committee. 2009. Statement of Richard Stana, Director of Homeland Security Issues, Government Accountability Office. 111th Cong., 1st sess. March 4, 2009.

U.S. Immigration and Customs Enforcement. 2009. "Secretary Napolitano Announces New Agreement for State and Local Immigration Enforcement Partnerships and Adds Eleven New Agreements." Washington: U.S. Department of Homeland Security. Available at: http://www.dhs.gov/ynews/releases/pr_1247246453625.shtm (accessed July 10, 2009).

U.S. Department of Homeland Security, Office of Inspector General. 2007. "An Assessment of United States Immigration and Customs Enforcement's Fugitive Operations Teams." OIG-07-34. Washington: U.S. Government Printing Office.

Wishnie, Michael J. 2001. "Laboratories of Bigotry? Devolution of the Immigration Power, Equal Protection, and Federalism." *NYU Law Review* 76(2): 493.

———. 2004. "State and Local Police Enforcement of Immigration Laws." *University of Pennsylvania Journal of Constitutional Law* 6(6): 1084–115.

Part II

Trends in Benefit Use and Reform's Impacts

—— Chapter 4 ——

Immigrant Welfare Receipt: Implications for Immigrant Settlement and Integration

Jennifer Van Hook and Frank D. Bean

Evidence cannot resolve the underlying conflict between those who believe more should be done to help the working poor and their children and those who resent subsidizing illegitimacy, family desertion, and consumption of leisure among able-bodied adults.
—Gary Burtless, "The Economist's Lament"

THE RECEPTION that newcomers face in host societies shapes the nature and degree of immigrant incorporation (Bloemraad 2006; Portes and Rumbaut 2001). Recent research, for example, has found that more favorable and welcoming social contexts increase the probability of naturalization (Van Hook, Brown, and Bean 2006). Such findings imply that providing assistance to immigrants, in whatever form, might foster immigrant economic integration, especially among the disproportionately large number of immigrants with scant education who have come to the United States over the past three decades, primarily to work. Of course, the United States has not traditionally provided settlement assistance to immigrants, except refugees. But this reasoning and these findings suggest that even forms of backdoor help, such as cash and noncash assistance, may provide bridge support to immigrants that facilitates their transition from arrival to subsequent labor market attachment, from episodes of joblessness to periods of gainful employment. However, many observers and policy analysts clearly think otherwise, tending to view immigrant welfare receipt in negative rather than positive terms. They assume it reflects not only lack of initiative and the development of dependency, but also the failure of the U.S. immigrant admission system to prevent public charges from entering the country (Borjas 2001; Brimelow 1995).

Thus the social science literature contains two views about the consequences of receiving welfare assistance, and in particular about its implications for immigrants' economic incorporation. On the one hand, some say it impedes immigrant economic incorporation and leads to the types of outcomes Gary Burtless noted in 1990. This line of argument is a variation on the theme that receiving support from the government discourages hard work and personal responsibility (Murray 1984). These observers see relatively higher levels of welfare receipt among recently arrived immigrants as evidence that newcomers disposed to welfare use are increasingly drawn to the United States (Borjas 1990). They also see apparently rising levels of welfare use with time in the United States as proof that generous public assistance programs create incentives that discourage work and promote dependency (Borjas and Hilton 1996). Such arguments were used to justify the sweeping 1996 changes in welfare policy that limited immigrants' eligibility for public assistance (Edwards 2001).

On the other hand, sociological theories suggest that successful immigrant integration most likely occurs in welcoming and supportive environments (Van Hook, Brown, and Bean 2006). Recent accounts of the poor further suggest that an infusion of resources—for investments such as cars, work clothing, job training, and rental deposits—may help the economically disadvantaged escape poverty and welfare (Ehrenreich 2001). Ethnographic research notes that public assistance often makes it possible for immigrant families to share resources, thus advancing long-term family-level goals of upward mobility through the schooling and occupational success of the next generation (Menjivar 1997; Zhou and Bankston 1998). Research further implies that persistent welfare recipiency among immigrants the longer they are in the United States—to the extent it occurs—may result in part from the lack of adequate settlement assistance (Bean, Stevens, and Van Hook 2003). Thus sociological perspectives would predict that high welfare benefit levels will hasten socioeconomic incorporation, perhaps eventually leading to lower levels of welfare use over time and across generations.

Previous research has focused extensively on immigrant-native differentials in welfare recipiency and to a lesser extent on immigrants' trajectories in welfare recipiency with time in the United States. Most of this research implicitly interprets immigrant welfare recipiency generally as an indicator of economic marginality and specifically as a portent of downward economic assimilation into a permanent poverty class. To place these ideas within the larger literature on welfare and immigrant assimilation, we first describe the dominant theoretical perspectives scholars have used to interpret or understand welfare recipiency in general and among immigrants in particular. We follow this discussion by outlining a series of research findings that, together, suggest an alternative interpretation of immigrant welfare recipiency in which public assistance functions as settlement assistance for the United States' newest arrivals. Some of the evidence comes from our own research and that of other researchers over the past decade or so. More comes from new findings based on the U.S. Census Bureau's Survey of Income and Program Participation presented here for the first time.

THEORIES RELEVANT TO IMMIGRANT WELFARE RECEIPT

Theoretical perspectives relevant to predicting immigrant welfare receipt appear in both the welfare and immigration literatures. Although these theories have apparently been formulated independently of one another, they agree on some points and differ on others. Interestingly, neither adequately considers that the immigrant experience may vary appreciably among different kinds of immigrants, particularly between labor migrants and other immigrants. In addition, these theories do not account for varying experiences and circumstances of natives and immigrants.

General Perspectives about Welfare

The three dominant approaches in the welfare literature used to explain public assistance receipt are *material deprivation, eco-*

nomic choice, and *cultural* theories. The material deprivation perspective sees welfare recipiency simply as a consequence of dire economic need originating from problems largely outside the control of recipients (such as layoffs, domestic abuse, mental illness, physical illness, lack of health insurance, and so on).

In contrast, economic choice theory focuses on the individual's calculation of the relative costs and benefits of welfare receipt weighed against alternative options (Bane and Ellwood 1994; Moffitt 1992). This approach thus predicts that individuals will be more likely to receive welfare in states where benefits are high relative to wages (less the costs of working outside the home and taxes on earnings, which economists call the benefit reduction rate). Consistent with economic choice theory, research shows that higher welfare guarantees generally lead to lower employment among single mothers (Burtless 1990; Moffitt 1992), more families on welfare (Ashenfelter 1983; Plotnick 1983), longer welfare spells (Bane and Ellwood 1994; Plotnick 1983; Robins, Tuma, and Yaeger 1980), and reduced earnings-related exits from welfare (Bane and Ellwood 1994). The extent to which these tendencies also characterize immigrant receipt remains unclear, however.

Finally, cultural theories view welfare behavior as resulting from values and orientations that promote benefits usage. According to these theories, people learn the value of welfare dependency, and living among others with such values—and being isolated from the more economically advantaged—reinforces their view of welfare (Bane and Ellwood 1994).

Perspectives on Immigrant Welfare Recipiency

Interestingly, all three of the dominant perspectives on welfare recipiency view welfare negatively, that is, as a behavior that arises from personal or group-level problems such as dire need, low wages, or dependency. Thus it is unsurprising that welfare recipiency among immigrants is deemed an indicator of immigration policy's failures. If immigrants are using welfare, the logic goes, then the wrong kinds of immigrants are coming to the United States (legally or illegally), or policies designed to provide assistance to immigrants may have been too generous and thus failed to reward work. We focus here on assessing the two major ideas that have motivated much of policy debate and research literature on immigrant welfare recipiency: the *magnet hypothesis* and the *negative acculturation hypothesis.*

The magnet hypothesis holds that U.S. welfare policy has attracted welfare-prone immigrants to the United States. This idea invokes all three welfare theoretical perspectives. The major argument is that because welfare benefits in the United States may be larger than wages in some foreign countries, such benefits provide a significant draw for immigrants living in low-wage countries (Borjas 1999, 2001). As George Borjas and Stephen Trejo observed, "There is also the fear that a relatively generous welfare system increases the attractiveness of immigration to the United States, especially for those persons most likely to use the available benefits" (1991, 195–96). Additionally, welfare availability may enable immigrants who are less successful in the labor market to stay rather than return home (Brimelow 1998). These ideas are consistent with economic choice perspectives in that immigrants are likely to move to and remain in places that offer greater opportunity, whether through work or through welfare. Forces identified in cultural and material deprivation theories may also play a role. In other words, those who prefer welfare over work, or who may need public assistance due to their personal problems, such as victims of abuse, may be more motivated to move to or remain in the United States. As a result, immigrants may comprise a selected group that is more welfare prone than other groups, even more than those with similar economic circumstances and prospects.

A second idea, which we term the negative-acculturation hypothesis (Gans 1992; Waters and Eschbach 1995; Waters 1994), holds that as immigrants become more familiar with American society, they learn certain U.S. behaviors and practices that have negative implications for their social, physical, or economic well-being—increased rates of smoking and drinking among Mexican immigrant women, for example (Brindis et al. 1995; Portes and Zhou 1993; Rumbaut 1994). The prevalence of these behaviors owes in part to the sectors of U.S. society into which many low-education immigrants assimilate. These tendencies are thought to be more characteristic of lower socioeconomic status or nonwhite immigrants because their social and economic standing provides fewer incentives to forgo those aspects of American life that offer short-term gratification but long-term harm.

With respect to welfare recipiency, the negative-acculturation perspective focuses on the same sort of factors as cultural theories of welfare, and has been extensively invoked by some economists in their work on immigrant welfare recipiency (Borjas 1990, 1998; Borjas and Hilton 1996). The basic argument is that immigrants learn about access to welfare programs in the United States and increasingly view participation in welfare programs as acceptable. In particular, immigrants who are more residentially segregated in poor or high-welfare communities are hypothesized to rely more on welfare the more time they spend in the United States. Thus, from this perspective, the availability of welfare programs to immigrants reinforces negative cultural orientations, contributing to higher use of welfare, thus slowing (or even fostering downward) economic assimilation.

EVIDENCE ABOUT IMMIGRANT WELFARE RECEIPT

To what degree does research support these two perspectives? We present several major research findings that, when taken together, question both the magnet and negative-acculturation perspectives and point to another possible interpretation of immigrant welfare recipiency.

We focus primarily on research and data on participation in Aid to Families with Dependent Children (AFDC). Among programs that provide cash assistance, AFDC, now Temporary Aid for Needy Families (TANF), dispenses cash welfare payments for needy children and their caretakers (usually parents) in the event one parent is deceased, incapacitated, unemployed, or absent from the home continuously. In contrast, Supplemental Security Income (SSI) provides income assistance to poor elderly, blind, and disabled persons. General Assistance, the smallest of the three cash assistance programs, consists of a handful of state-run programs that provide cash payments to poor persons who do not qualify for either AFDC-TANF or SSI. We examine AFDC-

TANF because the work disincentives of cash assistance are likely to be stronger for this program (Moffitt 1992) and may therefore slow immigrant assimilation.

We also focus on the time period before 1996, the year Congress passed welfare reform legislation. Also known as the Personal Responsibility and Work Opportunity Reconciliation Act (PRWORA), welfare reform replaced AFDC with TANF, which provides block grants to states to operate their own welfare programs within a set of new federal guidelines. PRWORA introduced a restriction that bars legal immigrants entering after August 22, 1996, from receiving TANF for the first five years after entry. States are allowed to choose whether to grant eligibility to immigrants after five years of residency and to legal immigrants already in the United States. Legal immigrants who have worked for ten years retained their eligibility for TANF.

The prereform period may not seem important in today's policy context. However, only by studying welfare-related behaviors during the prereform period can we evaluate the larger issue of whether state-provided financial support for newly arrived immigrants leads to higher or lower welfare receipt levels. Before PRWORA, legal immigrants were eligible for AFDC on largely the same terms as citizens (Huber and Espenshade 1997; Zedlewski and Giannarelli 2001), and undocumented immigrants were barred. After PRWORA, immigrant use of welfare fell dramatically (Borjas 2001; Fix and Passel 2002; Lofstrom and Bean 2002) in response to improving economic conditions and welfare policy changes (Chernick and Reimers 2004; Haider et al. 2004; Lofstrom and Bean 2002; Swingle 2000). If we were to include the postreform period in our analyses, it would appear as if immigrants used welfare substantially less the longer they are in the United States, when in fact at least a portion of the decline is attributable to changes in welfare policy.

Evidence for the Magnet Hypothesis

Research does not support the magnet hypothesis because immigrants tend to be less likely to use welfare than natives. This conclusion emerges from several decades of research on immigrant welfare use. During the 1970s and 1980s, U.S. immigrants were no more or even less likely than natives to receive welfare once differences in income and other characteristics were taken into account (Blau 1984; Borjas and Hilton 1996; Jensen 1991; Tienda and Jensen 1986). By 1990, immigrant welfare recipiency had increased both absolutely and relative to natives (Bean, Van Hook, and Glick 1997). Borjas and Hilton found that by the early 1990s, even after controlling for other factors, immigrants were more likely to use welfare than their native counterparts, whether welfare is defined as cash assistance only or various combinations of cash, noncash assistance, and vouchers (1996). Although some scholars have interpreted such changes as evidence of magnet effects, it is critical to distinguish between welfare programs. Borjas and Hilton combined a wide variety of programs without distinguishing between expensive and inexpensive programs, and programs that supplement versus replace earnings. In fact, much of the nativity differential Borjas and Hilton documented can be attributed to greater immigrant participation in programs that provide low-valued, noncash benefits, chiefly school meals programs (1996). The prospect of participating in such programs is unlikely to have drawn immigrants to the United States or led to reduced labor force participation (Bean, Stevens, and Van Hook 2003; Fix and Passel 1994).

Still other research covering the same period, the early 1990s, indicates that receipt of SSI increased over time, whereas receipt of AFDC, the program most relevant for assessing the tendency to favor welfare over work, remained steady at lower levels than that of natives (Bean, Van Hook, and Glick 1997; Ono and Becerra 2000). We demonstrate this point here using data from the Survey of Income and Program Participation (SIPP). We analyzed several SIPP panels from the period just before welfare reform: 1990, 1991, 1992, and 1993. SIPP is a longitudinal survey that follows up with respondents every four months for roughly three years (for more detail about the data, sample, and measures, see the appendix).

Among all mothers with children seventeen and younger, the foreign-born are significantly more likely to receive AFDC than the U.S.-born, 10.6 versus 8.5 percent (see table 4.1). However, this analysis compares all immigrants with all natives, regardless

TABLE 4.1 AFDC Recipiency, Early 1990s

	All Mothers	Single Mothers, High School or Less
Percentage receiving AFDC		
Immigrants	10.6	50.0
Natives	8.5	56.8
Difference	2.1**	−6.8
Adjusted percentage receiving AFDC		
Immigrants	9.8	52.4
Natives	9.2	56.6
Difference	0.6	−4.2

Source: Authors' compilation based on Survey of Income Program Participation (U.S. Bureau of the Census 1990, 1991, 1992, 1993), mothers of children aged seventeen and younger.
Note: The adjusted percentages control for nativity differences in age, marital status, household structure, disability, non-wage income, education, and state-level economic and policy characteristics.
*$p < .05$, **$p < .01$, ***$p < .001$.

of whether they are likely to be eligible for welfare. Policy critics worry more about less-educated immigrants coming to use welfare than about higher-skilled immigrants (Borjas 1990). In terms of education, the immigrants tend to be bimodal, that is, have either little education (a high school degree or less) or a great deal (a professional degree) (Bean and Stevens 2003). Those with a professional degree are highly unlikely to have immigrated to use welfare, but less educated, unmarried mothers may have done so. Thus the magnet hypothesis would predict that welfare recipiency would be particularly high for this group relative to natives.

However, when we examine welfare use among single mothers with a high school degree or less (the principal target of welfare reform), we find exactly the opposite. Rather than receiving more welfare than natives, these immigrants are likely to receive less, though the difference does not reach statistical significance. As an additional check, we estimate adjusted percentages of AFDC recipiency that control for nativity differences in a wider set of characteristics related to eligibility. These include age, marital status, household structure, disability, nonwage nonpublic-assistance income, education, and a variety of state-level characteristics, such as the unemployment rate, occupational structure, and generosity of welfare benefits. The regression models used to generate these estimates are shown in the appendix. After we make these adjustments, we find that immigrants are no more likely to use AFDC than natives, whether we examine all mothers or single mothers with a high school degree or less. Immigrants, even those the magnet hypothesis predicted to be the most welfare prone, are therefore no more likely to receive AFDC than natives. Such findings significantly challenge the idea that poor immigrants are drawn to the United States simply to draw on welfare benefits.

Another line of research has attempted to find evidence of welfare-magnet effects by examining whether immigrants disproportionately settle and live in states with generous welfare benefits. For example, Borjas concluded that the United States is in fact a welfare magnet because recently arrived immigrants and female-headed households with children are more heavily clustered in states with high welfare benefits than natives are (1999). Other studies also suggest that immigrants are more likely to move to states with high welfare-benefit levels (Dodson 2001), particularly refugees (Zavodny 1999).

However, such findings are not conclusive evidence. First, a wide variety of state-level characteristics other than welfare affect immigrant decisions of when and where to move. For example, research on Mexican migration flows suggests new immigrants go where they know other immigrants (Leach and Bean 2007; Massey and Espinosa 1997). In this way, migration streams and immigrant communities tend to be self-reinforcing. States with relatively high welfare benefits also tend to have historically high levels of immigration, such as California and New York, but the concentration of immigrants in these states long predated the growth in welfare caseloads.

Second, although previous research has suggested that immigrants are more likely to live in high-benefit states, it does not provide any evidence that immigrants living in high-benefit states are more likely to actually receive welfare. Given that high-benefit states tend to have historically larger immigrant populations and may have more social support and employment opportunities for immigrants, it certainly seems possible that the association between state welfare-benefit levels and immigrant populations is spurious.

Third, this research fails to address the differing expectations of international and interstate migration for welfare-related motives. If welfare availability increases the likelihood that immigrants decide to move to the United States, one could conclude that welfare's availability may have persuaded some to immigrate when they otherwise would not. If, on the other hand, state-level differences affect where immigrants settle once they have made the decision to move, it has little bearing on the types of immigrants initially drawn to the country, only on their distribution once they arrive. Although the finding that immigrants tend to settle in high-benefit states has important implications for the costs of immigration across states, it does not mean that people are immigrating expressly to receive benefits. As Borjas argued, immigrants have already made the initial investment to come to the United States (1999). The additional costs of choosing one location over another (say, states with high benefits) are comparatively small. In other words, evidence of state-level differences is not evidence of international magnet effects.

Evidence for the Negative-Acculturation Hypothesis

No research to date conclusively supports the view that working-age immigrants are drawn to the United States to receive welfare. Some, however, seems to support the idea that certain immigrants are subject to the kinds of forces that the negative-acculturation model emphasizes. In analyzing aggregated group-level data, George Galster, Kurt Metzger, and Ruth Waite found that, between 1980 and 1990, immigrant groups living in neighborhoods with high public assistance use in 1980 tended to experience increases in the jobless rate among those of working age, sixteen to sixty-four (1999). Lingxin Hao and Yukio Kawano also found a strong positive relationship between the average level of economic inactivity among coethnics in a neighborhood and single mothers' use of AFDC for both immigrants and natives (2001). Finally, George Borjas and Lynette Hilton concluded that the type of welfare used by immigrants who entered at an earlier time had some bearing on the type more recent arrivals from the same country used (1996). "This correlation suggests that there might be information networks operating within ethnic communities which transmit information about the availability of particular types of benefits to newly arrived immigrants" (602).

Yet it is important to recognize that these studies focus on outcomes among immigrants who have not moved out of high-poverty, ethnically segregated neighborhoods. Many newcomers are likely to do so (Brown 2007; Iceland and Scopilliti 2008). By focusing on less-advantaged subsets, those left behind in poverty neighborhoods, studies ignore the relatively more successful immigrants.

The negative-acculturation perspective predicts that immigrants who arrived as children or who have lived in the United States longer will be more welfare dependent than other immigrants. What happens when we examine evidence of welfare behaviors for all immigrants by age at arrival and duration of U.S. residence?

At first glance, some research does appear to suggest that rates of public assistance use rise the longer the immigrant is in the United States (Borjas 1990, 1998). This work, however, has not considered shifts in the demographic and age composition of immigrants and immigrant families that occur (Hu 1998). Over time, immigrants tend to age out of categories that make them eligible for AFDC and into categories that make them eligible to receive SSI. Because more immigrants receive SSI than AFDC, the net effect is a trend of increasing welfare use over time (Bean, Stevens, and Van Hook 2003; Van Hook and Bean 1999). We present evidence about the association of duration with AFDC recipiency only, rather than all sources of welfare combined. Because the negative-acculturation perspective emphasizes learned behaviors and attitudes, we also examine another indicator of welfare dependency: how long people stay on AFDC (what we call AFDC spells). We examine the percentage of recipients who leave welfare before their next interview four months later to provide an indication of how fast people leave the system. We distinguish among immigrants who arrived at age fifteen or older (the first generation) and those who came as children up to age fourteen (the 1.5 generation). We further differentiate the first generation by length of residence (zero to four years, five to nine years, ten to fourteen years, and fifteen years or older).

TABLE 4.2 **AFDC Receipt and Exit, Early 1990s**

	AFDC Recipiency	Exit from AFDC within Four Months
Percentage		
First generation immigrants		
0 to 4 years	13.8***	5.7
5 to 9 years	12.9***	4.3**
10 to 14 years	8.8aa	5.8
15 or more years	9.3aa	6.2
1.5 generation	9.6a	6.8
Natives	8.5	8.0
Adjusted percentage		
First generation immigrants		
0 to 4 years	10.3	6.0
5 to 9 years	12.3**	4.0**
10 to 14 years	10.0	6.8
15 or more years	10.8	7.4
1.5 generation	7.2a	8.1
Natives	9.2	8.0

Source: Authors' compilation based on Survey of Income Program Participation (U.S. Bureau of the Census 1990, 1991, 1992, 1993), mothers of children aged seventeen and younger.
Note: The adjusted percentages control for nativity differences in age, marital status, household structure, disability, non-wage income, education, and state-level economic and policy characteristics.
*$p < .05$, **$p < .01$, ***$p < .001$ (difference from natives).
a$p < .05$, aa$p < .01$, aaa$p < .001$ (difference from first generation immigrants, 0 to 4 years in country)

As shown in table 4.2, immigrants' high rates of welfare use and low rates of exit are concentrated among newly arrived immigrants. Among those with fewer than five years residence, 13.8 percent report receiving AFDC, versus 8.5 among the U.S.-born. However, AFDC prevalence quickly declines and exit rates increase with more time spent in the United States, reaching levels much closer to those of natives, even among adult immigrants with ten or more years in the United States. Comparing the upper panel with the lower panel of table 4.2 makes it clear that even when we control for welfare eligibility and state-level characteristics, the results do not support the idea the negative-acculturation model predicts, that immigrants assimilate into welfare dependency behaviors. Rather, welfare receipts start relatively high but decline from the first to the 1.5 generation (from rates of over 10 percent to 7.2 percent); the rate for the 1.5 generation is 2.0 percentage points below that for natives. Moreover, rates of exit from welfare increase within the first generation the longer immigrants stay in the country, and in the 1.5 generation, the rate is virtually the same as that for natives when other factors are controlled.

AN ALTERNATIVE PERSPECTIVE

Despite decades of research on immigrant welfare recipiency, the evidence for the magnet and negative-acculturation hypotheses remains weak, if not nonexistent. In several cases, research directly contradicts the predictions of both perspectives. It does not appear that welfare, when it was available to immigrants before welfare reform, slowed incorporation. As we explain, recent research further suggests that for some immigrants, welfare functioned as settlement assistance. Not only may welfare have done no harm, it may actually have helped at least some immigrants integrate economically.

Our idea is that the long-term structural conditions some immigrants face heighten their expectations about employment and mobility. These expectations, in turn, affect welfare and employment behaviors in positive ways. Because of the circumstances that lead people to decide to immigrate and the challenges they must overcome to do so, some immigrants may comprise a self-selected group of individuals who are likely to be more willing to take risks (such as crossing the U.S.-Mexico border), and endure hardships (such as being separated for long periods from family members) to achieve personal and familial goals. Consistent with this view, Barry Chiswick found that immigrants have been favorably selected: "One of the persistent findings regarding immigrants to the United States is that after a period of adjustment of about 10 to 15 years, male economic migrants earn more than adult men born in the United States of the same racial/ethnic origin, level of schooling, and other measured characteristics" (2000, 70). Analyses of longitudinal data also show that newly arrived immigrants make larger investments in human capital and at older ages than natives (Duleep and Regets 1999), and that immigrants coming into the country with lower earnings than natives eventually converge with natives over time (Duleep and Dowhan 2002; Duleep and Regets 1997, 1999).

Given strong orientations favoring work, newly arrived immigrant women might initially be more likely to receive welfare because they lack familiarity with their immediate surroundings. But because they and their husbands or partners are generally confident about finding employment, they tend to have stronger expectations of being employed than of being on welfare. Immigrant welfare recipiency would thus be predicted to decline with time in the country, just as we observe in the SIPP data.

These orientations may be particularly prevalent among the foreign-born from Mexico and Central America, who come to the United States primarily as labor migrants from countries that offer little prospect of employment (Bean and Stevens 2003; Stark 1991). Compared with other groups, their high employment rates (Bean, Gonzalez Baker, and Capps 2001) and faster wage growth (Hu 2000) testify to the presence and strength of positive expectations about finding employment. These expectations undoubtedly go a long way toward accounting for the fact that poor Mexican immigrants are less likely to participate in public-assistance programs than poor natives (Bean, Stevens, and Van Hook 2003).

Even more important, welfare may function as a form of settlement assistance that extends beyond simply helping make ends meet (Menjivar 1997). In particular, welfare may be primarily a way station to finding employment. Some evidence suggests that higher welfare guarantees may in fact help the poor escape poverty. Amy Butler found that higher welfare benefits hasten poverty exits for those who become single mothers as adults (age twenty-plus) when welfare is counted as part of family income (1996). Both Barbara Ehrenreich (2001) and David Shipler (2004) described how the poor incur additional costs, often in the form of higher interest rates and fees, that contribute to feelings of never being able to get ahead or to escape poverty. For example, low-income restaurant workers here claimed that they continued to live in hotels rather than rent an apartment (which would be considerably cheaper), because they could not save enough to pay the up-front costs of renting an apartment (two month's rent plus a deposit). Income from welfare may give newly arrived immigrants just enough to cover investments necessary for successful settlement, including rental deposits, phone hookups, language classes, and other educational costs.

Preliminary evidence from the Los Angeles Family Neighborhood Study (LA-FANS) lends some support to this idea of welfare as settlement assistance. Newly arrived immigrants appeared to have relatively favorable attitudes about the value of work versus welfare. Immigrant women age eighteen to forty-nine tended to disapprove of welfare more than their native counterparts, and the level of disapproval increased with time in the United States.[1] These attitudes were likely to be associated with a tendency to make the most of trying circumstances, including using welfare income only as a stopgap during periods of unemployment or difficulties associated with settlement.

Research on refugees and asylees supports this alternative perspective. Refugees were (and still are) immediately eligible for welfare, whereas regular immigrants are not (Gordon 1987). In many respects, newly arrived refugees are encouraged to use welfare as a form of settlement assistance. Tellingly, those who entered the country as refugees saw greater earnings growth during the 1980s than other immigrants (Cortes 2004). Kalena Cortes attributed this growth to differences in time horizons; refugees know they are staying and are therefore more likely to make human-capital investments (2004). But refugees' earnings growth may also be attributable to the reception and integration support they received. Raj Tiaja and Mark Leach, who replicated Cortes' basic findings about refugees for the 1990 through 1999 period, also found that group welfare use among nonrefugees was positively associated with subsequent earnings growth (2007).

Other research further suggests that welfare income may help immigrants secure employment, particularly among Mexican immigrants. We have been conducting research on the effects of living in states with relatively high or low welfare benefits in which we find several unique patterns concerning welfare and work among Mexican immigrants (Van Hook and Bean 2009). We found that AFDC recipiency among immigrants was lower in high-benefit than in low-benefit states. This pattern was particularly strong among Mexican immigrants and nonexistent among natives. Even more important, we also found that Mexican immigrants tended to transition from AFDC to employment faster in high-benefit than in low-benefit states. Higher welfare benefits thus appear to facilitate employment among Mexican immigrants.

Finally, other research suggests the benefits of welfare recipiency among Hispanic immigrants may extend even to the second generation (the children of immigrants). Using the 1997 cohort of the National Longitudinal Survey of Youth (NLSY-1997 cohort), Kelly Balistreri conducted research on the effects of growing up in a welfare-receiving household (2008). Similar to other research on this topic, her findings indicated that growing up in a welfare-receiving household has negative effects on completing high school, even after adjusting for differences in poverty, family, and neighborhood-level characteristics between welfare and nonwelfare households. However, she found that children of Hispanic immigrants exhibited a different pattern. For this group, receiving welfare in childhood and early adolescence was positively associated with high school completion.

CONCLUSIONS

The issue of immigrant welfare use has fueled debates about immigration and welfare policy for a century or more. Politicians have often embraced the position that immigrants should not receive public assistance. As early as 1891, U.S. immigration law permitted immigrants who became public charges to be deported. In the 1980s, a growing number of immigration-policy critics focused on what appeared to be rising levels of immigrant welfare dependency and expressed fears that immigrants were coming to the United States because of the welfare system.

In such contexts, much social science research has focused on whether immigrants are particularly welfare prone. This body of research, at least in its tone, has tended to assume that welfare receipt generally, and immigrant receipt in particular, is a negative and undesirable phenomenon. Its proponents adopted the viewpoint that immigrant welfare receipt reflects weak attachment to the labor force and low levels of self-initiative, ultimately leading to unsuccessful assimilation. Not surprisingly, a series of policy changes in the 1990s resulted in newly arrived, nonnaturalized immigrants being barred from receiving welfare in many circumstances.

In evaluating this characterization of immigrants who receive public assistance, we presented and discussed research that on balance refutes the magnet hypothesis by showing that the availability of welfare benefits does not attract welfare-prone immigrants. This result is consistent with other research findings, specifically that Mexican and often other Hispanic immigrants are labor migrants who choose particular U.S. states on the basis of information about jobs in those areas they get from their personal contacts, not on the welfare benefits the state provides (Kaushal 2005).

Further, the availability of welfare programs does not appear to encourage dependency among immigrants, which the negative-acculturation hypothesis would predict. In contrast, we find that when other variables are not controlled, although immigrants tend to receive more welfare than natives, their use rates decline from the first to the 1.5 generation, dropping below that of comparable natives.

Research also finds that receiving public assistance can exert a positive effect on economic integration, functioning as a surrogate for settlement assistance, or at least as a way to help immigrants work their way out of poverty and off welfare (Van Hook and Bean 2009). We suggest this is true because the circumstances leading immigrants to welfare are different and often more ephemeral than those that usually lead natives to welfare. For example, researchers have found that working-poor natives characterize welfare and former welfare recipients as sometimes fearful of leaving their neighborhoods in search of work or new experiences. Further, it has been claimed that native recipients and former recipients do not have the cultural skills to obtain and keep a job, such as "punctuality, diligence, and a can-do attitude" (Shipler 2004). Immigrants, on the other hand, especially female labor migrants, often demonstrate precisely the opposite tendencies (Bean and Stevens 2009). Their reasons for going on welfare are undoubtedly different. They may do so simply because, as newcomers, they are unfamiliar with the labor market, do not have well-developed nonfamilial social networks, and have either less ability to change or less control over their circumstances in the United States. Although native welfare use may derive largely from persistent social structural difficulties, immigrant welfare use may be more likely to arise from temporary challenges associated with being societal newcomers.

These research-based possibilities raise serious concerns about the country's policies (or lack of policies) with respect to immigrant integration. Welfare reform appears to have been formulated under the assumption that immigrant and native welfare recipiency share the same origin. If policymakers have wrongly assumed that immigrants are drawn to the United States by welfare, or that immigrants assimilate into welfare, then welfare reform is not only unlikely to deter future immigration, it may also delay economic assimilation, thus increasing hardship for many already poor children and adults, particularly among those newly arrived immigrant families who could most benefit from any form of settlement assistance.

APPENDIX

In this chapter, we have presented results based on our analysis of the Survey of Income Program Participation (SIPP). The data, measures, and statistical analyses we used are described in this appendix.

Data and Sample

We pooled multiple panels of the U.S. Census Bureau's Survey of Income and Program Participation (1990, 1991, 1992, and 1993), a nationally representative longitudinal survey, to study the temporal dynamics of AFDC recipiency. Each SIPP panel has several interviews (waves) occurring every four months for roughly three to four years. The SIPP includes welfare history, month-to-month information on welfare recipiency, and standard social, demographic, and economic variables. By combining five SIPP panels, we amassed a large enough sample to examine in depth the dynamics of welfare exit. Because the pooled samples included many more natives than immigrants, and far more than necessary for the analyses, we created an extract that includes 10 percent of native non-Hispanic whites randomly selected from the pooled sample and 100 percent of the other respondents. We adjusted the sampling weights appropriately.

To avoid any possible confounding effects from the very few cases involving differences in welfare receipt for husband-wife families, we restricted the sample to women who were age eighteen to forty-nine at the time of the first interview and had a valid wave-2 interview (the variables related to migration and nativity are

112 Immigrants and Welfare

asked only at wave 2). We included only original respondents, thus excluding those who joined sample households after the wave-1 interview. We eliminated from the sample those born in Puerto Rico or other U.S. outlying areas because they may not be justifiably classified as native, though they share many characteristics of legal immigrants, but they also do not fit in the immigrant category because as U.S. citizens by birth they are not subject to the same legal restrictions as immigrants. We also eliminated refugees. Even before welfare reform, U.S. immigration policy established different welfare-eligibility rules for those entering as refugees versus those entering as permanent resident aliens. Refugees were (and still are) immediately eligible, whereas regular immigrants are not. We identified as refugees those coming from eleven nations that were mainly refugee-sending countries during the 1980s.[2] Finally, we excluded those who did not have a valid interview at wave 2, because the variables related to migration and nativity are asked only at that stage. Our final sample included 4,071 immigrant women and 9,265 native women. We constructed a longitudinal data file that includes an observation for each individual for each interview they are in SIPP (every four months for three to four years). The number of interviews in the combined SIPP panels is 94,205. Attrition is remarkably low after wave 2 and similar for immigrants and natives. Of the original respondents interviewed in the second wave, about 90 percent of immigrants and natives were interviewed (or other family members were interviewed) at all waves.

Welfare Receipt

SIPP collects monthly information about AFDC. We measured AFDC use for the four-month period before each interview, coding women as receiving welfare if they either reported receiving benefits or were reported as being covered by the program. This strategy ensures that AFDC beneficiaries who did not personally receive or report a welfare payment are still counted as recipients. Previous research shows quite a bit of "seam bias" in welfare reporting in which respondents tend to assert that they received welfare all four months or none in the reference period, suggesting that month-to-month reporting on AFDC is not accurate. We therefore did not code AFDC as a monthly measure, but instead counted women as recipients if they received welfare during any month of the reference period.

We also examined the percentage of AFDC recipients who left the program. Exit is measured as the percentage who reported leaving welfare among those who reported receiving AFDC in the previous interview, conditional on the duration of the ongoing spell. Respondents reported the month and year they started receiving AFDC for current spells, and we used this information to estimate and statistically control for the duration of all welfare spells, even those already ongoing at the time of the first interview.

Nativity-Generational Status-Time in United States

SIPP collects information on naturalization status and migration history at the second interview. We constructed a categorical variable that distinguishes among the U.S.-born (reference category), the foreign-born who arrived as children up to age fourteen (the 1.5 generation), and the foreign-born who arrived as adults at age fifteen-plus. We further subdivided the third group by duration in the United States (zero to four, five to nine, and ten-plus years).

Control Variables

We controlled for the influence of socioeconomic status, family composition, and other demographic characteristics in our multivariate models, and the results of these models are used to generate the adjusted percentages shown in tables 4.1 and 4.2. As is common in research on welfare recipiency, we control for nonwage, nonwelfare income in the previous four months (logged) to take into account differences in income from assets, gifts, or inheritance. We also adjusted for educational attainment (less than high school, high school, and some college or technical school versus college graduate) to account for differences in potential wages. Other sociodemographic controls include marital status, living arrangements (residing with extended kin versus other), disability status, and age at baseline. All time-varying independent variables (income, education, living arrangements, and disability) are lagged by four months (one interview) from the time the dependent variable is measured.

We also included various contextual controls. To capture geographical variations and trends in opportunities for employment, we used estimates from the Bureau of Labor Statistics, based on the Current Population Survey, of the seasonally adjusted monthly unemployment rate by state. The unemployment rates were attached to individual women's records matching on state, year, and month. To account for possible variation in employment opportunities by sector, we controlled for the percentages of the labor force in the state and year in agricultural, forestry, or fishing and in service occupations, again using estimates from the Bureau of Labor Statistics. To partially adjust for geographic variations in group-level influences, such as social support from ethnic group members, we controlled for the percentage of the respondent's nativity-race-ethnic group in the state, based on 1990 census estimates. To adjust for policy variations in the compatibility of welfare and work, we controlled for the state-level benefit reduction rate (the AFDC income reduced for each additional dollar of earnings), which deviated from federal guidelines in states that obtained waivers during the prereform period (Blank and Haskins 2001). We used the same formula as David Stapleton, Gina Livermore, and Adam Tucker to estimate the marginal tax and benefit reduction rate (1997). Finally, we included a set of dummy variables indicating calendar year to account for period effects.

Analyses

The analytic sample for analyses of AFDC recipiency includes all observations from all available interviews. The samples for exit and employment following an AFDC spell include all interviews during which a former AFDC recipient reported receiving AFDC up until and including the interview within which AFDC is no longer reported or the individual is censored. To produce the adjusted percentages shown in tables 4.1 and 4.2, we estimated logistic regressions of AFDC recipiency and exit. These models included indicators of nativity (for the results in table 4.1) and predicted probabilities of recipiency and exit by nativity and duration. We then plugged the means of the control variables for the entire sample (immigrants and natives combined) into the predic-

TABLE 4.A1 Models of AFDC Recipiency and Exit from AFDC, Early 1990s

	Model 1	Model 2	Exit from AFDC
Immigrant	0.098		
First generation			
0 to 4 years		0.170	−0.319
5 to 9 years		0.469**	−0.750**
10 to 14 years		0.125	−0.186
15 or more years		0.251	−0.113
1.5 generation		−0.368	−0.001
Duration on AFDC (years)	—	—	−0.022
Age	−0.044***	−0.046***	0.006
Married	−2.710***	−2.716***	1.171***
Living with extended family members	0.156	0.162	−0.073
Disabled	1.211***	1.213***	−0.190
Non-transfer, non-wage income (lagged)	0.000***	0.000***	−0.004
High school	0.185	0.222	−0.060
Some college	−1.140***	−1.106***	0.146
College or higher	−2.090***	−2.055***	0.593***
1991	−0.059	−0.050	−0.157
1992	−0.189	−0.181	−0.034
1993	−0.043	−0.036	−0.129
1994	0.069	0.068	0.099
Unemployment rate for state and year	0.146***	0.145***	−0.065
Welfare guarantee (AFDC+food stamps, family of three)	0.110***	0.110***	−0.174***
Benefit reduction rate	−0.132	−0.135	−0.438*
Race-ethnic-nativity group concentration in state	−0.488	−0.490	0.026
Percentage of state labor force in agriculture	0.005	0.005	0.036
Percentage of state labor force in service sector	0.014	0.013	0.090
Intercept	−0.234	−0.267	−4.031***
Pseudo R^2	0.337	0.338	0.076
N (person-interviews)	74,047	74,047	14,437

Source: Authors' compilation based on Survey of Income Program Participation (U.S. Bureau of the Census 1990, 1991, 1992, 1993), mothers of children aged seventeen and younger.
*$p < .05$, **$p < .01$, ***$p < .001$.

tion equations to estimate the predicted probabilities of recipiency, exit, and employment by nativity and duration. Thus, the adjusted percentages capture the shares of each group that would receive welfare or exit welfare, controlling for other factors affecting welfare receipt and exit. We adjusted the standard errors in the models for clustering of observations within persons, states, and primary sampling units using STATA survey commands (Chakrabarty 1989; Huber 1967; White 1980, 1982). The models for the sample of all mothers are shown in table 4.A1.

This paper is based on research supported in part by a grant by the National Institutes of Health [R01-HD-39075-1], in part by the Center for Family and Demographic Research, Bowling Green State University, where Van Hook was previously located and which has core funding from the National Institute of Child Health and Human Development (R21HD042831-01), and in part by the Center for Research on Immigration, Population, and Public Policy at the University of California, Irvine.

NOTES

1. We examined attitudes about welfare among immigrants and natives, again using LA-FANS data. LA-FANS includes a seven-item scale measuring the extent to which respondents disapprove of welfare. Each item describes a hypothetical situation involving welfare (for example, a divorced woman goes on welfare to stay home with her children, or a father who cannot find a job goes on welfare to support his family). Respondents were asked the extent to which they approved or disapproved (five-point Lickert scale), with disapproval scored with higher values. The standardized mean scores for this scale were −.042, .158, and −.106 for new arrivals, other immigrants, and natives, respectively, and these differences remained large and significant when age and education were controlled.
2. These countries are the former Soviet Union, Cuba, Vietnam, Laos, Romania, Iran, Ethiopia, Cambodia, Poland, Afghanistan, and Nicaragua. Countries from the Balkans were added to this list to include

refugees who arrived in the 1990s. This classification strategy is viable because refugees have tended to come from only a relatively small number of countries (Fix and Passel 1994). In addition, countries that send refugees usually do not send large numbers of other legal immigrants. The eleven refugee-sending countries sent almost 90 percent of all refugee arrivals to the United States during the 1980s, and more than 91 percent of the persons they supplied came as refugees (Bean, Stevens, and Van Hook 2003).

REFERENCES

Ashenfelter, Orley. 1983. "Determining Participation in Income-tested Social Programs." *Journal of American Statistical Association* 78(383): 517–25.

Balistreri, Kelly S. 2008. "Welfare and the Children of Immigrants: Transmission of Dependence or Investment in the Future?" *Center for Family and Demographic Research* working paper 2008–03. Bowling Green, Ohio: Bowling Green State University.

Bane, Mary Jo, and David T. Ellwood. 1994. *Welfare Realities*. Cambridge, Mass.: Harvard University Press.

Bean, Frank D., Susan Gonzalez Baker, and Randy Capps. 2001. "Immigration and Labor Markets in the United States." In *Sourcebook on Labor Markets: Evolving Structures and Processes*, edited by Ivar Berg and Arne Kalleberg. New York: Plenum Press.

Bean, Frank D., and Gillian Stevens. 2003. *America's Newcomers and the Dynamics of Diversity*. New York: Russell Sage Foundation.

Bean, Frank D., Gillian Stevens, and Jennifer Van Hook. 2003. "Immigration and Immigrant Welfare Receipt." In *America's Newcomers and the Dynamics of Diversity*, edited by Frank D. Bean and Gillian Stevens. New York: Russell Sage Foundation.

Bean, Frank D., Jennifer Van Hook, and Jennifer E. Glick. 1997. "Country-of-Origin, Type of Public Assistance and Patterns of Welfare Recipiency Among U.S. Immigrants and Natives." *Social Science Quarterly* 78(2): 432–51.

Blank, Rebecca M., and Ron Haskins. 2001. *The New World of Welfare*. Washington, D.C.: Brookings Institution Press.

Blau, Francine D. 1984. "The Use of Transfer Payments by Immigrants." *Industrial and Labor Relations Review* 37(2): 222–39.

Bloemraad, Irene. 2006. *Becoming a Citizen: Incorporating Immigrants and Refugees in the United States and Canada*. Berkeley: University of California Press.

Borjas, George J. 1990. *Friends or Strangers: The Impact of Immigrants on the U.S. Economy.* New York: Basic Books.

———. 1998. "Immigration and Welfare: A Review of the Evidence." In *The Debate in the United States over Immigration*, edited by Peter J. Duignan and Lewis H. Gann. Stanford, Calif.: Hoover Institution Press.

———. 1999. "Immigration and Welfare Magnets." *Journal of Labor Economics* 17(4): 607–37.

———. 2001. "Welfare Reform and Immigration." In *The New World of Welfare*, edited by Rebecca M. Blank and Ron Haskins. Washington, D.C.: Brookings Institution Press.

Borjas, George J., and Lynette Hilton. 1996. "Immigration and the Welfare State: Immigrant Participation in Means-Tested Entitlement Programs." *Quarterly Journal of Economics* 111(2): 575–604.

Borjas, George J., and Stephen J. Trejo. 1991. "Immigrant Participation in the Welfare System." *Industrial and Labor Relations Review* 44(2): 195–211.

Brimelow, Peter. 1995. *Alien Nation: Common Sense About America's Immigration Disaster.* New York: Random House.

———. 1998. "The Case for Limiting Immigration." In *The Debate in the United States over Immigration*, edited by Peter J. Duignan and Lewis H. Gann. Stanford, Calif.: Hoover Institution Press.

Brindis, Claire, Amy L. Wolfe, Virginia McCarter, Shelly Ball, and Susan Starbuck-Morales. 1995. "The Associations between Immigrant Status and Risk-Behavior Patterns in Latino Adolescents." *Journal of Adolescent Health* 17(2): 99–105.

Brown, Susan K. 2007. "Delayed Spatial Assimilation: Multigenerational Incorporation of the Mexican-Origin Population in Los Angeles." *City and Community* 6(3): 193–209.

Burtless, Gary. 1990. "The Economist's Lament: Public Assistance in America." *Journal of Economic Perspectives* 4(1): 57–78.

Butler, Amy C. 1996. "The Effect of Welfare Benefit Levels on Poverty Among Single-Parent Families." *Social Problems* 43(1): 94–115.

Chakrabarty, Rameswar P. 1989. *Multivariate Analysis by Users of SIPP Micro-Data Files.* Washington: U.S. Department of Commerce, U.S. Bureau of the Census.

Chernick, Howard, and Cordelia Reimers. 2004. "The Decline in Welfare Receipt in New York City: Push vs. Pull." *Eastern Economic Journal* 30(1): 3–29.

Chiswick, Barry R. 2000. "Are Immigrants Favorably Selected?" In *Migration Theory: Talking Across Disciplines*, edited by Caroline B. Brettell and James F. Hollifield. New York: Routledge.

Cortes, Kalena E. 2004. "Are Refugees Different from Economic Immigrants? Some Empirical Evidence on the Heterogeneity of Immigrant Groups in the United States." *Review of Economics and Statistics* 86(2): 465–80.

Dodson, Marvin E. 2001. "Welfare Generosity and Location Choices among New United States Immigrants." *International Review of Law and Economics* 21(1): 47–67.

Duleep, Harriet Orcutt, and Dan Dowhan. 2002. "Insights from Longitudinal Data on the Earnings Growth of U.S. Foreign-Born Men." *Demography* 39(3): 485–506.

Duleep, Harriet Orcutt, and Mark C. Regets. 1997. "Measuring Immigrant Wage Growth Using Matched CPS Files." *Demography* 34(2): 239–49.

———. 1999. "Immigrants and Human Capital Investment." *American Economic Review* 89(2): 186–91.

Edwards, James R. 2001. "Public Charge Doctrine: A Fundamental Principle of American Immigration Policy." Washington, D.C.: Center for Immigration Studies.

Ehrenreich, Barbara. 2001. *Nickel and Dimed: On (Not) Getting By in America*. New York: Henry Holt and Co.

Fix, Michael E., and Jeffrey S. Passel. 1994. *Immigration and Immigrants: Setting the Record Straight*. Washington, D.C.: The Urban Institute.

———. 2002. "The Scope and Impact of Welfare Reform's Immigrant Provisions." *Assessing the New Federalism* discussion paper 02–03. Washington, D.C.: The Urban Institute.

Galster, George C., Kurt Metzger, and Ruth Waite. 1999. "Neighborhood Opportunity Structures and Immigrants' Socioeconomic Advancement." *Journal of Housing Research* 10(1): 95–127.

Gans, Herbert J. 1992. "Second-Generation Decline: Scenarios for the Economic and Ethnic Futures of the Post-1965 American Immigrants." *Ethnic and Racial Studies* 15(2): 173–92.

Gordon, Linda W. 1987. "Southeast Asian Refugee Migration to the United States." In *Pacific Bridges: The New Immigration from Asia and the Pacific Islands*, edited by J. T. Fawcett and B. V. Carino. New York: Center for Migration Studies.

Haider, Steven J., Robert F. Schoeni, Yuhua Bao, and Caroline Danielson. 2004. "Immigrants, Welfare Reform, and the Economy." *Journal of Policy Analysis and Management* 23(4): 745–64.

Hao, Lingxin, and Yukio Kawano. 2001. "Immigrants' Welfare Use and Opportunity for Contact with Co-Ethnics." *Demography* 38(3): 375–89.

Hu, Wei-Yin. 1998. "Elderly Immigrants on Welfare." *The Journal of Human Resources* 33(3): 711–41.

———. 2000. "Immigrant Earnings Assimilation: Estimates from Longitudinal Data." *American Economic Review* 90(2): 368–72.

Huber, Gregory A., and Thomas Espenshade. 1997. "Neo-Isolationism, Balanced-Budget Conservatism, and the Fiscal Impacts of Immigrants." *International Migration Review* 31(4): 1031–54.

Huber, P. J. 1967. "The Behaviour of Maximum Likelihood Estimates Under Non-Standard Conditions." In *Proceedings of the Fifth Berkeley Symposium in Mathematical Statistics and Probability*. Berkeley: University of California Press.

Iceland, John, and Melissa Scopilliti. 2008. "Immigrant Residential Segregation in U.S. Metropolitan Areas, 1990–2000." *Demography* 45(1): 79–94.

Jensen, Leif. 1991. "Secondary Earner Strategies and Family Poverty: Immigrant-Native Differentials, 1960–1980." *International Migration Review* 25(1): 113–37.

Kaushal, Neeraj. 2005. "New Immigrants' Location Choices: Magnets without Welfare." *Journal of Labor Economics* 23(1): 59–80.

Leach, Mark A., and Frank D. Bean. 2007. "The Structure and Dynamics of Mexican Migration to New Destinations in the United States." In *New Faces in New Places: The Changing Geography of American Immigration*, edited by Douglas S. Massey. New York: Russell Sage Foundation.

Lofstrom, Magnus, and Frank D. Bean. 2002. "Assessing Immigrant Policy Options: Labor Market Conditions and Post-Reform Declines in Welfare Receipt among Immigrants." *Demography* 39(4): 617–37.

Massey, Douglas S., and Kristen E. Espinosa. 1997. "What's Driving Mexico-U.S. Migration? A Theoretical, Empirical, and Policy Analysis." *American Journal of Sociology* 102(4): 939–99.

Menjivar, Cecilia. 1997. "Immigrant Kinship Networks: Vietnamese, Salvadorans, and Mexicans in Comparative Perspective." *Journal of Comparative Family Studies* 28(1): 1–20.

Moffitt, Robert. 1992. "Incentive Effects of the U.S. Welfare System: A Review." *Journal of Economic Literature* 30(1): 1–61.

Murray, Charles. 1984. *Losing Ground: American Social Policy, 1950–1980*. New York: Basic Books.

Ono, Hiromi, and Rosina M. Becerra. 2000. "Race, Ethnicity and Nativity, Family Structure, Socioeconomic Status and Welfare Dependency." *International Migration Review* 34(3): 739–65.

Plotnick, Robert. 1983. "Turnover in the AFDC Population: An Event History Analysis." *Journal of Human Resources* 18(1): 65–81.

Portes, Alejandro, and Min Zhou. 1993. "The New Second Generation: Segmented Assimilation and Its Variants." *The Annals of the American Academy of Political and Social Science* 530(1):74–96.

Portes, Alejandro, and Rubén G. Rumbaut. 2001. *Legacies: The Story of the Immigrant Second Generation*. New York: Russell Sage Foundation.

Robins, Philip K., Nancy Brandon Tuma, and K. E. Yaeger. 1980. "Effects of SIME/DIME on Changes in Employment Status." *The Journal of Human Resources* 15(4): 545–74.

Rumbaut, Rubén G. 1994. "The Crucible Within: Ethnic Identity, Self-Esteem, and Segmented Assimilation among the Children of Immigrants." *International Migration Review* 28(4): 748–94.

Shipler, David K. 2004. *The Working Poor: Invisible in America*. New York: Alfred A. Knopf.

Stapleton, David, Gina Livermore, and Adam Tucker. 1997. "Determinants of AFDC Caseload Growth." In *Report for the Office of the Assistant Secretary for Planning and Evaluation, Department of Health & Human Services*. Washington, D.C.: The Lewin Group.

Stark, Oded. 1991. *The Migration of Labor*. Oxford: Blackwell Publishing.

Swingle, Digna Betancourt. 2000. "Immigrants and August 22, 1996: Will the Public Charge Rule Clarify Program Eligibility?" *Families in Society* 81(6): 605–10.

Tiaja, Raj, and Mark Leach. 2007. Immigrant Welfare Receipt and Earnings Growth: Evidence Among Two Arrival Cohorts in the 1990s. *Center for Research on Immigration, Population and Public Policy Working Paper Series*. Irvine: University of California–Irvine.

Tienda, Marta, and Leif Jensen. 1986. "Immigration and Public Assistance Participation: Dispelling the Myth of Dependency." *Social Science Research* 15(4): 372–400.

U.S. Bureau of the Census. 1990. *Survey of Income and Program Participation*. Washington: Government Printing Office.

———. 1991. *Survey of Income and Program Participation*. Washington: Government Printing Office.

———. 1992. *Survey of Income and Program Participation*. Washington: Government Printing Office.

———. 1993. *Survey of Income and Program Participation*. Washington: Government Printing Office.

Van Hook, Jennifer, and Frank D. Bean. 1999. "The Growth in Non-Citizen SSI Caseloads 1979–1996: Aging Versus New Immigrant Effects." *Journal of Gerontology: Social Sciences* 54(1):S16-23.

———. 2009. "Explaining the Distinctiveness of Mexican-Immigrant Welfare Behaviors: The Importance of Employment-Related Cultural Repertoires." *American Sociological Review* 74(3): 423–44.

Van Hook, Jennifer, Susan K. Brown, and Frank D. Bean. 2006. "For Love or Money? Welfare Reform and Immigrant Naturalization." *Social Forces* 85(4): 643–66.

Waters, Mary. 1994. "Ethnic and Racial Identities of Second-Generation Black Immigrants in New York City." *International Migration Review* 28(4): 795–820.

Waters, Mary, and Karl Eschbach. 1995. "Immigration and Racial and Ethnic Inequality in the United States." *Annual Review of Sociology* 21: 419–46.

White, Halbert. 1980. "A Heteroskedasticity-Consistent Covariance Matrix Estimator and a Direct Test for Heteroskedasticity." *Econometrica* 48(4): 817–30.

———. 1982. "Maximum Likelihood Estimation of Misspecified Models." *Econometrica* 50(1): 1–25.

Zavodny, Madeline. 1999. "Determinants of Recent Immigrants' Locational Choices." *International Migration Review* 33(4): 1014–30.

Zedlewski, Sheila, and Linda Giannarelli. 2001. "Diversity among State Welfare Programs: Implications for Reform. New Federalism: Issues and Options for States." Washington, D.C.: The Urban Institute.

Zhou, Min, and Carl L. Bankston III. 1998. *Growing Up American: How Vietnamese Children Adapt to Life in the United States*. New York: Russell Sage Foundation.

— Chapter 5 —

Trends in Immigrants' Use of Public Assistance after Welfare Reform

Randy Capps, Michael E. Fix, and Everett Henderson

THE PERSONAL Responsibility and Work Opportunity Reconciliation Act of 1996 (PRWORA) significantly changed the eligibility of legal immigrants for means-tested federal public assistance (Public Law 104-193). Twelve years after the law was enacted, ample evidence shows that the use of these assistance programs has declined markedly among low-income families, including legal immigrants. But the trends in legal immigrant use patterns have varied across the five federal assistance programs we consider in this chapter: Temporary Assistance for Needy Families (TANF), Supplemental Security Income (SSI), the Food Stamp Program (FSP), Medicaid, and the State Children's Health Insurance Program (SCHIP).

As earlier chapters in this volume make clear, welfare reform substantially reduced legal immigrants' eligibility for a range of federal means-tested public benefits. The framers did so based on assumptions that immigrants were predisposed toward welfare, that benefits posed a moral hazard to newcomers, and that welfare would promote negative assimilation by discouraging work. Eligibility changes were introduced not just for cash transfer programs such as TANF and SSI, but also for work support programs such as food stamps, Medicaid, and SCHIP.

The law's immigrant provisions proved to be among the most politically unstable elements of the 1996 law. In the years following enactment, substantial restorations of eligibility to children

TABLE 5.1   Citizenship and Legal Status of Immigrants

Noncitizens

- *Legal permanent residents (LPRs)* are legally admitted to live permanently in the United States after qualifying for immigrant visas abroad or adjusting to permanent resident status in the United States. LPRs are issued documentation commonly referred to as green cards, though the cards have not been green for many years. A large majority of LPRs are sponsored (that is, supported for admission to the United States) by close family members or employers. LPRs are the main group that PRWORA restricted from receiving public assistance.
- *Refugees and asylees* are granted legal status on the basis of persecution or a well-founded fear of persecution in their home countries. Refugee status is granted before entry to the United States. Unlike refugees, asylees usually arrive in the country without authorization (or overstay a valid visa), later claim asylum, and are granted their legal status while in the United States. After one year, refugees and asylees are generally eligible for permanent residency; after five years, they are eligible to naturalize. Almost all adjust their status and become LPRs. This group retains certain rights—for instance, eligibility for major public-assistance programs. We categorize all immigrants who enter as refugees or are granted asylum as refugees even after they become LPRs or citizens. Refugee and asylee eligibility for assistance was restricted somewhat by PWRORA, with eligibility for TANF and SSI essentially capped at five years and later extended to seven years.
- *Temporary legal migrants* have been admitted to the United States for a temporary or indefinite period but have not attained permanent residency. Most have entered to work or to study, or because of political disruption or natural disasters in their home countries. Some seek to stay for a permanent or indefinite period. These migrants have a pending status that allows them to remain in the country and often to work, but does not carry the same rights as lawful permanent residency. Temporary legal migrants are ineligible for the assistance programs on which we focus, and so we excluded them from our analysis.

---

were enacted for SSI, for food stamps, and for Medicaid and SCHIP. That said, even following the tenth anniversary of the law, recently arrived adult legal immigrants remained outside the key programs that make up the U.S. social safety net.

This chapter adds to a small literature that documents trends in benefit use following reform. We disaggregate these trends by program and the legal status of low-income families, distinguishing among lawful permanent residents (LPRs), refugees, naturalized citizens, and native-born citizens (see table 5.1). Each of

TABLE 5.1 *(Continued)*

Noncitizens

- *Unauthorized immigrants* do not have a valid visa or other immigration document because they entered the United States illegally (usually across the Mexican border), stayed longer than their temporary visas permitted, or otherwise violated the terms under which they were admitted. Some eventually adjust their status and attain legal residency after a relative, spouse, or employer files a sponsorship petition. Unauthorized immigrants are also ineligible for the types of assistance discussed and are excluded from our analysis.

Citizens

- *Naturalized citizens* are former LPRs who have become U.S. citizens through naturalization. Typically, LPRs must be in the United States for five or more years to qualify for naturalization. However, immigrants who marry citizens can qualify for citizenship in three years. LPRs must pass a language and civics test—in English—and pass background checks before qualifying to naturalize. PRWORA did not include any categorical eligibility restrictions for naturalized citizens, who remain eligible for public assistance on the same terms as native-born citizens.
- *Native-born citizens* include all people born in the United States, regardless of their parents' birthplace or legal status. These include people born in Puerto Rico, the U.S. Virgin Islands, and other U.S. territories and possessions, as well as in foreign countries to a U.S. citizen parent.

Source: Authors' compilation.

these populations' eligibility for benefits was affected by welfare reform differently, the deepest cuts by far being absorbed by LPR families. Unauthorized immigrants are excluded from our analysis because they were ineligible for these programs before welfare reform and remained so afterwards. We also compare the study populations while controlling for income—in so doing presumably better informing such contested theoretical issues as immigrant versus natives' propensity to welfare (for methodology, see the appendix).[1]

The results of these analyses, like others reported in this volume, call into serious doubt claims that immigrants had a higher propensity than natives to use public benefits—either before or after welfare reform. Our results also suggest that welfare reform led to steep drops in legal immigrants' use of TANF and food stamps, but not to parallel declines in Medicaid or SCHIP. Low levels of private health coverage and high levels of uninsurance among legal immigrant children underscore the vulnerability of this population and reinforce the policy logic of the 2009 restoration of Medicaid and SCHIP to many of them.

PREVIOUS RESEARCH

The analysis in this chapter builds on research by the Urban Institute and others that documented both drops in immigrants' use of TANF, SSI, food stamps, Medicaid, and SCHIP after PRWORA as well as broader chilling effects on immigrants' use of public benefits and services.[2] An earlier Urban Institute study of trends in these five benefit programs also showed substantial declines in benefit use by low-income legal immigrant families with children between 1994—two years before PRWORA—and 1999—three years after enactment (Fix and Passel 2002). A study of food stamp participation over the same period showed substantial declines not only for noncitizens but also for U.S.-born citizen children with noncitizen parents (Cunnyngham 2003). Another study found declines in noncitizens' food stamp use during the late 1990s, especially in states that did not create programs to extend food assistance to noncitizens no longer eligible for FSP because of PRWORA (Borjas 2001).[3] This study also found that, in California, legal immigrant food stamp use declined despite the fact that the state had enacted a program to replace food stamps for LPRs. The author attributed this decline to immigrant fears of participating in public-assistance programs in the aftermath of Proposition 187, which California voters passed in 1994 to exclude unauthorized immigrants (not LPRs) from state-funded assistance programs.[4] Other research showed post-PRWORA declines in noncitizen applications for public assistance in California during the late 1990s (Zimmermann and Fix 1998), declines in food stamp and Medicaid use among legal immigrant families in Los Angeles and New York City (Capps et al. 2002), and a chilling effect on legal immigrant applications for food stamps and Medicaid in Texas (Hagan, Rodriguez, and Capps 1999).

We update these earlier studies by addressing trends in legal immigrant use of public-assistance programs from 1994 through

2004 at four points in time. The first is 1994, two years before PRWORA was enacted. The second is 1999, three years after enactment and a period of strong economic performance. The third is 2002, the year Congress passed the Farm Bill restorations of FSP eligibility to certain groups of legal immigrants and a year following a mild recession. The fourth is 2004, a year after the Farm Bill restorations were fully implemented and a year of strong economic expansion.

FINDINGS

It is difficult to interpret the success of welfare reform policies unless they are viewed against the backdrop of the performance of the economy and income shifts within the native and immigrant populations. Without this context, reduced public outlays, increased work, and diminished hardship could be inaccurately ascribed to policy and not to larger economic trends. As Ron Haskins points out in chapter 2, PRWORA came into effect during the late 1990s, a time of economic prosperity and falling poverty rates for all children and families. In fact, the positive economic climate from 1996 through 1999 made the two central accomplishments of PRWORA—increasing labor force participation and decreasing cash-welfare dependency— much easier (Haskins 2006).

Changes in Immigrants' Family Incomes, 1994 to 2004

During the late 1990s, as the economy strengthened, the proportion of low-income families with children fell, but leveled off after 2000. In 1994, 41 percent of all families with children had incomes below twice the federal poverty level. By 2002, this figure had fallen to 37 percent, and there was virtually no change between 2002 and 2004.

Native and LPR families Economic conditions lifted the incomes of both native and legal immigrant families during the late 1990s but not after 2000 (figure 5.1). In 1994, 41 percent of native fami-

FIGURE 5.1 Low-Income Share Families with Children

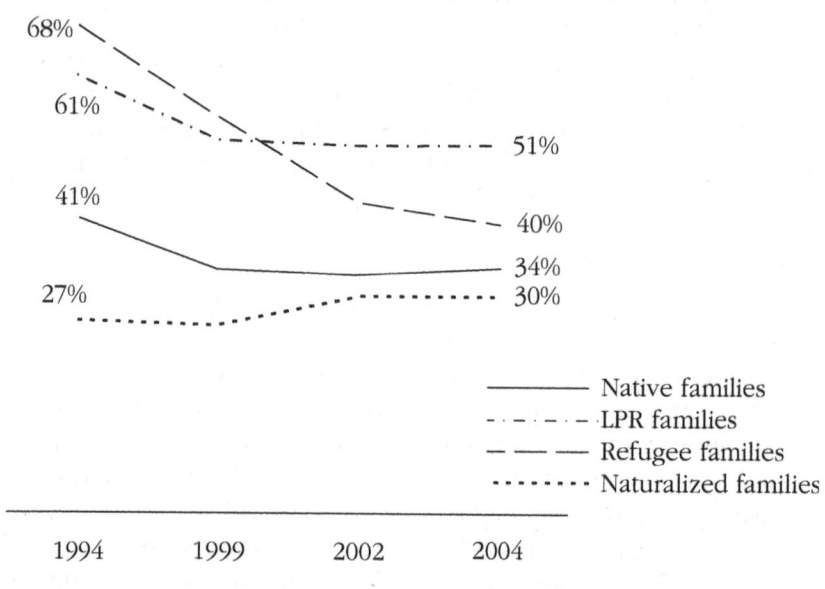

Source: Urban Institute analysis of U.S. Current Population Survey data (U.S. Bureau of the Census, various years), augmented with assignment of legal status to noncitizens.
Note: Low-income threshold is 200 percent of federal poverty level.

lies with children were low income. By 1999, this figure had fallen to 34 percent, where it remained through 2004. LPR families with children were much more likely than natives to be low income (61 percent) in 1994, but that rate also fell—to 51 percent by 1999—and remained unchanged through 2004 (for a detailed description of how we classify families by the citizenship and legal status of their members, see the appendix).

Refugee families The proportion of low-income refugee families with children fell much more sharply, a trend that persisted through 2004. In 1994, 68 percent of refugee families with children were low income, versus 61 percent of LPR families. The refugee proportion continued to decline to 40 percent in 2004, substantially below the 51 percent for LPR families and a striking turnaround over the decade. Incomes thus rose more sharply among refugees than other legal immigrants or even the native-born, both during the economic expansion of the late 1990s and after 2000.

There are several possible explanations for the steeper, long-run rise in refugee family incomes. One is that the dominant sending regions shifted in the 1990s from Southeast Asia to eastern Europe and the former Soviet Union. As a result, refugee education levels increased, which likely helped boost family incomes (Singer and Wilson 2006). Second, between 2002 and 2004, new refugee flows fell sharply, exaggerating the effect of longer-term, presumably better educated refugees on average refugee family incomes. Many of these longer-term refugees have naturalized.[5] Shifting settlement patterns and migration after initial settlement toward locations with better labor markets could be another potential explanation. Finally, since the early 1990s, the Office of Refugee Resettlement (ORR) has adopted policies that combine an initial grant of cash and health benefits with a work-oriented program that emphasizes refugee self-sufficiency through employment and English-language services. One possible result of this policy mix, implemented shortly before PRWORA, was that over time more refugees worked and fewer relied on cash assistance (Office of Refugee Resettlement 2006).

A recent evaluation of the federal refugee employment program in three major cities suggests that employment rates were high, exceeding 70 percent among refugees within their first five years in the United States in all three cities (Office of Refugee Resettlement 2008).[6] However, average refugee family income was still near the federal poverty level, even after five years in the United States. Thus the decline in the proportion of low-income refugee families is likely attributable to income improvements among longer-term refugees, that is, those in the United States at least five years.

Despite rises in incomes between 1994 and 2004, LPR and refugee families with children remained significantly more likely to be low income than their native counterparts at all points analyzed.

Naturalized citizen families Income trends for naturalized families with children differ from the three other groups we examined.

Naturalized families are less likely to be low income, even when compared with native families. The low income proportion of naturalized families actually rose during the late 1990s. In the late 1990s, a record number of immigrants naturalized, partly because the number of LPRs eligible to naturalize rose steeply. Many of those who naturalized had originally come from Mexico illegally and gained legal status after the 1986 Immigrant Reform and Control Act (Passel 2007; Fix, Passel, and Sucher 2003). This cohort tended to have somewhat lower incomes than other naturalizing populations, which depressed average family incomes. Although it is possible that increasing numbers of immigrants naturalized after PRWORA in order to receive public assistance, researchers have found that factors such as economic opportunities and the climate of reception affect naturalization behavior more than public assistance (Bloemraad 2006; Van Hook, Brown, and Bean 2006). Nonetheless, naturalized immigrants were the least likely of any family group—including native citizens—to be low income in 2004.

In sum, several income trends are notable between 1994 and 2004: broad declines in the share of low-income families across most legal status groups, especially steep declines among refugees, and a modest rise among naturalized citizens.

PUBLIC ASSISTANCE USE BY IMMIGRANT FAMILIES

With this context in mind we now turn to our analysis of public assistance use by low income immigrant families, disaggregating results by users' citizenship and legal status.

LPR versus Native-Born

Our analysis of trends in public benefit use shows lower use of all benefits except Medicaid-SCHIP among legal immigrants than among U.S.-born families at all time points—strong evidence that immigrants do not have a higher propensity to welfare use than natives. When we control for legal status and for low incomes, we find that legal immigrant families with children had lower TANF,

FIGURE 5.2 Use of Public-Assistance Programs, Low-Income Lawful Permanent Resident and Native-Born Citizen Families

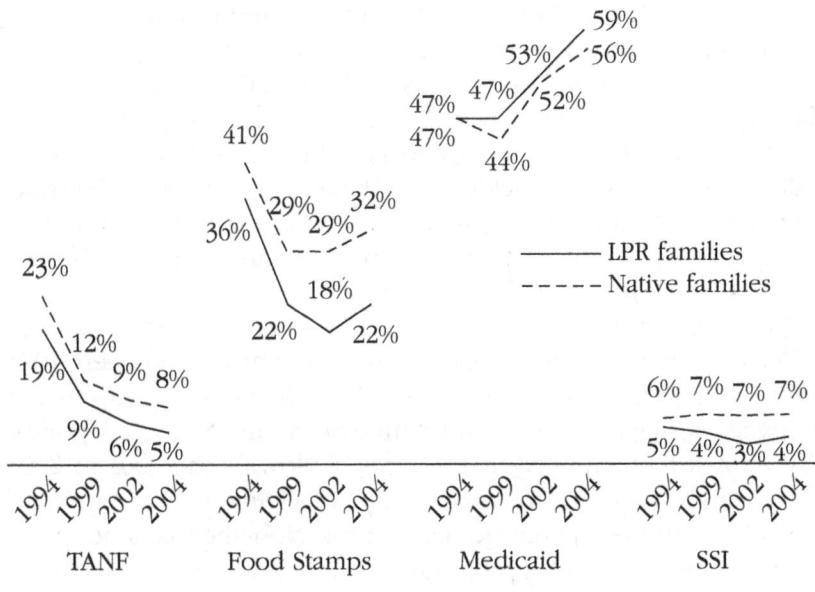

Source: Urban Institute analysis of U.S. Current Population Survey data (U.S. Bureau of the Census, various years), augmented with assignment of legal status to noncitizens.
Note: Low-income threshold is 200 percent of federal poverty level.

food stamp, and SSI use rates than citizens in 1994, two years before PRWORA was enacted—despite public and political perceptions to the contrary. Legal immigrant use rates for each of these programs remained lower than those of native citizens in 2004, eight years after welfare reform.

Among low-income LPR families with children, use of TANF, food stamps, and SSI declined steeply between 1994 and 2002, with TANF use decreasing by 13 percentage points. During the same period, TANF use dropped 14 percentage points among native citizen families (figure 5.2). Between 2002 and 2004, it fell slightly further—by about 1 percentage point—for both LPR and native families. The trend in TANF participation for low-income LPR families with children thus largely matched the pattern for native families, though LPR families participated less throughout the 1994 to 2004 period.

Food stamp use also declined sharply for both LPR and native families with low incomes during the late 1990s—declines that can be partially ascribed to welfare reform and to improved economic conditions. However, the drop in food stamp use was steeper for LPR families, and use rebounded sooner for native families. Among families with U.S.-born parents, use fell 12 percentage points between 1994 and 1999 but began slowly rising in 2002. The decrease coincided with large drops in the TANF rolls and with administrative efforts to reduce errors in payments that made it harder to prove eligibility for food stamps (Holcomb et al. 2003; America's Second Harvest 2001).[7]

Food stamp use among LPR families fell by 18 percentage points (50 percent more than for native families) between 1994 and 2002, with a small rebound by 2004. In 1994, the gap in use between low-income LPR and native-born families was 5 points. By 2002, it had widened to 11 points. Following the 2002 to 2003 Farm Bill restorations to some groups of LPRs, the gap narrowed slightly to 10 percentage points in 2004. Nonetheless, among the major public-assistance programs we analyzed, the Food Stamp Program appears to show a greater decline among legal immigrant families than among the native-born.

SSI use did not decline as sharply as TANF or food stamps, but was much lower among both native and LPR families with children in 1994. For low-income LPR families with children, it fell by 2 percentage points between 1994 and 2002.[8] Although the change is relatively small in terms of percentage points, it is substantial in relative terms, dropping by about half (from 5 to 3 percent) among presumably vulnerable families. There was no parallel drop in SSI use among low-income, native-born families with children.

Trends in Medicaid and SCHIP (analyzed together here), on the other hand, reveal a quite different pattern, with use rates increasing noticeably for both LPR and native-born families between 1994 and 2004. Use of Medicaid and SCHIP (by any family member) remained at 47 percent for low-income LPR families with children between 1994 and 1999, but fell slightly, from 47 to 44 percent, for their native-born counterparts.[9] It is likely that the creation of SCHIP in 1997, along with expanded outreach for both Medicaid and SCHIP during the late 1990s, offset PRWORA eligibility restrictions and declines associated with dramatically lower TANF use.[10] By 2004, LPR use of Medicaid-SCHIP had risen to 59 percent, exceeding the 56 percent rate for native-born families.

Thus, neither welfare reform nor the relatively benign economic climate of the study period appear to have affected Medicaid-SCHIP receipt the same way they affected TANF and food stamp receipt. As discussed later in this chapter and by Leighton Ku in chapter 6, increasing reliance on Medicaid and SCHIP by low-income families appears linked to declining employer and other private health insurance coverage, even during economic expansions.

Other less obvious programmatic changes in Medicaid and SCHIP may also explain rising enrollment. Urban Institute fieldwork in several states suggests that a combination of simplifying applications, additional access points in immigrant neighborhoods, improved interpretation and translation services, and targeted outreach to immigrant communities helped expand noncitizens' access to Medicaid and SCHIP since 2000 (Holcomb et al. 2003). Since 2000 there have also been broad outreach efforts in the Food Stamp Program directed toward immigrants (Capps et al. 2004; Food and Nutrition Service 2006). No parallel efforts have been taken in the TANF or SSI programs.

Refugees

The use of benefits—including Medicaid-SCHIP—by refugee families fell much more dramatically than that of other families during the study period, which is surprising given that refugee eligibility for these programs was largely unaffected by PRWORA. Between 1994 and 2004, refugee families' TANF use fell 32 percentage points, far outpacing the decline among native families (figure 5.3).[11] At the same time, refugee families' SSI participation also dropped sharply, from 12 to 5 percent, between 1994 and 2004, though only after 1999. These declines among refugees are notable not only because refugees were a comparatively protected population under PRWORA, but also because public benefit use among immigrants in the early 1990s had been highly concentrated among two subpopulations: refugees and the elderly (Fix and Passel 2002).

Refugees are the only population examined in this chapter to experience steep drops in both food stamps and Medicaid-SCHIP

134 Immigrants and Welfare

FIGURE 5.3 Use of Public-Assistance Programs, Low-Income Refugee and Native-Born Citizen Families with Children

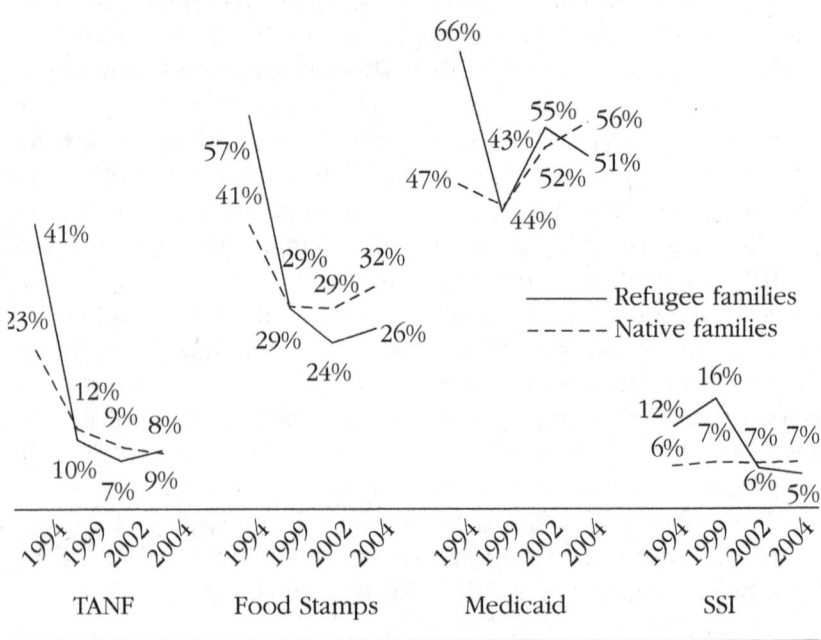

Source: Urban Institute analysis of U.S. Current Population Survey data (U.S. Bureau of the Census, various years), augmented with assignment of legal status to noncitizens.
Note: Low-income threshold is 200 percent of federal poverty level.

use following PRWORA. Between 1994 and 2004, FSP participation among refugees dropped more than 30 percentage points, from 57 to 26 percent. Medicaid-SCHIP also fell between 1994 and 2004, from 66 to 51 percent. Most of this decline occurred when use was rising considerably for both native-born and LPR families.

Naturalized Citizens

One concern regarding making public benefits more dependent on citizenship was that it might provide an incentive for low-income immigrants to naturalize to receive welfare and health insurance. Did these concerns appear justified?

Although we see rising use of food stamps and Medicaid-SCHIP

FIGURE 5.4 **Use of Public-Assistance Programs, Low-Income Naturalized and Native-Born Citizen Families with Children**

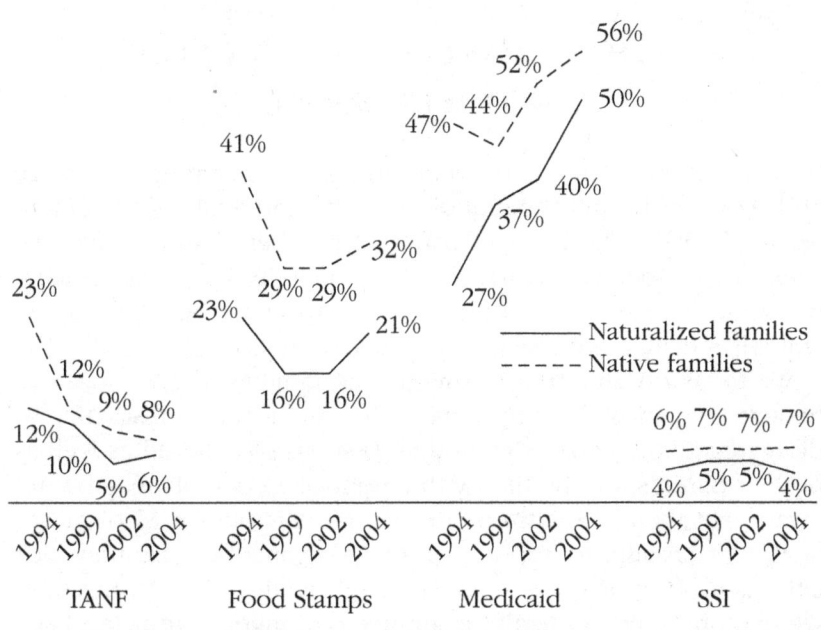

Source: Urban Institute Analysis of U.S. Current Population Survey data (U.S. Bureau of the Census, various years), augmented with assignment of legal status to noncitizens.
Note: Low-income threshold is 200 percent of federal poverty level.

after 2000, naturalized citizen families have lower rates than native-born families, suggesting that they, too, have a relatively low propensity to rely on welfare. Given the rising number of low-income naturalized citizen families, it should not be surprising that we see different patterns in public assistance use among low-income, naturalized-citizen families with children than among LPR or refugee families. In comparison, their use of TANF and food stamps dropped less than for these other groups between 1994 and 2004; their SSI use was unchanged; and their Medicaid-SCHIP use increased more rapidly (figure 5.4). We see similar patterns when we compare low-income naturalized citizens and native families, that is, smaller declines in TANF and food stamps and larger increases in Medicaid and SCHIP use. Nonetheless, naturalized citizens' use substantially trails that of natives across all programs examined—

TANF, food stamps, Medicaid-SCHIP, and SSI. Moreover, the lower use levels persist despite the fact that naturalized citizens are eligible for these programs on the same terms as native-born citizens.

HEALTH INSURANCE COVERAGE OF LOW-INCOME CHILDREN

In this section we focus on children's health insurance coverage and accordingly shift the unit of eligibility and analysis from families to children. There are, of course, a number of substantive reasons for the focus on children. These include the possible negative and to some extent unanticipated impacts of benefits cuts on children's health, well-being, and development.

We focus on children in low-income families, those most vulnerable and most broadly eligible for Medicaid and SCHIP. We disaggregate the citizenship and legal status of children as well as of their parents, on the theory that noncitizen parents may be unaware that their U.S. citizen children are eligible for Medicaid or SCHIP, or hesitant to apply for these programs because they lack citizenship (Capps et al. 2002: Holcomb et al. 2003). To this end, we explore trends in health insurance coverage for four legal status groupings: citizen children with citizen parents, citizen children with LPR parents, LPR children, and refugee children. We also describe trends in employer-provided and other insurance coverage to help address trends in Medicaid and SCHIP coverage.

Any discussion of health insurance coverage is necessarily complicated by the fact that people can receive coverage from a variety of sources—including employer-provided coverage, insurance bought on the private market, and public programs such as but not limited to Medicaid and SCHIP. To thoroughly examine trends in health-care coverage for children, we first discuss public coverage, then private or employer-provided coverage, and finally trends in the share of children who are uninsured.

Medicaid and SCHIP Coverage

With the exception of refugees, Medicaid and SCHIP coverage rose for all children studied here between 1994 and 2004, with es-

FIGURE 5.5 Medicaid-SCHIP Coverage of Low-Income Children

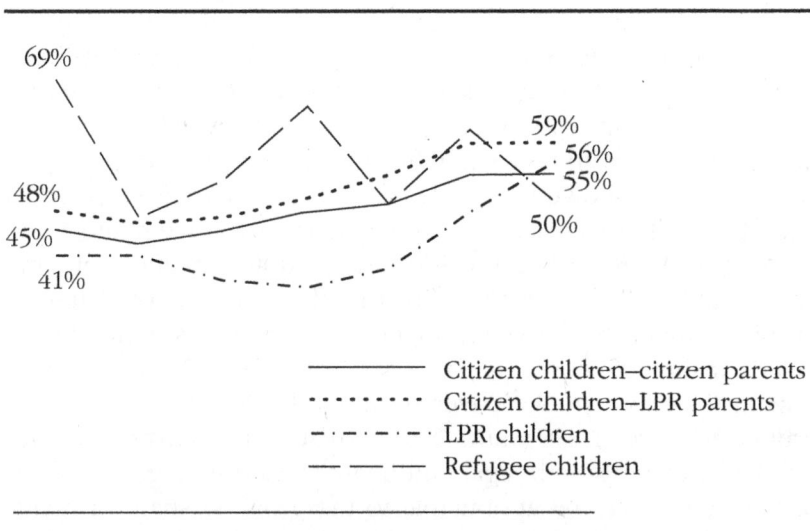

Source: Urban Institute analysis of U.S. Current Population Survey data (U.S. Bureau of the Census, various years), augmented with assignment of legal status to noncitizens.
Note: Low-income threshold is 200 percent of federal poverty level.

pecially notable increases among LPR children. In 1994, low-income LPR children had the lowest rates of Medicaid coverage (just 41 percent) of any of the four legal status groups discussed here, and their coverage fell somewhat between 1994 and 2001 (figure 5.5).[12] But their use levels began to rise fairly rapidly, and by 2004, their Medicaid-SCHIP coverage (56 percent) had closed the gap with low-income citizen children with citizen parents (55 percent). It seems likely that the initial drop in LPR children's coverage attributable to PRWORA eligibility restrictions was later offset by state-funded replacement programs in twenty-two states (National Immigration Law Center 2002) and outreach efforts aimed at immigrant communities (Holcomb et al. 2003).

Low-income citizen children show a similar trend whether their parents were LPRs or citizens. Yet Medicaid-SCHIP coverage is consistently about 3 to 4 percentage points higher for children with LPR parents than those with citizen parents—probably because the latter have a significantly higher rate of employer-based coverage (see figure 5.6). Low-income refugee children are the only group to show a decline in Medicaid-SCHIP coverage over this period, the sharpest drop occurring between 1994 and 1999 (see figure 5.5).[13] Refugee children start out with the highest rate of coverage in 1994 (69 percent) but wind up with the lowest (50 percent) by 2004. This finding is consistent with trends in refugee families' receipt of public assistance, which showed steep declines for all programs during this period as well as increases in their family incomes (see figure 5.1).

Our finding regarding the increasing public coverage of low-income LPR children seems at first to differ from that of chapter 6 in this volume. In Chapter 6 Leighton Ku examines trends in the health insurance coverage of low-income noncitizen children, finding that their public coverage through Medicaid and SCHIP dropped between 1995 and 2005. Because noncitizens are defined as including both legal and unauthorized immigrants, some of the trends may be attributable to the growing share of unauthorized immigrants in the noncitizen population. Our findings in this chapter focus separately on LPRs and refugees—the two main categories of legal noncitizens. We exclude the unauthorized. Thus, though coverage through Medicaid-SCHIP rose during the period for LPR children, the LPR proportion of noncitizen children fell overall. The rising share of unauthorized children—who are entirely ineligible for Medicaid-SCHIP—largely explains the declining coverage among noncitizen children overall.

Employer and Other Private Coverage

Despite the fact that the study period was one of relative economic growth and prosperity, certainly compared to 2008 and 2009, we see employer and other private coverage of low-income children generally falling from already low rates (figure 5.6). The increases in children's public coverage through Medicaid and SCHIP for all children except refugees shown earlier (see figure 5.5) mostly offset drops in employer and other private coverage.

Our results also indicate that employer and other private coverage varies widely by the citizenship of children and their parents. Coverage rates for LPR children, citizen children with LPR parents,

FIGURE 5.6 **Employer and Other Health Insurance Coverage of Low-Income Children**

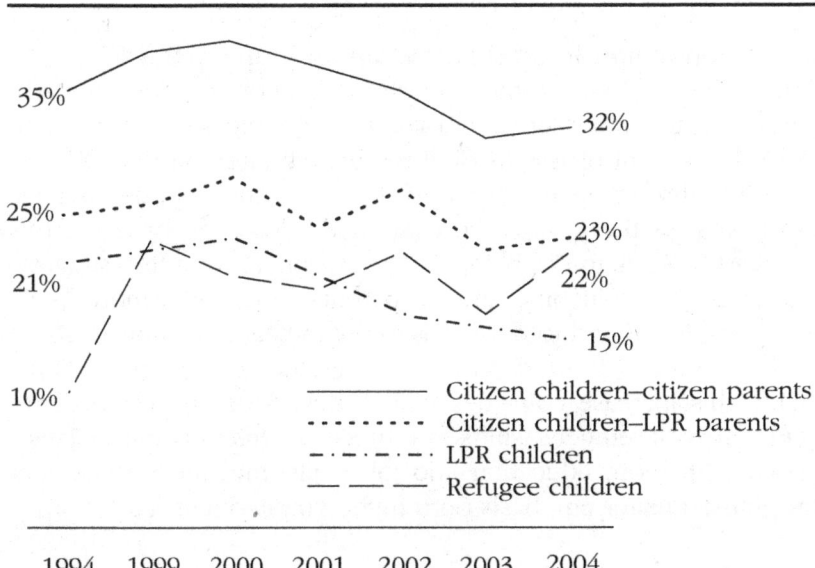

Source: Urban Institute analysis of U.S. Current Population Survey data (U.S. Bureau of the Census, various years), augmented with assignment of legal status to noncitizens.
Note: Low-income threshold is 200 percent of federal poverty level.

and refugee children were quite low in 1994. Seen in this light, the restrictions on LPR children's eligibility for Medicaid-SCHIP were likely to threaten coverage of an already vulnerable population.

In fact, low-income LPR children saw their coverage through parental employers and other sources fall considerably, from 21 to 15 percent, between 1994 and 2004. Parental employer and other coverage also dropped slightly among low-income citizen children with citizen parents, from 35 to 32 percent, suggesting that declining employer coverage affected demand for Medicaid and SCHIP among low-income children generally, not just among immigrants. Nonetheless in 2004, employer and other private coverage remained significantly higher for children with citizen rather than LPR parents. These results suggest that health-care reforms premised on employer contributions—as opposed to expansion of public coverage unlinked to employers—could disadvantage low-income children in LPR families. Declining employer and other private health insurance coverage is a trend common to both the LPR children, discussed in this chapter, and the larger population of noncitizen children, discussed in chapter 6.

Refugee children are the sole group to show improvements in employer and other private coverage over the study period. In 1994, 10 percent of low-income refugee children had health-care coverage through parental employers and other private sources, the lowest of the groups we examined. However, by 2004, this rate had more than doubled, to 22 percent. This finding suggests that in 2004 low-income refugee parents were much more likely to be employed and to have jobs carrying health insurance—both express goals of the federal refugee resettlement program. Once again, this increase coincides with a decline in the share of recently arrived refugees, shifts in refugee origins to countries associated with more education and job skills, and the resettlement program's greater emphasis on refugee employment.

Low-Income Children without Health Insurance

Despite the growth in Medicaid-SCHIP coverage of low-income children in immigrant families, the proportion of these children without insurance remained high in 2004 (see figure 5.7). Studies have correlated the lack of health insurance coverage to a lack of a usual source of medical care, lower use of primary care, and higher use of the emergency room (Ku 2009). Between 1994 and 2004, the proportion of uninsured low-income LPR children fell from 38 to 30 percent.[14] Nonetheless, their 2004 uninsurance rate was nearly twice as high as that for citizen children with LPR parents (30 to 18 percent), and more than twice that for citizen children with citizen parents (30 to 14 percent). Thus, a large gap in insurance coverage remained for low-income LPR children in 2004 despite gains through the SCHIP program, simplification of Medicaid, and outreach to immigrants for both programs (Holcomb et al. 2003). This persisting gap, coupled with evidence of hardship provided in chapter 7 of this volume, reinforces the merits of restoring all LPR children's eligibility for Medicaid and SCHIP as the Congress enacted in the 2009 SCHIP reauthorization bill. At the same time, though, declining rates of uninsurance among

Figure 5.7 Low-Income Children without Health Insurance

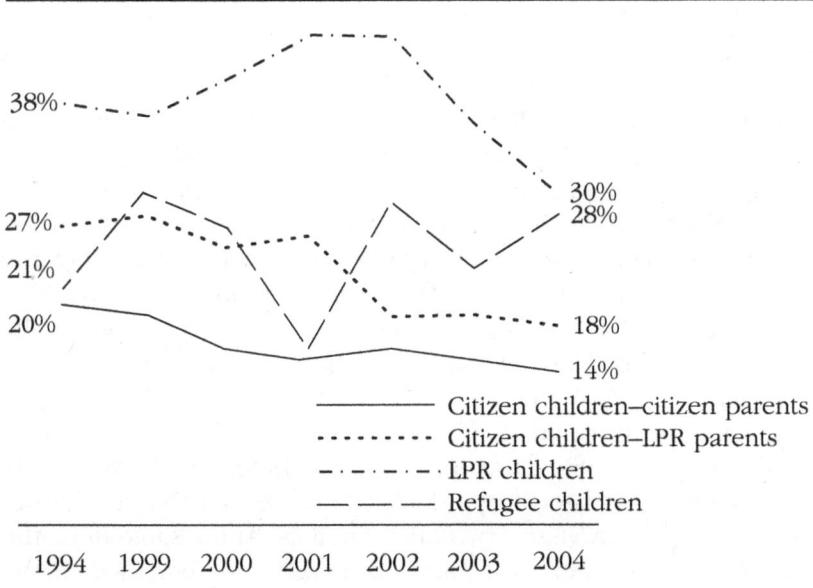

Source: Urban Institute analysis of U.S. Current Population Survey data (U.S. Bureau of the Census, various years), augmented with assignment of legal status to noncitizens.
Note: Low-income threshold is 200 percent of federal poverty level.

LPR and citizen children also demonstrate that reforms and outreach programs in the Medicaid and SCHIP programs effectively reached their target populations.

Refugees again show a different pattern. Their uninsurance rate actually rose between 1994 and 2004, from 21 to 28 percent. By 2004, their uninsurance rate was almost as high as that for LPR children. It may be that more refugee parents were working by 2004, but many of their jobs—like the jobs of LPR parents—did not carry health insurance.

SUMMARY AND DISCUSSION

We have analyzed trends between 1994 and 2004 in the use of means-tested public-assistance programs by low-income LPR, refugee, naturalized, and native-born citizen families with children. We used the same period to examine the public and employer-private health insurance coverage of four groups of low-income children: citizens with citizen parents, citizens with LPR parents, LPRs, and refugees.

Among families in all citizenship and legal status groups, the low-income proportion fell from 1994 through 1999, a period of strong economic growth. These income improvements flattened out after 1999 as the nation entered a mild recession followed by a slow economic recovery. Although between 1994 and 1999, the low-income share of naturalized immigrant families rose, by 2004 LPR and refugee families with children remained substantially more likely to be low income than native or naturalized families.

Contrary to public perceptions, we find that low-income LPR families were no more likely than native families to use TANF, food stamps, or SSI, either in 1994, just before PRWORA, or in 2004, eight years later. In particular, LPR use of TANF fell further and faster than TANF use by native families. At the same time, the widest gaps between LPR and citizen use rates emerged in the Food Stamp Program. In light of these findings, it is hard to argue that LPRs and other legal immigrants have or ever had a greater propensity to use public-assistance programs than citizens.

Subsequent reforms in the Food Stamp program and in public health insurance programs, at both the federal and state levels, further complicate the already complex policy story of the 1996 welfare reform. An economic slowdown, coupled with the restoration of food stamps to selected LPR subpopulations seem to have boosted LPR's food stamp use after 2002. Although the federal five-year bar on Medicaid or the SCHIP program did not change for children and some adults until 2009, a number of factors led to rising rates of public coverage among children with legal immigrant parents—at least through 2004. These include the emergence of state-funded health insurance programs, the spillover effects of SCHIP enactment, substantial state and private outreach, and eased access policies and practices. The expansions have proven especially critical given declines in private insurance among immigrant families. Even so, low-income LPR and refugee children, along with citizen children of LPRs, remain more likely to be uninsured than children with citizen parents.

Low employer and other private coverage, coupled with limitations on LPR children's eligibility for Medicaid and SCHIP, account in part for these high uninsurance rates.

The data also reveal two powerful trends among other immigrant subgroups. The first trend is a significant decline in the share of low-income refugees and an even steeper drop in their use of TANF, SSI, food stamps, Medicaid, and SCHIP. Use rates for refugees were far higher than natives before welfare reform. By 2004, refugee use rates were lower for every program except TANF. What explains these sharp decreases? We suspect they derive in part from aggressive placement in low-wage work; ORR's sustained integration efforts, including initial cash and health benefits; shifts in the origins and increased education of arriving refugees; and time limits on refugees' eligibility for SSI and Medicaid. Declines in new arrivals of refugees, shifting settlement patterns, and internal migration to locations with better job opportunities may also play a role. However, we did not systematically assess how these factors influenced assistance use among refugee families.

A second notable trend is a modest rise in the percentage of low-income naturalized citizens and their increased use of food stamps, Medicaid, and SCHIP. Nevertheless, these families, as with other populations, sharply decreased their TANF use. Further, despite the fact that they face no eligibility restrictions, naturalized-citizen families use benefits at a lower rate than their native counterparts.

In sum, despite income gains, legal immigrants and refugees remain more likely to be low income, and they have used and continue to use cash assistance less than citizens. Although their use of public health insurance has risen, they remain substantially more likely than their native counterparts to be uninsured.

APPENDIX: METHOLOGY

To measure changes in benefits use, we relied on the official data set with largely comparable measures of public-assistance program use across the years: the Current Population Survey (CPS) Annual Social and Economic Supplement (ASEC), which is conducted in March of every year. We augmented the CPS data with techniques for assigning legal status to noncitizens, techniques that researchers at the Urban Institute and Pew Hispanic Center pioneered (Passel and Clark 1998; Passel 2006; Passel, Van Hook, and Bean 2004).

Data Source

The March CPS ASEC includes variables for program participation of individuals and families, including three of the benefit programs in our analyses: TANF, SSI, and the Food Stamp program. The data also include detailed information about whether an individual's health insurance coverage is through employers, other private sources, Medicaid, SCHIP, or other public sources.[15] We used four years of CPS data for our family-level analysis: 1994, 1999, 2002, and 2004. Data in the March CPS ASEC are collected for the previous year—data for calendar year 1994 from the March 1995 survey, for example.

CPS data on benefits use are reported by the survey's respondents. Both welfare use and welfare income are known to be underreported, possibly substantially, in CPS (Wheaton and Giannarelli 2000). We did not correct for either type of underreporting in our analysis. Further, the data have not been adjusted to take into account program-eligibility rules or the misreporting of public benefit use on the part of immigrants and native citizens.

Units of Analysis

The unit of program eligibility varies among TANF, SSI, FSP, and Medicaid-SCHIP. FSP eligibility is determined at the household level among all adults and children who "purchase and prepare food together" (Food and Nutrition Service 2006). TANF eligibility is determined among family units with children—usually either single parents with children or two parents with children, but in some cases children who live with other relatives or nonrelative caregivers. In some instances, TANF benefits are granted only to children. SSI, Medicaid, and SCHIP are individual-level benefits, though family income heavily influences eligibility for them.

We chose the family as the unit for our analysis so that we could compare use rates across the five programs. We defined families slightly more narrowly than CPS. We included all parents and minor children together in the same family but put other adult relatives (such as uncles, aunts, and grandparents) into separate families. Our definition is thus similar to the concept of a nuclear family (parents and children) as well as to the one used for TANF eligibility. Our family definition is narrower than that for determining FSP eligibility. Therefore, more than one of our family units may be receiving food stamps in the same FSP unit. For SSI and Medicaid-SCHIP, we defined recipient families as those in which at least one member is receiving benefits, thereby including families where some members receive benefits and others do not.

We focused on families with children because two of the benefit programs we analyzed—TANF and SCHIP—are available only to children or families with children, and because families with children were the focus of the 1996 welfare law and of the 2002 Farm Bill.

Definition of Low Income

We confined our analysis to low-income families, those with annual incomes below twice the federal poverty level (FPL). In 1994, the FPL for a four-person family was $14,800, and in 2004 it was $18,850; poverty levels were slightly lower for smaller families and higher for larger ones (U.S. Department of Health and Human Services 2009). Focusing on low-income LPR families with children allowed us to assess immigrants' versus natives' proclivity to receive public benefits, as immigrant families are more likely to be low income than native families. We chose 200 percent of FPL because, although income eligibility thresholds vary among the five programs we analyzed, the thresholds largely fall within the 100 to 200 percent range.

Assignment of Legal Status

It is essential to distinguish LPRs from the unauthorized population because the unauthorized are ineligible for the five public-assistance programs we examined. Indeed, PRWORA or subsequent policy changes did not affect the eligibility of unauthorized immigrants. We also believe it is important to distinguish refugees from other legal immigrants because refugees have broader eligibility for benefits, benefit from targeted integration services, and have high historic levels of program use (Fix and Passel 2002). Thus, our analyses differentiated among four groups: legal immigrants (LPRs), refugees and asylees, naturalized citizens, and native-born citizens. The CPS data separate immigrants from natives and differentiate between immigrants who are not citizens and those who have naturalized.[16] Among noncitizens, however, the CPS data do not differentiate among refugees, other legal immigrants, and the unauthorized.

The Urban Institute and Pew Hispanic Center have developed techniques for assigning legal status to noncitizens in the CPS data (Passel and Clark 1998; Passel 2006; Passel, Van Hook, and Bean 2004). These techniques yield four groups of noncitizens: refugees and asylees, legal temporary migrants, LPRs, and unauthorized immigrants (see figure 5.1). Refugees are defined based on their country of birth and year of arrival;[17] legal temporary residents are defined based on length of U.S. residency, school enrollment, labor force participation, or occupation and industry of employment. The remaining noncitizens are categorized as either LPRs or unauthorized immigrants, using a probabilistic procedure that takes into account their country of origin, length of U.S. residency, occupation, household composition, and other factors. The numbers of LPRs, refugees, and temporary migrants are adjusted to match control totals based on Department of Homeland Security admissions data. The number of unauthorized immigrants is determined by subtracting the noncitizens in the other three groups from the total noncitizens in the data. After classifying noncitizens into these four groups, we removed temporary legal migrants and unauthorized immigrants from our sample because neither group is eligible for the public benefit programs we analyzed.

Once we assigned citizenship and legal status to immigrants in the CPS data, we then created a family-level status variable. Because our family units are essentially nuclear families composed of parents and children (other adult relatives and nonrelatives are excluded), we assigned the legal status of the family based on the legal status of the parents.

In assigning legal status to a family, we adopted a hierarchy that bases a family's legal status on that of the parent who is least eligible for public benefits under the theory that families with ineligible noncitizen adults will be deterred from applying for benefits, even when other family members (usually the children) may be eligible.[18] To illustrate, where one parent is a naturalized citizen and another is an LPR, the family is classified as an LPR family. If either parent is unauthorized, the family is classified as unauthorized.

NOTES

1. Throughout the chapter, we focus on low-income families, which we conventionally define as those with incomes below twice the federal poverty level (FPL). In 1994, the FPL for a four-person family was $14,800, and in 2004 it was $18,850; poverty levels were slightly lower for smaller families and higher for larger ones.
2. SCHIP was enacted and implemented starting in 1997, a year after PRWORA. Although a separate program, we include SCHIP in our analysis of Medicaid because the two programs together substantially increased the public health insurance coverage of children in low-income families, and in part because respondents rarely distinguished between the two.
3. After PRWORA was enacted, several states created programs that used state-only funds to either replace food stamps or to supply similar assistance not unlike food stamps for families who included LPRs made ineligible for FSP by PRWORA (Zimmermann and Tumlin 1999).
4. Proposition 187 restricted the access of unauthorized immigrants to education, health care, and most social services across the state. Although courts struck down most of its provisions—and though it never targeted LPRs or other legal immigrants—the proposition conveyed a message that appears to have deterred legal immigrants from applying for benefits in California for several years after its passage.

5. Our assignment of refugee status includes former refugees who have become citizens.
6. The three cities included in the evaluation were Miami, Houston, and Sacramento.
7. For many families, food stamp eligibility has been linked to TANF and its predecessor program, Aid to Families with Dependent Children. Thus, when the TANF rolls dropped, many families lost food stamp eligibility as well. Because welfare reform changed the eligibility rules for the two programs, the tie between TANF and the Food Stamp Program has loosened, leading to greater differences in the use rates for the two programs.
8. Our focus on low-income families with children means that the SSI population we analyze largely excludes the elderly. The SSI recipients in our sample include disabled children and parents and, in some instances, elderly adults who serve as caregivers for children. Our sample does not include elderly SSI recipients who are not caregivers for children under age eighteen.
9. SCHIP was enacted in 1997, so participation rates for 1994 are for Medicaid only.
10. Like food stamps, Medicaid eligibility has historically been linked to TANF-AFCD receipt, and since welfare reform Medicaid has also become increasingly decoupled from TANF.
11. Note that our analysis of refugee families includes families in which refugees have become naturalized citizens.
12. In this section, we show data for all years from 1999 through 2004 because of significant year-to-year fluctuations for some groups of children, particularly refugees. The coverage rate for 1994 represents coverage through Medicaid only, because SCHIP had not yet been enacted; in all other years, it includes both Medicaid and SCHIP.
13. Because of relatively small sample sizes in the CPS for refugee children, their Medicaid-SCHIP coverage rate rises and falls from year to year. We show individual-year changes in order to display the volatility of these estimates. Despite these year-to-year variations, the coverage rate for refugees in 2004 is clearly much lower than in 1994, and is at or below the rates for the other groups of children displayed here.
14. Leighton Ku finds in chapter 6 that the uninsurance rate for low-income noncitizen children rose during this period, whereas our analysis here finds that it fell for low-income LPR children. The reason for this discrepancy is the same as the reason for the different trends observed for Medicaid-SCHIP coverage: our analysis is lim-

ited to LPR children, whereas that in chapter 6 includes both LPR and unauthorized children. Because the unauthorized are a growing share of noncitizen children and unauthorized children have relatively high uninsurance rates, their growing share raised the uninsurance rate for noncitizen children overall.

15. We combine Medicaid and SCHIP receipt under the assumption that some CPS respondents may not have known in which of these two programs their children were enrolled. Respondents may also have failed to distinguish between regular Medicaid—to which PRWORA restrictions apply—and emergency Medicaid—which is available to all immigrants, including the unauthorized. However, emergency Medicaid accounts for a very small share of total Medicaid recipients and spending, and therefore should not significantly influence our results.

16. Immigrants must generally have lived in the United States for at least five years before they can apply for citizenship; if they marry a U.S. citizen, the waiting period is three years. A small number of immigrants in CPS have not lived in the country long enough to meet the waiting-period criteria, and so we moved them from the naturalized citizen to noncitizen group.

17. We assigned refugee status to all immigrants who entered the United States since 1980 and were born in refugee or asylee countries, regardless of whether they have become citizens. We included both citizen and noncitizen refugees together in our analysis because the refugee experience and subsequent public services made available to refugees may affect participation in public-benefit programs beyond citizenship. In other words, we excluded refugees from our naturalized group.

18. Previous studies suggested that even one noncitizen adult in the family—whether the adult is legal or unauthorized—can deter the family from seeking public assistance (Hagan, Rodriguez, and Capps 1999; Holcomb et al. 2003; Zimmermann and Fix 1998).

REFERENCES

America's Second Harvest. 2001. *The Red Tape Divide: State-by-State Review of Stamp Applications.* Chicago: America's Second Harvest.

Bloemraad, Irene. 2006. *Becoming a Citizen: Incorporating Immigrants and Refugees in the United States and Canada.* Berkeley: University of California Press.

Borjas, George J. 2001. "Food Insecurity and Public Assistance." *Joint*

Center for Poverty Research working paper 243. Chicago: Northwestern University and University of Chicago.

Capps, Randolph, Michael E. Fix, Leighton Ku, Chris Furgiuele, and Daniel Perez-Lopez. 2002. *How Are Immigrants Faring after Welfare Reform? Preliminary Evidence from Los Angeles and New York City.* Washington: U.S. Department of Health and Human Services.

Capps, Randolph, Robin Koralek, Katherine Lotspeich, Michael E. Fix, Pamela Holcomb, and Jane Reardon-Anderson. 2004. *Assessing Implementation of the 2002 Farm Bill Legal Immigrant Food Stamp Restorations.* Washington, D.C.: The Urban Institute.

Cunnyngham, Karen. 2003. *Trends in Food Stamp Program Participation Rates: 1999 to 2001.* Washington, D.C.: Mathematica Policy Research.

Fix, Michael E., and Jeffrey S. Passel. 1994. *Immigration and Immigrants: Setting the Record Straight.* Washington, D.C.: The Urban Institute.

———. 2002. "The Scope and Impact of Welfare Reform's Immigrant Provisions." *Assessing the New Federalism* discussion paper 02–03. Washington, D.C.: The Urban Institute.

Fix, Michael E., Jeffrey S. Passel, and Kenneth Sucher. 2003. "Trends in Naturalization: Immigrant Families and Workers." *Facts and Perspective Brief* no. 3. Washington, D.C.: The Urban Institute.

Food and Nutrition Service. 2006. *Characteristics of Food Stamp Households: Fiscal Year 2005.* Alexandria, Va.: U.S. Department of Agriculture, Food and Nutrition Service, Office of Analysis, Nutrition and Evaluation.

Hagan, Jacqueline, Nestor Rodriguez, and Randy Capps. 1999. "Effects of the 1996 Immigration and Welfare Reform Acts on Communities in Texas and Mexico." *WPS* working paper 99-5. Houston: University of Houston, Center for Immigration Research.

Haskins, Ron. 2006. *Work over Welfare, The Inside Story of the 1996 Welfare Reform Law.* Washington, D.C.: Brookings Institution Press.

Holcomb, Pamela A., Karen C. Tumlin, Robin Koralek, Randolph Capps, and Anita Zuberi. 2003 *The Application Process for TANF, Food Stamps, Medicaid and SCHIP: Issues for Agencies and Applicants, Including Immigrants and Limited English Speakers.* Washington: The Urban Institute / U.S. Department of Health and Human Services.

Ku, Leighton. 2009. "Restoring Medicaid and SCHIP Coverage to Legal Immigrant Children and Pregnant Women: Implications for Community Health and Health Care for Tomorrow's Citizens." Geiger Gibson / RCHN Community Health Foundation Research Collaborative issue no. 7. Washington, D.C.: The George Washington University, School of Public Health and Health Services, Department of Health Policy.

National Immigration Law Center. 2002. "State Funded Medical Assistance Programs." In *Guide to Immigrant Eligibility for Federal Programs*, updated July 2007. Washington, D.C.: National Immigration Law Center. Available at: http://www.nilc.org/pubs/Guide_update.htm (accessed August 2008).

Office of Refugee Resettlement. 2006. "Refugee Resettlement Program: Basis and Purpose of the Program," In *Title 45—Public Welfare*. 45CFR400.1, Available at: http://www.acf.hhs.gov/programs/orr/policy/45cfr400_06.htm (accessed November 2008).

———. 2008. *The Evaluation of the Refugee Social Service (RSS) and Targeted Assistance Formula Grant (TAG) Programs: Synthesis of Findings from Three Sites*. Washington: U.S. Department of Health and Human Services, Administration for Children and Families.

Passel, Jeffrey. 2006. *The Size and Characteristics of the Unauthorized Migrant Population in the United States: Estimates Based on the March 2005 Current Population Survey*. Washington, D.C.: Pew Hispanic Center.

———. 2007. *Growing Share of Immigrants Choosing Naturalization*. Washington, D.C.: Pew Hispanic Center.

Passel, Jeffrey, and Rebecca L. Clark. 1998. *Immigrants in New York: Their Legal Status, Incomes, and Taxes*. Washington, D.C.: The Urban Institute.

Passel, Jeffrey, Jennifer Van Hook, and Frank D. Bean. 2004. *Estimates of Legal and Unauthorized Foreign Born Population for the United States and Selected States, Based on Census 2000*. Report to the Census Bureau. Washington, D.C.: The Urban Institute.

Singer, Audrey, and Jill H. Wilson. 2006. *From 'There' to 'Here': Refugee Resettlement in Metropolitan America*. Washington: Brookings Institution Press.

U.S. Bureau of the Census. Various years. *Current Population Survey, Annual Social and Economic Supplement, March*. Washington: Government Printing Office.

U.S. Department of Health and Human Services. Administration for Children and Families. 2009. "HHS Poverty Guidelines," Washington: Government Printing Office. Available at: http://aspe.hhs.gov/poverty/figures-fed-reg.shtml (accessed May 2007).

Van Hook, Jennifer, Susan K. Brown, and Frank D. Bean. 2006. "For Love or Money? Welfare Reform and Immigrant Naturalization." *Social Forces* 85(4): 643–66.

Wheaton, Laura, and Linda Giannarelli. 2000. "Coverage of Social Benefit Programs in the Current Population Survey." Paper presented at the annual meeting of the American Statistical Association. Indianapolis, Ind. (August 13–17).

Zimmermann, Wendy, and Michael E. Fix. 1998. *Declining Immigrant Applications for Medi-Cal and Welfare Benefits in Los Angeles County.* Washington, D.C.: The Urban Institute.

Zimmermann, Wendy, and Karen Tumlin. 1999. "Patchwork Policies: State Assistance for Immigrants under Welfare Reform." *Assessing the New Federalism* occasional paper no. 24. Washington, D.C.: The Urban Institute.

—— Chapter 6 ——

Changes in Immigrants' Use of Medicaid and Food Stamps: The Role of Eligibility and Other Factors

Leighton Ku

CONGRESS RESTRICTED the eligibility of legal immigrants for means-tested benefits by passing two laws in 1996, the Personal Responsibility and Work Opportunity Reconciliation Act (PRWORA) and the Illegal Immigration Reform and Immigrant Responsibility Act (IIRIRA). These changes were designed to limit the use of means-tested federal benefits by immigrants, to shift responsibility for immigrants' needs to their sponsors or to the states and to achieve federal cost savings (Fix and Passel 2002). In so doing, Congress altered the previous social contract, under which immigrants who were legally admitted as lawful permanent residents (LPRs)—and who were subject to civic responsibilities like paying taxes—were eligible for public benefits on terms similar to those of citizens.

This chapter examines how the use of Medicaid and food stamps—the two most commonly used means-tested benefits—changed for noncitizen immigrants over the past decade. Part of the changes in participation can be attributed to the restrictions in the eligibility criteria established by Congress in 1996 or to changes made in subsequent years. But some of the changes were influenced by other economic, social, and programmatic factors over the years. I compare trends in Medicaid and Food

Stamp Program (recently renamed the Supplemental Nutrition Assistance Program, or SNAP) use by noncitizen immigrants with trends for citizens as well as for citizen children with U.S.-born versus noncitizen parents.[1] I also review evidence regarding how changes in Medicaid or Food Stamp Program participation may have affected hardship levels among immigrants as measured by changes in uninsurance, medical care use, and food insecurity.

INTERPLAY OF SOCIAL FACTORS

Public benefits like Medicaid and food stamps are designed to reduce the hardships of poor families and individuals, immigrants and citizens alike. But immigrants often face higher barriers to such services. Immigrants' access to and use of public benefits are governed by multiple factors. The most visible and easily identifiable of these from a public policy perspective are the eligibility criteria, that is, the formal federal or state rules that determine who qualifies. But there is typically a large gap between the number of people who are eligible and those who actually participate, and a number of social and policy factors may also affect participation. Numerous economic, social, and structural factors affect immigrants' participation in public benefit programs and, more broadly, the use of services that meet their needs (see table 6.1).

Eligibility Criteria

Elements of eligibility rules established for public benefits include income limits, immigration status, categorical restrictions, and so on. The 1996 legislation modified immigrant-related eligibility criteria, but subsequent amendments eased some of those restrictions, restoring eligibility for some legal immigrants. Key provisions of the 1996 law and subsequent modifications for Medicaid and the Food Stamp Program (FSP)—including the 2002 restorations of FSP eligibility under the Farm Bill (Public Law 107-17) and 2009 restorations of Medicaid and the State Children's Health Insurance Program (SCHIP) under the Children's Health Insurance Program Reauthorization Act (Public Law 111-3)—are summarized in table 6.2.

Table 6.1 Types of Factors Affecting Immigrants' Use of Public Benefits

Eligibility criteria
- Immigration-citizenship status (for example, citizen, lawful permanent resident (LPR), refugee, undocumented)
- Income and assets
- Category and family composition (for example, family, child, elderly person, person with disability)
- Other special factors (for example, worked for ten years in qualified employment, military veteran)
- Residence (duration, place)
- Documentation-verification requirements

Economic and social trends
- Poverty or unemployment rates
- Demographic trends
- Immigration and naturalization rates (for example, growth in undocumented population)

Social and community factors
- Awareness of public benefit programs and understanding about immigrant eligibility
- Social isolation and integration, including acculturation and time in the United States
- Language barriers
- Fears about consequences of participation
- Perceived need for assistance
- Alternative forms of assistance or services (for example, relatives or sponsors, free clinics, and food banks)

Program access
- Availability of governmental or nongovernmental outreach or assistance services
- Perceived immigrant friendliness, including language assistance and cultural competence
- Simplicity of enrollment (for example, shortened forms, less documentation)

Source: Author's compilation

Requirements that applicants submit certain types of documents or that their status be verified also affect who can be determined eligible. When specific documentation is mandated, those who are unable to provide the necessary paperwork may be barred. Thus, for example, under legislation enacted for Medicaid in 2006 (the Deficit Reduction Act, Public Law 109-171), citizens who could not prove their citizenship by submitting a passport,

TABLE 6.2 Key Changes in Immigrants' Eligibility for Medicaid and the Food Stamp Program

Before 1996
- Lawful permanent residents (LPRs) and refugees were eligible for public benefits on the same terms as citizens in Medicaid and on similar terms in the Food Stamp Program (FSP). For the FSP, a portion of sponsors' income was "deemed available" to the immigrants for the first three years in the United States, increasing their apparent income and reducing benefits.
- Undocumented migrants were ineligible for the FSP and Medicaid, except for Medicaid coverage of emergency medical conditions.

PRWORA and companion immigration legislation
- *Medicaid*. LPRs admitted after August 1996 became ineligible during their first five years in the United States. Restrictions were not applied to refugees, those with forty quarters (ten years) of qualified work, veterans, and other small groups of legal immigrants.
- *Food stamps*. Denied food stamp eligibility to most LPRs, regardless of date of entry into the United States. LPRs with forty quarters of qualified work, refugees, veterans, and others remained eligible.
- *Sponsorship*. Required sponsors of newly admitted LPRs to have family incomes of at least 125 percent of the federal poverty level. Sponsors must sign affidavits stating they will be financially responsible for the immigrants until they become citizens or work for forty quarters (ten years). If immigrants use public benefits, sponsors can be liable to repay the value of the benefits. States are allowed to deny eligibility to LPRs if sponsors' incomes lift their family incomes over eligibility thresholds.

After 1996
- *1997*. Eligibility was restored for certain immigrants in SSI. Medicaid eligibility was also restored to those who gained SSI coverage. The State Children's Health Insurance Program (SCHIP) was created and most Medicaid immigrant eligibility rules were applied to SCHIP.
- *1998*. Food stamp eligibility was restored to LPR children, elderly, and disabled who were admitted before August 1996.
- *2002*. Food stamp eligibility was restored to LPRs who have lived in the United States for more than five years and to all LPR children and disabled regardless of their dates of admission to the United States.
- *2009*. States are given the option to restore Medicaid and SCHIP eligibility to all LPR children and pregnant women regardless of their date of admission.

Source: Author's compilation.
Note: These changes refer to eligibility for federal benefits. Many states provide state-funded medical or food assistance for immigrants who are not eligible under federal criteria (for information about state-funded assistance, see National Immigration Law Center 2002).

birth certificate, or similar document no longer qualified. Before these rules were repealed, preliminary evidence showed that Medicaid enrollment had fallen in many states and suggested that those losing coverage because of inadequate documentation were primarily U.S. citizens, who ought to have remained eligible (Ross 2007).

Although the federal legislation specifies eligibility for the federally funded benefit programs, a number of states opted to create medical or food-assistance replacement programs that use state funding to continue to provide benefits to some or all of the legal immigrants who lost coverage in 1996 (Zimmermann and Tumlin 1999; National Immigration Law Center 2002). Many, particularly state officials, have interpreted the 1996 immigrant restrictions as effectively constituting a cost-shift from the federal government to states, given that federal funds for participation were no longer available. A number of states, such as California or Illinois, instituted these programs soon after the 1996 legislation was enacted. Some states, such as Florida, subsequently terminated or reduced their state-funded programs in recent years, mainly because of state budget problems.

Economic and Social Trends

When the number of poor people rises, as it did between 2001 and 2005, we would expect that receipt of Medicaid or food stamps would grow simply because more are eligible. Changes in the flows of legal and unauthorized immigrants also affect the pool of those who might be eligible.

Social and Community Factors

Only a fraction of eligible immigrants and native-born citizens actually use public benefits. Many families are unaware that public benefits are available, or may not understand if they are eligible.

Other concerns may further impede immigrants from obtaining public benefits even if they are eligible (Schwartz 2001). Evidence suggests that the 1996 law had a chilling effect: a large number of immigrant households—including those with U.S.-born citizen children—incorrectly believed they had lost eligibility and their coverage (Fix and Passel 2002). Sometimes immigrant families erroneously believed that all family members were ineligible, even though children in noncitizen families are often U.S.-born and thus eligible on the same terms as any other native-born citizens (Fix and Zimmerman 2001). Similarly, the immigrant eligibility restrictions imposed in 1996 are complicated and differ across programs. Because a post-1996 LPR child is not eligible for Medicaid, the family may believe she or he is also not eligible for food stamps. Simply because an immigrant has lived in the United States for more than five years does not mean that she or he will be aware of eligibility for Medicaid. Nonetheless, such misunderstandings and fears may ease with the passage of time as immigrants become more aware of the rules and realize that they or their children are in fact eligible for assistance.

Some noncitizens worry that receiving public benefits might jeopardize their legal status or future rights. This concern arises because of long-standing policies under which the U.S. Citizenship and Immigration Service or State Department may deny admission to an immigrant who is likely to become a public charge. Public charge policies apply to those who received cash welfare benefits but not to those who receive noncash benefits such as food stamps or Medicaid, except long-term care (Fremstad 2004). In a study of immigrants in Texas, for example, though a large number of LPR immigrants lost benefits because of eligibility restrictions, some eligible immigrants dropped Medicaid voluntarily because they feared that receipt might have adverse consequences, such as making it harder to sponsor the entry of relatives in the future (Hagan et al. 2003).

For immigrants, numerous factors add barriers to participation beyond those the U.S.-born face. Language barriers make it harder for immigrants to understand the programs and may make it more difficult to apply. Means-tested programs often have complex eligibility rules and require the ability to read and complete complicated application forms in English if translated forms or interpreters are not available. Cultural differences may also create confusion. For example, many immigrants come from countries with universal health care and may find concepts such as securing health insurance or navigating managed care systems difficult to grasp.

A final factor that affects participation in government assistance programs is the availability of alternative sources of the needed services. Immigrants may be able to use their earnings to buy health insurance or food for their families, although this would be more challenging for low-income immigrants. If the immigrants were sponsored, they might be able to turn to their sponsors for assistance; indeed, the 1996 legislation sought to place primary financial responsibility on immigrants' sponsors. Finally, if low-income immigrants are unable to get assistance from either their sponsors or government programs, they may seek help from other more comfortable sources, such as charitable medical clinics or hospitals, food banks, or soup kitchens.

Program Access

Public agencies and nongovernmental organizations can take steps to promote participation by those who are eligible, including immigrants and members of their families. The availability of multilingual program materials and application forms along with multilingual eligibility staff or interpreters make it possible for immigrants to both understand the programs and successfully apply for them. A federal presidential order issued in August 2000 required that federal agencies assess the needs of clients who are limited English proficient (LEP) and develop plans to meet their needs to deter discrimination against people based on their national origin.[2] As a result, federal, state, and local agencies—including welfare offices—stepped up their efforts to ensure that program materials, such as applications and outreach materials, were available in multiple languages and that language and interpretation assistance were available. Similarly, many hospitals and clinics offer language assistance to improve access to care and quality of care among LEP patients. It is clear, though, that language barriers remain serious despite these efforts (Andrulis, Goodman, and Pryor 2002; Holcomb et al. 2003).

Outreach, particularly by community groups that immigrants trust, can improve immigrant families' awareness and facilitate enrollment (Aizer 2006; Holcomb et al. 2003). Finally, simplifying enrollment procedures—shortening applications or lengthening certification periods, or both—can make it easier for eligible immigrants and the native-born alike to become enrolled and to retain enrollment.

One impressive demonstration of the effect of strengthened outreach efforts was seen in a recent project focusing on uninsured Latino children, primarily of low-income immigrants, conducted by Glenn Flores and his associates (2005). Children randomly assigned to an intensive community-based outreach and case management effort attained a 96 percent insurance coverage rate, versus 57 percent among children receiving standard outreach. The case managers—Spanish-speaking women from the communities—received special training and worked closely with parents. They helped the parents understand the insurance program and helped them complete the child's application. The case managers also acted as advocates with eligibility staff to ensure that the children were enrolled. In Massachusetts, where this study was conducted, children in both the intervention and control groups were eligible for some form of publicly funded health insurance coverage; the key difference was the outreach approach. Insurance coverage of low-income Latino children—a population with low coverage that is often hard to reach—almost doubled.

CHANGES IN COVERAGE

In this chapter we analyze trends in Medicaid, SCHIP, and other health insurance coverage for citizens versus noncitizens, as well as for citizen children with U.S.-born versus noncitizen parents.[3] We compare these trends across three points in time: 1995 (the year before PRWORA was enacted), 2000, and 2005. Separate analyses for children, nonelderly adults, and the elderly are included. Our analyses are based on Medicaid or SCHIP participation at the individual level, based on individuals' eligibility, consistent with the way that Medicaid benefits are conferred. As noted, in 2009, federal legislation gave states the option to restore Medicaid and SCHIP coverage to LPR children and pregnant women during their first five years in the United States, but data indicating the possible impact of this change will not be available for at least a couple of years.

In our analyses, we used data from the March supplements of the Current Population Survey (CPS), which offers large sample sizes and information about nativity, citizenship, income, and health insurance coverage in the previous year. The March 2006 survey, for example, asks about insurance coverage and income in 2005. Because the CPS includes information about all types of health insurance, we can determine whether a person uses Medicaid or another form of health insurance coverage, including private coverage. Our analysis sample is limited to low-income families—those with family incomes below 200 percent of the federal poverty level.

There are four noteworthy limitations to our analyses of CPS data. First, we are unable to differentiate noncitizens by legal status. Other researchers, such as Capps, Fix, and Henderson, impute legal status to immigrants using methods we lack (chapter 5, this volume). Trends described here for all noncitizens may differ between LPRs and unauthorized immigrants because changes in the size or composition of the unauthorized population (for instance, their family incomes) may differ from changes in the legal immigrant population. PRWORA restricted benefit eligibility for LPRs and some other groups of legal immigrants but not for unauthorized immigrants, who were already ineligible for Medicaid before the 1996 legislation was enacted. Second, the CPS, compared with administrative data, underreports Medicaid participation. Third, there have been modest methodological changes in the way the CPS asks respondents about their health insurance coverage, and thus the 1995, 2000, and 2005 survey data are similar but not completely comparable.[4] Fourth, the CPS data do not distinguish between federally funded Medicaid-SCHIP benefits and state-funded replacement programs for noncitizens that were made ineligible by PRWORA; beneficiaries typically are not aware of the differences. Several states, including the major immigrant destinations of California and New York, began funding health insurance coverage for noncitizens after PRWORA was enacted (Zimmermann and Tumlin 1999). Because they leave out the state-level restorations of benefits, the changes in Medicaid-SCHIP participation we observed in the CPS data tend to underestimate the impact of the federal eligibility restrictions in PRWORA.

Children

The proportion of uninsured noncitizen children rose from 1995 to 2005—the year welfare reform was enacted and the nine years that followed—from 44 percent in 1995 to 48 percent by 2005, and the percentage covered by Medicaid or SCHIP fell (figure 6.1). In contrast, for citizen children whose parents were born in the United States, the uninsured proportion fell from 19 percent in 1995 to 15 percent by 2005, largely because of increases in Medicaid and SCHIP participation. Insurance coverage of noncitizen children eroded over the period, but strengthened for children in native-born families. As is noted elsewhere in this volume, these results suffer somewhat from those in chapter 5, which found that Medicaid coverage rose for low-income noncitizen children in legal-immigrant families. The differing results can be ascribed to the fact that many of the noncitizen children included in the analysis shown in figure 6.1 are unauthorized and therefore ineligible for Medicaid-SCHIP.

The creation of SCHIP in 1998 and parallel expansions that states made to simplify or expand coverage for children in Medicaid led to large eligibility expansions for low-income children. At the same time, states developed substantial outreach programs and made it simpler to enroll children in both programs. Most states provide Medicaid or SCHIP to children of parents with incomes below 200 percent of poverty (Ross and Cox 2005).

As a result, for low-income citizen children of U.S.-born parents, Medicaid and SCHIP participation increased from 45.4 percent in 1995 to 53.2 percent in 2005 (see table 6.3). The net result was that the uninsured proportion of these low-income children fell by about 25 percent, from 19.4 percent to 14.9 percent.

Citizen children of noncitizen parents were eligible for Medicaid or SCHIP coverage in all these years on the same terms as citizen children of U.S.-born parents. Nonetheless, Medicaid-SCHIP coverage declined between 1995 and 2000 before rebounding dramatically in 2005. This pattern is consistent with other analyses (Zimmermann and Fix 1998; Ku, Fremstad, and Broaddus 2003;

Figure 6.1 Low-Income Children Uninsured or Covered by Medicaid-SCHIP

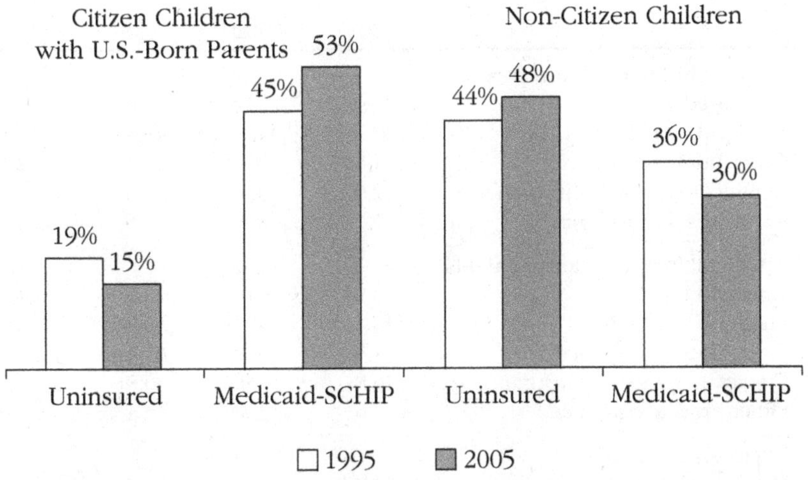

Citizen Children with U.S.-Born Parents
- Uninsured: 19% (1995), 15% (2005)
- Medicaid-SCHIP: 45% (1995), 53% (2005)

Non-Citizen Children
- Uninsured: 44% (1995), 48% (2005)
- Medicaid-SCHIP: 36% (1995), 30% (2005)

☐ 1995 ■ 2005

Source: Author's analysis based on Current Population Survey (U.S. Bureau of the Census, various years).
Note: Low-income means family income below 200 percent of the poverty line.

Capps, Kenney, Fix 2003). The rebound was probably related to coverage expansion as well as to extensive outreach to ethnic communities. That is, participation fell because of community confusion and fears about the new welfare reform rules and rebounded in part because of extensive efforts to communicate with immigrant parents to let them know that their U.S.-born children were still entitled, as citizens, to enroll in Medicaid or SCHIP.

By contrast, among noncitizen children, Medicaid-SCHIP participation fell from 36.4 percent in 1995 to 30.3 percent a decade later, even as the proportion of uninsured noncitizen children rose from 43.7 to 47.7 percent. Medicaid-SCHIP coverage for noncitizen children dropped between 1995 and 2000, but rose slightly from 2000 to 2005. The gain was likely due to the general expansion of Medicaid and SCHIP, including extensive outreach to citizen children as well as to noncitizen children who met the eligibility criteria. In several states, including the major immigrant destinations of California and New York, noncitizen children who

TABLE 6.3 Changes in Health Insurance Coverage of Low-Income Children

	2005	2000	1995	1995 to 2005
Citizen children, U.S.-born parents				
Uninsured	14.9%	16.5%	19.4%	−4.5%
Medicaid or SCHIP	53.2	44.4	45.4	7.7
Other public insurance	1.8	2.5	2.1	−0.3
Employer-sponsored insurance	22.9	28.5	25.5	−2.6
Other private insurance	7.2	8.1	7.6	−0.4
Citizen children, noncitizen parents				
Uninsured	23.8	27.9	28.6	−4.7
Medicaid or SCHIP	54.3	44.6	46.8	7.4
Other public insurance	1.5	0.9	1.4	0.1
Employer-sponsored insurance	16.8	23.8	20.8	−4.0
Other private insurance	3.6	2.8	2.4	1.2
Noncitizen children				
Uninsured	47.7	48.4	43.7	4.0
Medicaid or SCHIP	30.3	27.6	36.4	−6.0
Other public insurance	1.2	0.9	1.3	−0.1
Employer-sponsored insurance	17.1	20.5	16.4	0.7
Other private insurance	3.6	2.6	2.2	1.4

Source: Author's analysis of data from Current Population Survey (U.S. Bureau of the Census, various years).
Note: Numbers in percentages. Data are not fully comparable because of changes in survey methodology over time. Low-income means family income below 200 percent of the poverty line. To avoid double counting, we apply a hierarchy in which Medicaid coverage takes priority over other types of insurance, followed by employer coverage.

were legal immigrants were eligible for state-funded coverage throughout the period (see Zimmermann and Tumlin 1999).

Both noncitizen children and citizen children with noncitizen parents were much more likely to be uninsured than low-income children with U.S.-born parents. Much of the explanation for this gap lies in low employer and other private coverage of noncitizen parents. This is in fact the likely explanation for most if not all of the coverage gap between citizen children with noncitizen parents and their counterparts with U.S.-born parents. The consistently higher uninsurance rate for noncitizen children was attributable to relative shortfalls in both private coverage and Medicaid coverage. As a result, by 2005, low-income noncitizen children

Figure 6.2 Low-Income Parents Uninsured or Covered by Medicaid-SCHIP

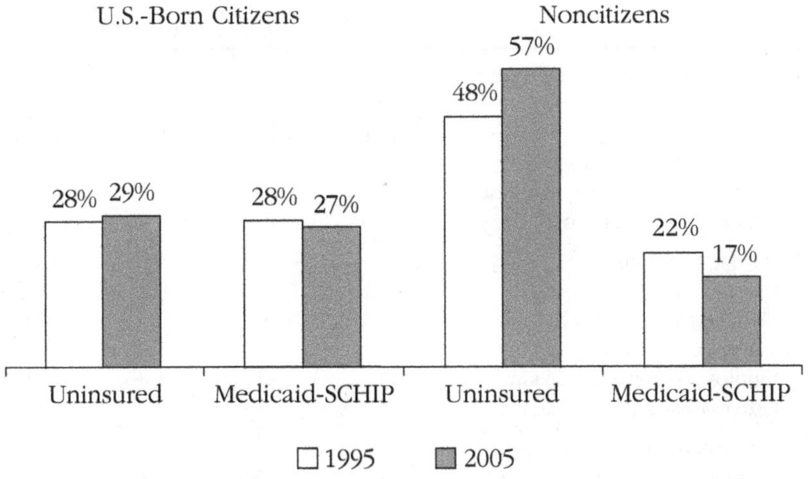

```
U.S.-Born Citizens                Noncitizens
                                     57%
                                  48%
 28% 29%      28% 27%
                                                22%
                                                    17%
 Uninsured   Medicaid-SCHIP    Uninsured   Medicaid-SCHIP

           □ 1995      ■ 2005
```

Source: Author's analysis of data from Current Population Survey (U.S. Bureau of the Census, various years).
Note: Low-income means family income below 200 percent of the poverty line.

(both legally and illegally present) were more than three times as likely to be uninsured as citizen children with U.S.-born parents.

Nonelderly Adults

Trends in health insurance coverage for noncitizen parents are similar to the trends observed for noncitizen children—that is, Medicaid coverage declined from 1995 to 2005, and the uninsured proportion rose. Most nonelderly adults covered by Medicaid are low-income parents; those without children are not usually eligible unless they are pregnant, severely disabled, or live in the handful of states that cover childless adults through Medicaid.[5] Insurance coverage of low-income U.S.-born citizen parents changed little from 1995 to 2005, but the proportion of uninsured low-income noncitizen parents rose from 48 to 57 percent, and the proportion covered by Medicaid fell (figure 6.2).[6]

When trends are reviewed in more detail, Medicaid coverage of

TABLE 6.4 Changes in Health Insurance Coverage of Low-Income Adults

	2005	2000	1995	1995 to 2005
Parents, U.S.-born minor children				
Uninsured	29.3%	27.1%	26.8%	2.5%
Medicaid	27.3	22.6	28.2	−.9
Other public insurance	3.7	3.4	3.6	.1
Employer-sponsored insurance	34.8	41.6	36.3	−1.5
Other private insurance	5.0	5.3	5.2	−.2
Noncitizen parents				
Uninsured	57.1	53.0	48.2	8.9
Medicaid	17.3	15.0	22.3	−5.0
Other public insurance	.9	.6	1.2	−.3
Employer-sponsored insurance	22.0	29.1	26.0	−4.0
Other private insurance	2.7	2.3	2.3	.4
U.S.-born childless adults				
Uninsured	38.7	34.4	39.4	−.8
Medicaid	20.9	19.1	17.7	3.3
Other public insurance	7.2	7.3	6.5	.8
Employer-sponsored insurance	23.0	27.3	26.1	−3.1
Other private insurance	10.2	11.9	10.3	−.2
Noncitizen childless adults				
Uninsured	65.2	66.8	64.5	.7
Medicaid	9.5	7.8	10.8	−1.3
Other public insurance	2.3	1.6	1.5	.8
Employer-sponsored insurance	16.6	18.1	15.8	.8
Other private insurance	6.3	5.7	7.4	−1.1

Source: Author's analysis of data from Current Population Survey (U.S. Bureau of the Census, various years)

Notes: Numbers in percentages. Data are not fully comparable because of changes in survey methodology over time. Low-income means family income below 200 percent of the poverty line. To avoid double counting, we apply a hierarchy in which Medicaid coverage takes priority over other types of insurance, followed by employer coverage.

low-income U.S.-born parents fell from 28.2 to 22.6 percent between 1995 and 2000 but rebounded to 27.3 percent by 2005. The primary driver of insurance coverage for parents during this period was change in employer-sponsored insurance rates. The economic boom of the late 1990s increased job-based insurance coverage and lessened the need for Medicaid, but the downturn of

2000 through 2005 reversed these trends: employer coverage fell and Medicaid rose. Some of the reduction in parents' Medicaid enrollment between 1995 and 2000 was probably also attributable to a general reduction in welfare caseloads that followed the 1996 legislation. Net, from 1995 to 2000, the proportion of uninsured low-income U.S.-born parents rose from 26.8 to 29.3 percent.

For low-income noncitizen parents, the trends were more dramatic (see table 6.4). Medicaid participation fell sharply from 1995 to 2000 but increased a little between 2000 and 2005. Employer-sponsored coverage improved slightly from 1995 to 2000 but fell steeply by 2005. For noncitizen parents, then, there was a substantial net loss in both Medicaid coverage and employer-sponsored insurance coverage over the decade, with their uninsurance rate rising from 48.2 percent in 1995 to 57.1 percent in 2005.

There are probably several reasons for the steep reduction in Medicaid participation. Restrictions in the eligibility of LPRs and other legal noncitizens after PRWORA was enacted in 1996 are almost certainly part of the explanation. But growth in the number of unauthorized immigrants—who were ineligible for Medicaid throughout the period of study—along with changes in immigrants' understanding of Medicaid eligibility and fears about the immigration consequences of enrolling in the program may also have played a role.

For low-income childless adults, there were no substantial changes in Medicaid coverage, but relatively few childless adults participated in Medicaid to begin with. For both citizens and noncitizens alike, the proportion covered by Medicaid or by employer-sponsored programs was substantially less than that for parents, and far more childless adults than parents were uninsured. Nonetheless, when compared with U.S.-born childless adults, noncitizen adults were about half as likely to be covered by Medicaid or employer programs. The uninsured share of childless noncitizens was consistently about twice as high as that among U.S.-born childless adults.

Although Medicaid is an important source of health insurance for low-income adults, it is important to remember that the larger source and the main driver of insurance trends is employment-based coverage. Noncitizens face serious barriers in getting job-based coverage. Research has shown that noncitizen workers, particularly Latinos, are less likely to be offered employer-sponsored coverage than their native-born counterparts. A California study, for example, found that 49 percent of unauthorized Latino workers—versus 62 percent of their legal immigrant counterparts and 82 percent of native-born Latinos—were offered health insurance at work. However, the take-up among those offered insurance was higher among immigrant workers—84 percent for the unauthorized and 83 percent for legal immigrants—than among native-born Latinos, at 72 percent (Marcelli 2004). Other analyses also found that Latino noncitizen workers are far less likely to be offered insurance at work (Schur and Feldman 2001; see also Buchmueller et al. 2005). Part of the reason for these gaps is that immigrants often work in poorer quality jobs that offer fewer benefits, such as health insurance, but some of the effect also appears to be related to immigration status.

Because low-income immigrant adults and their children have less access to both employer-sponsored and Medicaid coverage, they are much more likely to be uninsured than their native-born counterparts.

Elderly

Elderly noncitizens were also affected to some degree by PRWORA's restrictions on Medicaid eligibility, because in general the elderly often rely on Medicaid to supplement Medicare. In fact, elderly immigrants may depend more than elderly natives on Medicaid, because some have not lived and worked in the United States long enough to qualify for Medicare.

Medicare is the primary health insurance for most elderly people in the United States. Low-income elderly may also be eligible for Medicaid. Those who receive both Medicaid and Medicare, sometimes called dual eligibles, use Medicaid as supplemental coverage to help pay deductibles or copayments required in Medicare. Medicaid also covers services—such as long-term care or prescription drugs—that Medicare does not cover. Many elderly immigrants, including some who have become naturalized citizens, are not eligible for Medicare because they or their spouses did not have the required forty quarters of qualified employment generally required for eligibility for both Medicare and Social Security. Some elderly have private health insurance coverage, such as retiree health benefits or supplemental Medi-gap coverage that supplements Medicare.

Because Medicare is very nearly universal, few low-income native-born elderly were uninsured in 1995, 2000, or 2005 (table 6.5). Close to 100 percent had Medicare, but some 14 to 15 percent also had supplemental Medicaid. There was a marked reduction in the number with other supplemental coverage between 1995 and 2005 and, as a result, a parallel increase in the percentage with Medicare coverage only. Other research has confirmed that retiree health benefits dwindled greatly between 1995 and 2005 (Buchmueller, Johnson, and Lo Sasso 2006).

For naturalized citizens, although the overall percentage with Medicare changed little over the decade, the mix of Medicare, Medicaid, and other coverage changed greatly.[7] The proportion of elderly naturalized citizens with both Medicare and Medicaid rose from 18.3 percent in 1995 to 31.3 percent in 2005, but the proportion with Medicare and other insurance fell more—from 46.7 percent to 24.8 percent. Consequently, the percentage of naturalized citizen seniors who had only Medicare climbed from 30.9 percent in 1995 to 39.2 percent in 2005. One likely reason for the growth in Medicaid coverage is that large numbers of immigrant seniors naturalized during this period, in part to help retain their SSI and Medicaid coverage.

For noncitizen seniors, the trends were quite different. To begin with, noncitizen elderly were substantially less likely than either naturalized or native-born citizens to have Medicare, and the proportion of noncitizens with Medicare fell from 84 to 80 percent between 1995 and 2005. Noncitizen elderly also experienced substantial reductions in joint Medicare plus Medicaid coverage (from 47.6 percent in 1995 to 36.6 percent in 2005) along with Medicare plus other coverage (from 16.6 percent to 9.5 percent). As a result, the proportion of noncitizens who had Medicare only rose from 19.9 percent in 1995 to 33.8 percent by 2005. Because the percentage with any Medicare coverage decreased, the proportion of uninsured rose somewhat over the decade to a substantial 15 percent in 2005.

Health insurance coverage for low-income elderly noncitizens

TABLE 6.5 Changes in Health Insurance Coverage of Low-Income Elderly

	2005	2000	1995	1995 to 2005
U.S.-born				
Uninsured	1.2%	.6%	.8%	.4%
Medicare (any):	97.1	97.7	98.0	−1.0
Medicare only	38.3	36.1	31.0	7.2
Medicare and Medicaid	14.4	15.0	13.9	.6
Medicare and other insurance	44.4	46.6	53.1	−8.7
Medicaid only	.2	.2	0	.2
Other public insurance	.1	.2	.1	0
Employer-sponsored insurance	1.1	.9	.7	.4
Other private insurance	.3	.4	.3	0
(Memo: any Medicaid)	14.6	15.2	13.9	.7
Naturalized citizens				
Uninsured	3.2	.5	2.6	.7
Medicare (any):	95.3	96.7	95.8	−.6
Medicare only	39.2	44.7	30.9	8.2
Medicare and Medicaid	31.3	29.0	18.3	13.0
Medicare and other insurance	24.8	23.0	46.7	−21.8
Medicaid only	.3	.3	0	.3
Other public insurance	.2	.2	0	.2
Employer-sponsored insurance	1.0	1.4	1.4	−0.4
Other private insurance	.1	.8	.2	−.2
(Memo: any Medicaid)	31.5	29.4	18.3	13.3
Noncitizens				
Uninsured	14.9	13.6	11.9	3.0
Medicare (any):	79.9	76.8	84.1	−4.2
Medicare only	33.8	32.7	19.9	14.0
Medicare and Medicaid	36.6	32.5	47.6	−11.1
Medicare and other insurance	9.5	11.6	16.6	−7.1
Medicaid only	2.4	2.5	.6	1.8
Other public insurance	2.2	0	0	2.2
Employer-sponsored insurance	.5	4.8	2.7	−2.3
Other private insurance	0	2.4	.7	−.7
(Memo: any Medicaid)	39.0	35.0	48.2	−9.2

Source: Author's analysis of data from Current Population Survey (U.S. Bureau of the Census, various years)
Notes: Numbers in percentages. Data are not fully comparable because of changes in survey methodology over time. Low-income means family income below 200 percent of the poverty line. To avoid double counting, we apply a hierarchy in which Medicaid coverage takes priority over other types of insurance, followed by employer coverage.

declined considerably over the decade. Small but rising numbers of elderly noncitizens had neither Medicare nor Medicaid, and were uninsured. In part because of PRWORA's eligibility restrictions, some elderly noncitizens lost supplemental coverage from Medicaid, forcing them to shoulder additional cost-sharing burdens in Medicare. Losing supplemental coverage also meant no more coverage for prescription drugs and long-term care.[8]

The Role of Sponsors

PRWORA's drafters believed that immigrants' sponsors should serve "as the primary line of defense" in meeting immigrants' needs, rather than the government (Haskins, Greenberg, and Fremstad 2004). Congressman Lamar Smith (R-Tex.), at that time the chairman of the House Immigration Subcommittee, explained that "immigrants, who were never supposed to receive public benefits, should turn to their sponsors—their families—for support" (U.S. Congress 1997). The 1996 companion immigration legislation (IIRIRA) required sponsors of newly admitted immigrants to sign affidavits of support stating they would be financially responsible for the immigrant and would be liable for repaying any benefits the immigrant received. If this policy worked as intended, we would expect sponsors to pay for immigrants' private health insurance in at least some cases, partially offsetting noncitizens' loss of Medicaid in the wake of welfare reform.

Unfortunately, the data on sponsored immigrants are limited, and so it is difficult to analyze whether sponsors paid for a significant level of new private health insurance.[9] Census data and other comparable national data sets do not indicate which immigrants are sponsored, who immigrant sponsors are, or who paid for immigrant health insurance coverage. Indeed, relatively little is known about immigrant sponsors or the types of support they offer. Nonetheless, we can get preliminary insights by examining changes in public and private health coverage of immigrants.

The primary groups of sponsored immigrants are spouses and unmarried children of U.S. citizens or LPRs (U.S. Department of Homeland Security 2005, table 6; Wheeler and Taylor 2000). If the spouses and children gained private coverage from their sponsors, it would most likely be because the sponsoring spouse or parent extended his or her employment-based health insurance to include dependents. In some cases, there are cosponsors. For example, a husband may sponsor his wife's admission, but someone else, such as a friend, may also cosponsor the wife.

Thus the first place to look for data on the impact of sponsorship rules is trends in coverage for noncitizen children and parents. The health insurance data presented in figures 6.1 and 6.2 show that both noncitizen children and noncitizen parents lost ground in insurance coverage between 1995 and 2005. For noncitizen children, who include sponsored immigrant children, there were very mild increases in employer-sponsored (.7 percentage points) and other private insurance coverage (1.4), but these apparent gains were much smaller than the 6 percentage point reduction in Medicaid-SCHIP coverage. Very slight gains in the share of noncitizen children with private coverage provided by sponsors were possible, but any potential gains were offset by larger losses in Medicaid-SCHIP coverage.

For noncitizen parents, who include sponsors and their spouses, there was a marked reduction in both employment-based coverage (4 percent) and Medicaid (5 percent) and a trivial change in other private coverage (.4 percent). Although some of the decline in employer coverage could be ascribed to the growing share of noncitizens with unauthorized status who generally work at jobs that don't carry health coverage, there is no evidence that noncitizen parents received more private coverage through their sponsors in 2000 or 2005 than they did in 1995.

Small numbers of sponsored immigrants are parents, married children, or the adult siblings of citizens. We can investigate the coverage of sponsored immigrant parents by examining trends for noncitizen elderly (because most newly admitted parents are elderly), and the coverage of sponsored married children and siblings by examining trends for childless adults. The data in tables 6.2 and 6.3 show that noncitizen childless adults and the elderly experienced slight reductions in private health insurance coverage from 1995 to 2005. Once again, there is no evidence that sponsors provided coverage for many of the parents, married children, or siblings they sponsored.[10]

An underlying question is whether most sponsors could afford to purchase health insurance for the new immigrants. Children and spouses might be able to gain coverage as dependents under a sponsor's employment-based insurance policy. But if the sponsor does not have employment-sponsored insurance or if the sponsor's employer does not offer dependent coverage, this is not an option. Census Bureau data suggest that only a small minority of low-income noncitizen adults have employment-based coverage: 22 percent for parents and 17 percent for childless adults in 2005 (see table 6.4). More low-income naturalized citizens have job-based coverage—39 percent for parents and 23 percent for childless adults in 2005 (data not shown)—but they are still in the minority. Thus, most new immigrants cannot look to their sponsors for employment-based coverage.

Even when a sponsor is eligible to purchase dependent coverage for his spouse or children, the cost may be a problem. In 2005, it cost a worker an average of $2,300 per year to cover dependents; this is the employee's share of the additional cost to expand an employment-based policy from single to family coverage (Kaiser Family Foundation 2005). For many low- and moderate-income workers, the additional cost might not be affordable.

The alternative is for the sponsor to buy individual (nongroup) health insurance for the immigrant. The cost of individual health insurance is typically far higher than the cost of equivalent employment-based insurance, however, because the employer is not contributing to the coverage and because individual policies have higher administrative costs. One recent analysis estimated that the average cost in 2002 of an individual health insurance policy for an uninsured person ranged from $1,600 for a person eighteen to twenty-four years old to $4,300 for a person fifty-five to sixty-four years old, though the actual cost may vary widely depending on the person's health status, level of cost-sharing in the insurance plan, the state of residence, and other factors (Auerbach and Ohri 2006). Getting comprehensive individual health coverage for elderly parents not covered by Medicare is particularly difficult and expensive.

Because we cannot link changes in health insurance coverage for immigrants to changes in coverage purchased by sponsors, it is not possible to say definitively whether sponsors provided more private coverage to compensate for the loss of public coverage. The evidence suggests, though, that there was no substantial improvement in private coverage and that the loss of Medicaid coverage outweighed any gains that might have occurred. Given the barriers that sponsors often face getting private coverage and the prohibitively high cost of additional private coverage, it is implausible that many sponsors could fill the gaps left by the loss of Medicaid coverage.

Language Access

One factor that has particularly important effects on immigrants' access to care and the quality of care that they receive is language access. If immigrants cannot communicate effectively with health-care providers, they receive less care and poorer quality care (Ku and Waidmann 2003; Flores et al. 2003; Flores 2006). Federal policies developed since 2000 indicate that, to prevent against discrimination based on national origin, health-care providers must offer interpretation services to patients who are limited English proficient. Nonetheless, language assistance is frequently unavailable in hospitals and other health-care facilities, as well as in offices where immigrants apply for Medicaid and other public health benefits.

Since a 2000 federal executive order on language assistance, state and local government and private initiatives have sought to reduce language barriers (Clinton 2000). These efforts include facilitating enrollment into public programs like Medicaid and SCHIP and improving language access when people use medical care. In August 2003, following up on the 2000 executive order, the Office of Civil Rights at the Department of Health and Human Services issued guidance relating to language services at state and local Medicaid-SCHIP eligibility offices as well as for health-care providers who receive federal funding (U.S. Department of Health and Human Services 2003). Thirteen states provide funding for language assistance and interpretation services for LEP patients as part of their Medicaid programs, but the majority of states have yet to do so (Youdelman 2007). A majority of hospitals offer at least some language assistance to LEP patients, but rarely receive reimbursement from insurers for these services (Hasnain-Wynia et al. 2006). Still, it remains clear that many organizations do not, on the basis of cost or logistical concerns, offer substantial assistance to those who are LEP. Finally, in some areas political pressures to avoid language aid or bilingual services sometimes come into play, owing to measures that declare English the official language of the United States. In 2008, for example, thirty states had laws stating English as the official language for state business.[11]

CONSEQUENCES OF THE LOSS OF MEDICAID AND OF HEALTH INSURANCE

Even if someone is uninsured, he or she may be able to get medical care in other ways, whether by paying out pocket or by getting free or reduced-price care from clinics or hospitals. Because so many immigrants are uninsured and have low incomes, they rely more on safety net sources of health care, such as publicly funded, charitable, and religiously affiliated clinics and hospitals (Ku and Freilich 2001). A recent study found that Spanish-speaking Latino access to medical care depends largely on the availability of community health centers (Hadley, Cunningham, and Hargraves 2006).

Even so, a substantial body of research indicates that being uninsured reduces a person's access to medical care (see, for example, Institute of Medicine 2001, 2002). Because those without health insurance must pay more for health care, they may not have enough money to buy food or pay their housing or utility bills (Long 2003). More specifically, research has shown that being uninsured reduces noncitizens' access to medical and dental care, but that noncitizens still have less access to and use of medical care, including emergency rooms, even when they have insurance coverage comparable to that of citizens (Ku and Matani 2001; Mohanty et al. 2005).

A recent study of nonelderly immigrants in Los Angeles County found that LPRs were less likely to have seen a physician in the past year than native-born citizens, 68 percent versus 80 percent (Goldman, Smith, and Sood 2006). Average per capita medical expenditures for LPRs were substantially less than for native citizens because LPRs had both lower public medical expenditures and lower private medical expenditures. However, out-of-pocket medical spending for LPRs was about the same as for native-born citizens, meaning that LPRs shouldered a much larger proportion—30 percent versus 20.

CHANGES IN IMMIGRANTS' USE OF FOOD STAMPS

Aside from Medicaid, the FSP is the largest remaining entitlement program to assist low-income families. PRWORA's restrictions in immigrants' eligibility for food stamps that were described earlier, along with other reductions in access to the program, may have two types of effects on immigrant households. First, immigrants may stop participating in the FSP when households become ineligible or when access barriers are high enough that eligible immigrants fail to apply. Second, it is possible that some immigrant households may have seen their benefits cut when a noncitizen member lost eligibility after PRWORA but other members of the household remained eligible. In other words, even in a household with U.S.-born citizen children, the size of the food stamp benefit—and therefore the money available to the household—could fall because noncitizen parents can no longer participate. One study found that children with noncitizen parents experienced greater food insecurity after PRWORA restricted their parents' eligibility and thus reduced food stamp allotments (Van Hook and Balistreri 2006).

This analysis looks only at individual-level participation in the FSP, not household-level participation or the food stamp benefits households received. We examine trends in the number of individuals who are eligible for and participate in the FSP by citizenship. We use a different analytical approach from that used in the previous Medicaid–health insurance analyses. The components of and data sources for our analysis include:

- Data about the characteristics of food stamp recipients, based on the Food Stamp Quality Control (QC) system administered by the Food and Nutrition Service (FNS) of the U.S. Department of Agriculture. The QC data are a product of an administrative monitoring system that checks for errors and fraud in the FSP and generates a nationally representative sample of food stamp recipients and their eligibility-related characteristics. A noncitizen who lives in a household that receives food stamps but does not himself or herself receive benefits is not counted as a recipient. The QC data include only those eligible for the federal FSP and not those who receive state-funded nutrition assistance.

- Microsimulation data that estimate the number and characteristics of those who are eligible based on FSP rules and CPS data. The microsimulation model, which is operated by Mathematica Policy Research, Inc., under contract to FNS, provides detailed estimates of the number and characteristics of people eligible for food stamps under current policies, though these estimates are subject to the limits of CPS data. The QC and microsimulation data have been used by Mathematica and FNS to create a series of reports about FSP participation rates (Barrett and Poikolainen 2006; Karen Cunnyngham 2005, 2004, 2002). There have been methodological changes in the microsimulation models over time (methods of trying to account for the undocumented, for example), so the data are not completely comparable across years. In addition, some components of eligibility (such as treatment of assets or sponsor deeming) are difficult or impossible to simulate accurately.

- CPS data about the number of people with incomes below 200 percent of poverty. We derive a denominator of the number of people who live in low-income families and are therefore mostly income-eligible for the FSP from the CPS data.

- Calculation of eligibility and participation rates for low-income people. We divide the number of eligible and participating people, as estimated by FNS and Mathematica, by the number of people who have low incomes, as calculated using the CPS data. We create eligibility and participation rates for low-income people generally, as well as the rate of eligible individuals who participated in the FSP. We disaggregate noncitizens as well as citizen children living with noncitizen adults in our analysis.

Findings

There was an overall drop in FSP participation among low-income individuals between 1994 and 2004, but the drop for noncitizens was greater than for low-income people generally.[12] Although the proportion of the overall eligible low-income population rose from 39 to 42 percent, the proportion who actually received benefits fell from 29 percent to 26 percent (see figure 6.3). When only low-income noncitizens are considered, there was a drop in the eligible proportion (from 29 to 19 percent) and an even steeper decline in the participant proportion (from 20 to 8 percent). In this chapter, noncitizens are not disaggregated into LPRs, unauthorized immigrants, and other status categories. As a result, the noncitizen group analyzed here includes LPRs who had their FSP eligibility changed by PRWORA, as well as unauthorized immigrants who were ineligible for the program both before and after the law was enacted.

Looking at more detailed results, we see that noncitizens' food stamp eligibility rates were strongly influenced by PRWORA's eligibility restrictions and subsequent restorations. The proportion of eligible low-income noncitizens fell by about half between 1994 and 2000, from 29.4 to 14.7 percent (see table 6.6). This period corresponds with the implementation of PRWORA restrictions on LPR food stamps eligibility described earlier. The proportion of eligible noncitizens, however, rebounded from 14.7 to 19.4 percent between 2000 and 2004. During this period, the 2002 Farm Bill restored eligibility to LPRs with five years of U.S. residency, to disabled LPRs, and to all LPR children regardless of length of residency. Neither PRWORA nor the Farm Bill affected the eligibility of citizen children of noncitizen parents, whose rate thus remained constant at 58 to 59 percent. Eligibility rates (without distinguishing by citizenship) dropped somewhat between 1994 and 2000, but rebounded by 2004—partially as a result of the decline in the size of the poverty population during the late 1990s and the subsequent slight rise in poverty since 2000. But it is also worth noting that PRWORA did not only restrict noncitizen eligibility for the

Figure 6.3 Changes in Food Stamp Eligibility and Participation

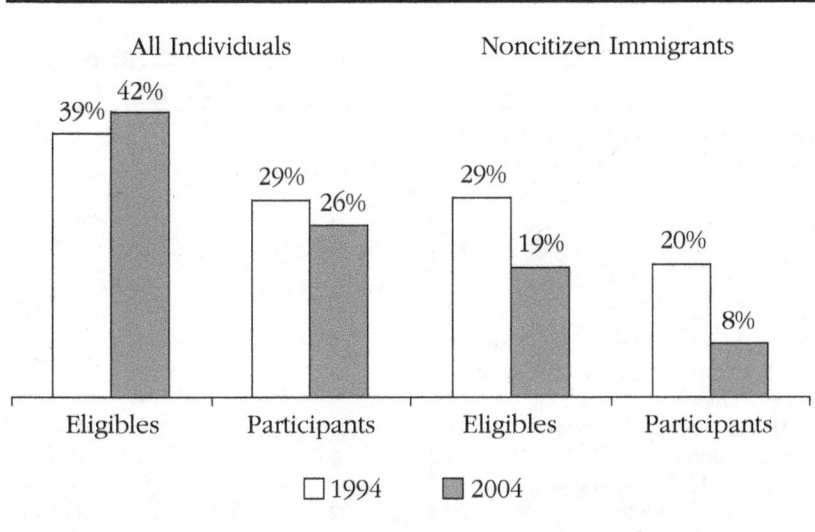

Source: Author's analysis of data from Current Population Survey (U.S. Bureau of the Census, various years).

FSP; there were a number of other across-the-board changes that restricted eligibility for citizens and noncitizens alike.[13]

Low-income noncitizens and their children were both less likely to participate in the FSP in 2004 than in 1994. Noncitizens' participation fell by about two-thirds, from 19.6 to 6.6 percent between 1994 and 2000, but then rose slightly to 8.2 percent by 2004. Although PRWORA included no eligibility changes for citizen children in noncitizen households, their participation fell by about half from 47.1 percent in 1994 to 22.5 percent in 2000, and then recovered somewhat to 29.8 percent by 2004. The overall food stamp participation rate for low-income families dropped more modestly between 1994 and 2000 (from 29.2 to 20.4 percent) but also recovered somewhat by 2004.

For all three groups—noncitizens, citizen children living with noncitizen adults, and all participants—the program participation rate (measured as the number of participants divided by the number of eligible individuals) dropped sharply between 1994 and 2000. The reductions were particularly steep for citizen children

TABLE 6.6 **Changes in Food Stamp Eligibility and Participation**

	2004	2000	1994	2004 As Percentage of 1994
Eligibles (percentage of those with incomes below 200 percent of poverty)				
All individuals	42.2	34.5	39.0	108.1
Noncitizens	19.4	14.7	29.4	65.8
Citizen children living with Noncitizen adults	58.0	59.0	58.6	99.0
Participants (percentage of those with incomes below 200 percent of poverty)				
All individuals	25.5	20.4	29.2	87.4
Noncitizens	8.2	6.6	19.6	41.8
Citizen children living with noncitizen adults	29.8	22.5	47.1	63.3
Participation rate (percentage of eligibles who participate)				
All individuals	60.5	59.3	74.8	80.8
Noncitizens	42.4	44.7	66.8	63.5
Citizen children living with noncitizen adults	51.5	38.1	80.5	64.0

Source: Author's analysis of data from Current Population Survey (U.S. Bureau of the Census, various years).
Note: Numbers in percentages.

in noncitizen households, where participation rates fell by about half. In the more recent years, participation by eligible citizen children in noncitizen households rose somewhat, from 38.1 percent in 2000 to 51.5 percent in 2004, but the participation rates for eligible people stayed about the same for noncitizens and all individuals between 2000 and 2004. These declines in the program participation from 1994 to 2000 suggest that factors other than changes in eligibility rules were also at play.

Effects of Eligibility Changes

Using the information in table 6.6, we can gain insights about the relative effects on noncitizen participation in the FSP of eligibility changes versus those of other factors such as economic changes, access barriers for limited English speakers, and noncitizens' fears about participating in the program. In any given year, the number of participants is equal to the number of eligible individuals multiplied by the participation rate. Changes in the number of participants are therefore affected by both changes in the number of eligible individuals and changes in participation rates. Mathematically this can be expressed as:

participants in 2004/participants in 1994 = (eligibles in 2004/eligibles in 1994)
× (participation rate in 2004/participation rate in 1994).

Using the data in the last column of table 6.6 (the 2004 level as a percent of the 1994 level), we can estimate this for noncitizens: noncitizens 41.8% = 65.9% × 63.5%.

The number of participating noncitizens in 2004 was 42 percent of the 1994 level. The number of eligible individuals in 2004 was about two-thirds (66 percent) as high as in 1994, as was the participation rate among eligibles (64 percent). That is, the FSP participation of eligible noncitizens fell by about two-thirds over the decade, and both eligibility and noneligibility factors had roughly equal effects in explaining the reduction in noncitizen participation.

For citizen children in noncitizen households, the equivalent result is: 63.3% = 99% × 64%. That is, there was virtually no change in eligibility, but about a one-third reduction in their participation rate over the decade. Thus none of the drop in participation for citizen children in noncitizen households was attributable to changes in eligibility criteria, PRWORA or otherwise.

On the other hand, declining participation rates are not a problem confined to noncitizens or to children in noncitizen households. Overall, food stamp participation rates fell by about 20 percent from 1994 to 2004. They fell even more, by about 30 percent, among noncitizens and their children, however.

A closer look shows one other important fact: participation rates fell between 1994 and 2000, but rose somewhat in 2004. This was true for both the overall population and for those in immigrant households.

It is relatively easy to provide explanations for eligibility changes over time; key legislative changes were summarized in table 6.2.

The reasons for changes in participation rates are less clear, but some stand out. First, the economy was very strong from 1994 to 2000, particularly in the late 1990s, but weakened from 2000 to 2004. Even though we have partially controlled for these changes by restricting our analysis to the number of people with incomes below 200 percent of poverty, the analysis may not accurately track changes in the relative depth of poverty, for example, the number of people with very low incomes who are the most likely to apply for food stamps. Second, there were separate changes being made in cash welfare programs throughout most of this period. Even though TANF changes do not directly change food stamp eligibility, policy shifts may alter poor families' perceptions of whether they are eligible or close pathways for them to access the program. In addition, during the past decade there have been changes in the residential decisions of immigrants, who have moved from traditional immigrant strongholds like California or New York to new growth states like Georgia or North Carolina. The new growth states are, as a group, less likely to have provided nutrition benefits for LPRs who lost federal FSP eligibility after PRWORA; they are also states that traditionally have had lower welfare benefits and more restrictive rules and systems for accessing public benefits (Zimmermann and Tumlin 1999).

Other social and community factors—such as immigrants' perceptions of their eligibility, fears about the consequences of participation, and special outreach efforts aimed at immigrants—also played a role. Data reported soon after 1996 indicate that immigrant families often believed they lost eligibility even when they did not and worried about potentially harsh consequences (Fix and Passel 2002; Zimmermann and Fix 1998). Subsequently, there were active efforts to reach out to immigrant households—in particular, after the 2002 Farm Bill restored FSP eligibility to all LPR children—by federal, state, and local agencies and community organizations to let children and other immigrants know that they were eligible (Capps et al. 2004). In addition, FNS and the state agencies gradually improved the availability of multilingual materials and the availability of language assistance to help LEP applicants access benefits.

Despite these substantial efforts, the data shown in table 6.6 suggest that participation rates in 2004 are still well below the rates of 1994, particularly for noncitizens and their children. Some of the explanation for this is that the 2002 Farm Bill only partially restored benefits to legal immigrants: most LPR adults with less than five years of U.S. residency remain ineligible. Another explanation is that many immigrants still fear applying for benefits for which they are entitled, and not all state and local food stamp offices do a good job of outreach. Finally, and perhaps most important, the data presented here do not disaggregate noncitizens by legal status. Unauthorized immigrants were a rapidly growing share of all noncitizens from 1994 to 2004 (Passel and Cohen 2008) and were never eligible for the FSP. As their share of noncitizens increased, so did the proportion of ineligible noncitizens. These findings thus suggest that further investigation and progress in restoring benefits to noncitizens are both warranted.

CONSEQUENCES OF THE LOSS OF FOOD STAMPS

Some studies have examined the potential implications of changes in food stamp receipt for immigrant households. In 1998, surveys of immigrant households in Los Angeles and San Francisco found that food insecurity was greater and hunger more common among children in immigrant households who lost food stamp benefits than among those not affected by eligibility changes (California Food Policy Advocates 1998).

Other studies looked at how state-funded food assistance programs for immigrants that replaced the federal FSP have affected food security. One study compared levels of food insecurity and other hardships across the states and suggested that food insecurity was more serious for children in immigrant families in states without replacement programs (Capps 2001). The economist George Borjas found that noncitizens in states with more generous state-funded assistance for noncitizens were much less likely to report food insecurity than those in states without these programs. A 10 percentage-point cut in the fraction of noncitizens receiving state-funded public assistance increased their food insecurity rate by about 5 percentage points (Borjas 2004).

Finally, as noted earlier, research suggests that reduced household participation in food stamps among immigrants may increase food insecurity in children in their households, even if they are citizens who remain eligible (Van Hook and Balistreri 2006).

CONCLUSIONS

Since 1996, Medicaid and food stamp participation among noncitizens and their citizen children has fallen considerably. The research literature indicates that the loss of health insurance and food stamps led to serious hardships for a number of low-income immigrant families, such as decreased access to medical care services and increased food insecurity.

Because levels of private health insurance coverage for noncitizen children, parents, and the elderly fell or did not change significantly after welfare reform, it seems that few sponsors were able to provide employer-based coverage to compensate for noncitizens' loss of Medicaid coverage. Similarly, evidence of higher food insecurity among immigrant households that lacked food assistance suggests sponsors did not fill that gap effectively either.

In the late 1990s, Medicaid and food stamp participation by noncitizens fell sharply, but rebounded after 2000. Soon after the 1996 changes, misperceptions and fears in the immigrant community led many eligible immigrants to drop out of the public benefit programs. Although citizen children in noncitizen households remained eligible, their use of public benefits dwindled.

Both eligibility criteria and other factors that may have affected noncitizens' participation in these programs changed over time. LPR eligibility for food stamps was partially restored by laws passed in 1998 and 2002. There have been no major restorations of Medicaid coverage to adults, but Medicaid-SCHIP coverage was extended to all LPR children in 2009.

Changes in other social factors have been more subtle. Both Medicaid-SCHIP and food stamp participation of citizen children in noncitizen families have recovered somewhat in recent years. Medicaid participation by noncitizens also improved slightly after 2000, although food stamp participation rates for noncitizens have remained low. Both governmental and nongovernmental organizations developed outreach efforts aimed at immigrant communities and increased efforts to reduce language barriers. These efforts, in conjunction with the passage of time, appear to have both increased understanding in immigrant communities and reduced fears.

Despite this modest progress, evidence indicates that immigrants continue to experience disproportionate levels of hardships, such as being uninsured, having difficulty affording medical care, and being unable to afford food for their families. There is substantial room for reforming policies that govern immigrants' eligibility for and use of services. The federal government could restore eligibility to means-tested benefits to all LPRs or extend the food stamp and Medicaid restorations afforded to LPR children to parents and other groups of needy noncitizens. The 2009 Children's Health Insurance Program Reauthorization Act gave states the option to restore Medicaid or SCHIP coverage to legal immigrant children and pregnant women during their first five years in the United States. As such, it is another example of devolving eligibility rule-setting to the states, but which states will take this option remains to be seen.

There is now substantial interest in major health-care reform at the federal level. One component of that may be to more broadly restore Medicaid coverage for legal immigrant adults, in light of the recent restorations for children. One broad coalition, which includes diverse organizations including advocacy groups, medical and hospital associations, the health insurance industry, prescription drug manufacturers, small businesses, and the U.S. Chamber of Commerce, has endorsed such a change.[14] Even more important, health reform proposals to expand health insurance coverage through "health insurance exchanges" and federal subsidies for low- and moderate-income people may include all legal immigrants, but not the undocumented. This could bolster access and affordability to private health insurance for legal immigrant families.

Other efforts to boost immigrants' Medicaid or food stamp participation could be strengthened. One demonstration project, for example, was able to virtually eliminate uninsurance among low-income Latino children through a strong program of linguistically and culturally appropriate community-based outreach and case management (Flores et al. 2005). We could do more to eliminate barriers and confusion that may deter immigrants from using services for which they are eligible, such as the citizenship documentation requirements that the 2006 Deficit Reduction Act imposed—requirements that may lead immigrants to believe they must be citizens to enroll. Finally, it should be possible to do more to help immigrants integrate into American society and to enhance progress in improving their wages and living conditions. Increased availability of English-language instruction and/or bilingual job training programs could help immigrants improve their earnings potential and quality of life. Along with these other improvements might also come employer-based health insurance coverage, which would reduce the need for Medicaid or SCHIP in many immigrant families.

Although noncitizens' use of benefits fell sharply for both programs from 1994 through 2000, the period during which PRWORA was enacted and implemented, there were signs of improvement after 2000, as time created distance from PRWORA's initial implementation. There were also some eligibility restorations in the FSP. It is possible that after 2000, because of outreach efforts, noncitizens came to better understand the programs and be less fearful about using government benefits. It is plausible, however, that since 2005, trends have reversed again. The combination of failure to pass comprehensive immigration reform legislation at the national level, increased immigration enforcement activities such as worksite raids, and the proliferation of state and local ordinances aimed at unauthorized immigrants may have influenced immigrants' attitudes once again, making them even more fearful of using the benefit programs for which they or their children are eligible. A poll in late 2007, for example, indicated that many Latinos were worried by these recent trends and had grown wary of using government services (Pew Hispanic Center 2007). On the other hand, as of 2009, policies of the new Obama administration, such as reduced arrests of unauthorized immigrants, may allay some immigrants' fears and restore their willingness to participate in public programs. Subsequent research will be needed to determine whether these actions will lead to substantial changes in immigrants' benefits use and hardship in the future and to appropriate public policy responses.

NOTES

1. Children with naturalized citizen parents are excluded from the analyses because they are a small group, with characteristics that lie between children with noncitizen parents and children with U.S.-born parents.
2. See the summary of Executive Order 13166 and related guidance materials from the Department of Justice and many other federal agencies at http://www.lep.gov.
3. Because of the limited Current Population Survey sample size, we do not present the analyses for citizen children with naturalized-citizen parents.
4. The Census Bureau recently revised CPS insurance estimates for 2004 and 2005 after identifying a technical error. However, because it has not yet made comparable corrections for earlier years, going back to 1995, we use the unrevised data to maintain better comparability across years.
5. The Medicaid income eligibility limit for parents with dependent children varies greatly from state to state, ranging from 19 percent of poverty in Alabama and Arkansas to 275 percent in Minnesota. In the median state, the Medicaid income limit is 67 percent of the poverty line (Ross and Cox 2005). During the late 1990s, a number of states began initiatives to expand coverage for parents, but these expansions largely stopped when state budgets faltered and were sometimes withdrawn.
6. Naturalized citizen parents are excluded from the analysis because they are a small group with insurance rates between those for noncitizen and U.S.-born parents, and because the sample of naturalized citizen parents in the CPS is too small for analysis.
7. A much higher proportion of elderly immigrants than working-age adults or children are naturalized, because so many elderly immigrants are long-term U.S. residents. As a result, we disaggregate results for naturalized elderly in this section of the chapter.
8. Effective January 2006, Medicare offers prescription drugs for dual eligibles and Medicaid is no longer responsible for them.
9. The only data set to provide detail on sponsorship of legal immigrants is the New Immigrant Survey (NIS), a sample of recent LPR admissions. The NIS also includes data on health insurance coverage, but these data have not yet been analyzed specifically for sponsored immigrants.
10. Employer-provided health insurance is generally only for depend-

ents who are spouses or minor children, and thus it is very difficult for individuals to obtain coverage through their employers for their parents, married children, or adult siblings. Thus it is likely that sponsors would have to purchase private coverage on the open market for sponsored parents, married children, or adult siblings—which for low-income sponsors would be prohibitively expensive.

11. U.S. English, "States with Official English Laws," available at: http://www.us-english.org/inc/official/states.asp (accessed November 15, 2008).
12. The Current Population Survey includes data for food stamp eligibility and participation during the calendar year before the survey, and so the 2005 CPS includes data on 2004, and the 1995 CPS includes data on 1994.
13. For example, the 1996 legislation limited the eligibility of able-bodied adults without dependents (that is, childless adults between eighteen and forty-nine who were able to work) to only three to six months of Food Stamps during any given year.
14. Health Reform Dialogue, "A Dialogue on U.S. Health Reform," *PhaRMA*, March 2009. Available at: http://www.phrma.org/files/HRD%20Common%20Ground.pdf (accessed April 16, 2009).

REFERENCES

Aizer, Anna. 2006. "Public Health Insurance, Program Take-up and Child Health." *NBER* working paper 12105. Cambridge, Mass.: National Bureau of Economic Research.

Andrulis, Dennis, Nanette Goodman, and Carol Pryor. 2002. "What a Difference an Interpreter Can Make: Health Care Experiences of the Uninsured with Limited English Proficiency." Boston, Mass.: The Access Project.

Auerbach, David, and Sabrina Ohri. 2006. "The Price and Demand for Nongroup Health Insurance." *Inquiry* 43(2): 122–34.

Barrett, Allison, and Anni Poikolainen. 2006. *Food Stamp Program Participation Rates: 2004*. Washington: U.S. Department of Agriculture, Food and Nutrition Service.

Borjas, George J. 2004. "Food Insecurity and Public Assistance." *Journal of Public Economics* 88(7–8): 1421–443.

Buchmueller, Thomas, Anthony Lo Sasso, Irene Lurie, and Sarah Senesky. 2005. "Immigrants and Employer-Provided Health Insurance." *Economic Research Initiative on the Uninsured* working paper 38. Ann Arbor: University of Michigan.

Buchmueller, Thomas, Richard W. Johnson, and Anthony T. Lo Sasso. 2006. "Trends in Retiree Health Insurance." *Health Affairs* 25(6): 1497–506.

California Food Policy Advocates. 1998. *Impact of Legal Immigrant Food Stamp Cuts in Los Angeles and San Francisco*. San Francisco: CFPA.

Capps, Randolph. 2001. *Hardship Among Children of Immigrants: Findings from the 1999 National Survey of America's Families*. Series B, no. B-29. Washington, D.C.: The Urban Institute.

Capps, Randolph, Genevieve Kenney, and Michael E. Fix. 2003. *Health Insurance Coverage of Children in Mixed-Status Immigrant Families*. Washington, D.C.: The Urban Institute.

Capps, Randolph, Robin Koralek, Katherine Lotspeich, Michael E. Fix, Pamela Holcomb, and Jane Reardon Anderson. 2004. *Assessing Implementation of the 2002 Farm Bill's Legal Immigrant Food Stamp Restrictions*. Washington, D.C.: The Urban Institute.

Clinton, William Jefferson. 2000. "Improving Access to Services for Persons with Limited English Proficiency." Executive Order 13166. *Federal Register* 65(159): 50121–122. Available at: http://www.usdoj.gov/crt/cor/Pubs/eolep.pdf (accessed April 16, 2009).

Cunnyngham, Karen. 2002. *Trends in Food Stamp Program Participation Rates: 1994 to 2000*. Washington: U.S. Department of Agriculture, Food and Nutrition Service.

———. 2004. *Trends in Food Stamp Program Participation Rates: 1999 to 2002*. Washington: U.S. Department of Agriculture, Food and Nutrition Service.

———. 2005. *Food Stamp Program Participation Rates: 2003*. Washington: U.S. Department of Agriculture, Food and Nutrition Service.

Fix, Michael E., and Jeffrey S. Passel. 2002. "The Scope and Impact of Welfare Reform's Immigrant Provisions." *Assessing the New Federalism* discussion paper no. 02–03. Washington, D.C.: The Urban Institute.

Fix, Michael E., and Wendy Zimmermann. 2001. "All Under One Roof: Mixed Status Families in an Era of Reform." *International Migration Review* 35(2): 397–419.

Flores, Glenn. 2006. "Language Barriers to Health Care in the United States." *New England Journal of Medicine* 355(3): 229–31.

Flores, Glenn, Milagros Abreu, Christine E. Chaisson, Alan Meyers, Ramesh C. Sachdeva, Harriet Fernandez, Patricia Francisco, Beatriz Diaz, Ana Milena Diaz, and Iris Santos-Guerrero. 2005. "A Randomized, Controlled Trial of the Effectiveness of Community-Based Case Management in Insuring Uninsured Latino Children." *Pediatrics* 116(6): 1433–441.

Flores, Glenn, M. Barton Laws, Sandra J. Mayo, Barry Zuckerman, Milagros Abreu, Leonardo Medina, and Eric J. Hardt. 2003. "Errors in Medical Interpretation and Their Potential Clinical Consequences in Pediatric Encounters." *Pediatrics* 111(1): 6–14.

Fremstad, Shawn. 2004. *The Applicability of "Public Charge" Rules to Legal Immigrants Who Are Eligible For Public Benefits*. Washington, D.C.: Center on Budget and Policy Priorities.

Goldman, Dana, James Smith, and Neeraj Sood. 2006. "Immigrants and the Cost of Medical Care." *Health Affairs* 25(6): 1700–711.

Hadley, Jack, Peter Cunningham, and J. Lee Hargraves. 2006. "Would Safety-Net Expansions Offset Reduced Access Resulting from Lost Insurance Coverage? Race/Ethnicity Differences." *Health Affairs* 25(6): 1679–687.

Hagan, Jacqueline, Nestor Rodriguez, Randolph Capps, and Nika Kabiri. 2003. "The Effects of Recent Welfare and Immigration Reforms on Immigrants' Access to Health Care." *International Migration Review* 37(2): 444–63.

Haskins, Ron, Mark Greenberg, and Shawn Fremstad. 2004. "Federal Policy for Immigrant Children: Room for Common Ground?" *Future of Children* policy brief. Princeton, N.J.: Princeton University Press; Washington, D.C.: Brookings Institution Press.

Hasnain-Wynia, Romana, Julie Yonek, Debra Pierce, Ray Kang, and Cynthia Hedges Greising. 2006. *Hospital Language Services for Patients with Limited English Proficiency*. Washington, D.C.: Health Research and Educational Trust.

Holcomb, Pamela, Karen C. Tumlin, Robin Koralek, Randolph Capps, and Anita Zuberi. 2003. "The Application Process for TANF, Food Stamps, Medicaid and SCHIP." Washington, D.C.: The Urban Institute. Available at: http://www.urban.org/UploadedPDF/410640.pdf (accessed April 16, 2009).

Institute of Medicine. 2001. *Coverage Matters: Insurance and Health Care*. Washington, D.C.: National Academies Press.

———. 2002. *Care without Coverage: Too Little, Too Late*. Washington, D.C.: National Academies Press.

Kaiser Family Foundation. 2005. *Employer Health Benefits, 2005*. Menlo Park, Calif.: Kaiser Family Foundation.

Ku, Leighton, and Alyse Freilich. 2001. "Caring for Immigrants: Health Care Safety Nets in Los Angeles, New York, Miami and Houston." Menlo Park, Calif.: Kaiser Family Foundation.

Ku, Leighton, Shawn Fremstad, and Matthew Broaddus. 2003. "Noncitizens' Use of Public Benefits Has Declined since 1996." Washington, D.C.: Center on Budget and Policy Priorities. Available at: http://www.cbpp.org/archiveSite/4-14-03wel.pdf (accessed April 16, 2009).

Ku, Leighton, and Sheetal Matani. 2001. "Left Out: Immigrants' Access to Health Care and Insurance." *Health Affairs* 20(1): 247–56.

Ku, Leighton, and Tim Waidmann. 2003. "How Race/Ethnicity, Immigration Status and Language Affect Health Insurance Coverage, Access to Care and Quality of Care among the Low-Income Population." Menlo Park, Calif.: Kaiser Family Foundation.

Long, Sharon. 2003. *Hardship among the Uninsured: Choosing Between Food, Housing and Health Insurance*. Washington, D.C.: The Urban Institute.

Marcelli, Enrico. 2004. "The Unauthorized Residency Status Myth: Health Insurance Coverage and Medical Care Use among Mexican Immigrants in California." *Migraciones Internacionales* 2(4): 5–36.

Mohanty, Sarita, Steffie Woolhandler, David U. Himmelstein, Susmita Pati, Olveen Carrasquillo, and David H. Bor. 2005. "Health Care Expenditures of Immigrants in the United States: A Nationally Representative Analysis." *American Journal of Public Health* 95(8): 1431–438.

National Immigration Law Center. 2002. "*Guide to Immigrant Eligibility for Federal Programs*, 4th ed., updated 2007. Washington, D.C.: National Immigration Law Center. Available at: http://www.nilc.org/pubs/Guide_update.htm (accessed April 16, 2009).

Passel, Jeffrey, and D'Vera Cohen. 2008. "Trends in Unauthorized Immigration." Washington, D.C.: Pew Hispanic Center.

Pew Hispanic Center. 2007. *2007 National Survey of Latinos: As Illegal Immigration Issue Heats Up, Hispanics Feel a Chill*. Washington, D.C.: Pew Hispanic Center.

Ross, Donna Cohen. 2007. "New Medicaid Citizenship Documentation Rules Are Taking a Toll: States Report Enrollment Is Down and Administrative Costs Are Up." Press Release. Washington, D.C.: Center on Budget and Policy Priorities. Available at: http://www.cbpp.org/files/2-2-07health.pdf (accessed April 16, 2009).

Ross, Donna Cohen, and Laura Cox. 2005. *In a Time of Growing Need: State Choices Influence Health Coverage Access for Children and Families*. Washington, D.C.: Kaiser Commission on Medicaid and the Uninsured.

Schur, Claudia, and Jacob Feldman. 2001. *Running in Place: How Job Characteristics, Immigrant Status, and Family Structure Keep Hispanics Uninsured*. New York: Commonwealth Fund.

Schwartz, Sonya. 2001. "Immigrant Access to Food Stamps: Overcoming Barriers to Participation." *Clearinghouse Review/Journal of Poverty Law and Policy* (Sept.–Oct.): 260–75.

U.S. Bureau of the Census. Various years. *Current Population Survey*. Washington: Government Printing Office.

U.S. Congress. House. Committee on Ways and Means. 1997. Testimony of Representative Lamar Smith. 105th Cong., 1st sess., February 13, 1997.

U.S. Department of Health and Human Services. 2003. "Guidance to Federal Financial Assistance Recipients Regarding Title VI Prohibition Against National Origin Discrimination Affecting Limited English Proficient Persons." *Federal Register* 68(153): 47311–323.

U.S. Department of Homeland Security. 2005. *2005 Yearbook of Immigration Statistics*. Washington: Government Printing Office.

Van Hook, Jennifer, and Kelly Stamper Balistreri. 2006. "Ineligible Parents, Eligible Children: Food Stamp Receipt, Allotments, and Food Insecurity among Children of Immigrants." *Social Science Research* 35(1): 228–51.

Wheeler, Charles, and J. Edward Taylor. 2000. *The Effects of the Affidavit of Support Requirements on Low-Income Families*. Washington, D.C.: Catholic Legal Immigration Network.

Youdelman, Mara. 2007. *Medicaid and SCHIP Reimbursement Models for Language Services, 2007 Update*. Washington, D.C.: National Health Law Program.

Zimmermann, Wendy, and Michael E. Fix. 1998. *Declining Immigrant Applications for Medi-Cal and Welfare Benefits in Los Angeles County*. Washington, D.C.: The Urban Institute.

Zimmerman, Wendy, and Karen Tumlin. 1999. "Patchwork Policies: State Assistance for Immigrants under Welfare Reform." *Assessing the New Federalism* occasional paper 24. Washington, D.C.: The Urban Institute.

Chapter 7

Welfare-Leaving and Child Health and Behavior in Immigrant and Native Families

Ariel Kalil and Danielle A. Crosby

CHILDREN OF immigrants are the fastest-growing segment of the child population. Although immigrants make up less than 13 percent of the total population, their children make up 22 percent of the total child population and 30 percent of the low-income child population in the United States.[1] Research indicating disparate access to resources and opportunities for immigrant families raises concerns about the health, economic well-being, and social and cognitive development of this significant segment of the child population. Children of immigrants are more likely than their native counterparts to be poor and to experience material hardships such as crowded housing conditions and difficulties affording food (Capps 2001). They are also much less likely to have health insurance, even after controlling for key demographic characteristics (Hernandez 2004), and the barriers immigrant families face in accessing health care often extend beyond those created by insurance coverage issues (Capps 2001). Moreover, the quality of care available to immigrants is likely to be less than that of their native counterparts (Ku and Matani 2001). That immigrant children are at increased risk for not having health insurance and a regular place for medical care partly explains why they are substantially more likely than their peers to be in poor health (Reardon-Anderson, Capps, and Fix 2002), despite better health outcomes at birth and during infancy (Ventura et al. 2000).

An important and unresolved issue concerns the extent to which changes in federal welfare policy have affected household economic security and the health and well-being of young children in immigrant families. Before the Personal Responsibility and Work Opportunity Reconciliation Act of 1996 (PRWORA), legal immigrants and their children were generally eligible for public benefits under the same terms as citizens. The main vehicle for welfare reform, PRWORA introduced broad restrictions on immigrants' eligibility for many health and social service programs, including cash welfare assistance (TANF), food stamps, and subsidized health insurance (Medicaid and the State Children's Health Insurance Program, or SCHIP). For example, the law restricted TANF and Medicaid eligibility among legal immigrants to those who are citizens, refugees, those in the country for at least five years, and other small groups. Food stamp eligibility was restricted to legal immigrants with ten years of work history, though this requirement was later softened to a five-year residency requirement for adults and no restriction for legal immigrant children. Unauthorized immigrants were ineligible for these major public assistance programs both before and after PRWORA was enacted (Capps and Fortuny 2006).

Caseloads for benefit programs fell dramatically in the wake of welfare reform (Blank 2002), but the declines were steeper for immigrants than for native-born citizens, even among immigrants who remained eligible for assistance because of their tenure and status in the United States or their child's U.S. citizenship (Fix and Passel 1999; Haider et al. 2004; Ku and Blaney 2000; Van Hook and Balistreri 2006). Several hypotheses have been put forth to explain these patterns. First, there is some indication that immigrants had different (and more favorable) responses to the robust economy of the late 1990s (Capps et al. 2003; Haider et al. 2004; Kaestner and Kaushal 2005; Lofstrom and Bean 2002). It has also been suggested that the new restrictions on immigrants may have induced some families to seek citizenship (Fix and Haskins 2002; Van Hook 2003), making it appear as if the noncitizenship welfare rolls were declining at an accelerated rate. The hypothesis most relevant to this chapter, however, concerns the so-called chilling effect, which maintains that immigrant families became reluctant to access public assistance after 1996 (even if eligible) because they were confused about the new policies and feared the potential consequences for family members (Shields and Behrman 2004). The new eligibility rules are complex, vary by state (depending on how states responded to the federal changes), and have continued to change over time. In addition, limited English proficiency may have contributed to immigrants' confusion about the new laws. Noncitizen parents may have been unaware of their U.S.-born children's eligibility for important benefits, or may have believed that seeking assistance for eligible children would hinder other family members' efforts to obtain citizenship or legal status, or their ability to reenter and stay in the United States (Capps 2001; Fix and Passel 1999; Holcomb et al. 2003).

LINKING PATTERNS OF USE TO HEALTH AND WELL-BEING

This chapter examines changes in young children's health and behavior over the period of PRWORA implementation as a function of native and immigrant parents' welfare transitions during this time. Much of what is known about the impact of welfare reform on children comes from studies of native families. This literature suggests that in the context of a robust economy, and with new pressures and incentives for employment, most parents who were able to exit the rolls did just that. In general, welfare recipients who left the system in the late 1990s increased their work hours and earnings and experienced less material hardship (Danziger et al. 2002), despite moving into largely low-wage jobs with no retirement or health benefits (Page and Simmons 2000). These changes appear to have had largely neutral to slightly positive net effects for children, with some exceptions for adolescents (Blank 2002).

For some policy analysts, immigrants' welfare leaving is an indicator of positive adjustment because it demonstrates an ability to integrate into the American economy—the integration hypothesis (Borjas 1998; Camarota 2001); like native leavers, these immigrants may also have experienced increased earnings and less hardship. However, if some immigrant parents left welfare because of confusion or fear, as suggested by the chilling effect hypothesis, they were likely to be worse off than both immigrants who continued to receive assistance and native welfare leavers.

Parents' reasons for leaving welfare and their experiences after doing so have implications for children's well-being; here, we speculate about these implications. First, if immigrant parents experienced welfare reform in ways similar to native parents and left welfare because of increased employment, the net impact on child outcomes may have been small, because increased earnings were largely offset by the loss of welfare benefits. If, however, families left welfare despite continued need, children could have faced adverse developmental consequences. Material hardship bodes negatively for young children's health and behavior (Duncan and Brooks-Gunn 1997). Indeed, following PRWORA, eligible children of immigrant noncitizens experienced more persistent and higher levels of food insecurity than the children of citizens, reflecting in part their lesser use of food stamps (Van Hook and Balistreri 2006). It is also true that welfare often serves as a gateway to accessing other public programs, such as subsidized child care, which may be especially important for immigrant families in allowing both parents to work. Child care outside the home could also be important to improve children's cognitive development and preparation for school—especially those children in the immediate preschool years. Thus, families who exited the system could have been cut off from child care and other services that would have promoted their children's health, economic well-being, and development. There is some evidence that immigrant parents (particularly those whose status was more precarious) were less likely (or potentially more reluctant) to take up public benefits in the wake of welfare reform despite their children's continued eligibility (Lurie 2008; Kaushal and Kaestner 2005).

THE RELEVANCE OF YOUNG CHILDREN'S HEALTH

The question of how policy changes affect young children's health is important for several reasons. First, health is increasingly recognized as an important component of development, with links to children's cognitive functioning and academic success (Crosnoe 2006; Currie 2005). Moreover, childhood health is a strong predictor of adult health and productivity (Marmot and Wadsworth 1997). Children born into less advantaged families have poorer health outcomes, which in turn contribute to less positive health and economic outcomes in adulthood (Case, Lubotsky, and Paxson 2002; Case, Fertig, and Paxson 2005). Influences on the health of immigrant children may be particularly important to examine, given their increased risk for health problems and inadequate health care and insurance coverage (Capps et al. 2004; Flores et al. 2002). Latino immigrant children, who constitute more than half of all immigrant children, are among the most vulnerable in terms of their health, well-being, and development (Hernandez 2004). For example, immigrant children of Mexican descent, roughly two-thirds of the Latino immigrant child population, are more likely than other children to be rated by their parents as being in fair or poor health and having poor dental health (Mendoza and Dixon 1999). Further, Latino children from certain high-risk countries are more likely than their peers to have tuberculosis, hepatitis B, parasitic infections, and elevated levels of lead in the blood (Mendoza and Dixon 1999).

Research on group-level differences in children's social behavior generally reveals more positive outcomes for immigrant youth, though research in this area is relatively sparse. Latino and Asian immigrant adolescents tend to exhibit fewer conduct problems than their native-born peers (Fuligni 1998; Valenzuela 1999). A recent study using longitudinal data for a representative sample of American kindergarteners found that immigrant Latino and Asian children had, on average, the lowest levels of behavior problems amongst the various racial-ethnic groups examined (Crosnoe 2006).

THE MODERATING EFFECTS OF CHILD AGE

There is good reason to think that any effects of welfare-leaving, especially if they correlate with material hardship, will have different effects on the well-being of younger versus older children

(Duncan and Brooks-Gunn 1997). A substantial number of studies document that family economic hardship has relatively more deleterious effects on preschool-age children than those in middle childhood or adolescence, especially in families at the lower end of the income distribution (Duncan and Brooks-Gunn 1997; Duncan et al. 1998). Particularly around health issues, young immigrant children may be more vulnerable than their older counterparts, in part because they are both not yet in school and less likely than native children to be attending an organized care and education program (Capps and Fortuny 2006; Nord and Griffin 1999; Takanishi 2004). School and other organized settings for children may provide some health monitoring (and require up-to-date vaccinations) and may help connect families to needed services. Moreover, preschool-age children whose parents' English is limited cannot facilitate communication between their parents and teachers, medical staff, and other service providers in the same ways as older children, who often serve as translators or language brokers (Orellana 2003).

STUDY OVERVIEW AND KEY FINDINGS

Using longitudinal data for a large sample of young children living in low-income families during the middle to late 1990s, we examined whether leaving welfare is associated with changes in children's health and behavior and the extent to which these associations vary for children of immigrants versus native-born parents. We also examined whether these associations differ by child age, reasoning that young children may be more affected by changes in parental income and employment than school-age children. Finally, we also performed a set of analyses to explore whether changes in families' economic conditions over the study period might explain any of the associations we observed between welfare use and child well-being. Whereas most related studies have examined children's physical health only, our analysis focuses on children's physical health as well as their emotional adjustment and behavior.

To investigate these questions, we drew on two waves of data from the longitudinal cohort component of the Project on Human

Development in Chicago Neighborhoods (PHDCN), a multilevel study of more than 6,000 children and adolescents. Designed to be representative of Chicago, the PHDCN sample is racially, ethnically, and socioeconomically diverse, and includes a sizable proportion of native and immigrant families. Although the single-community sample potentially limits the extent to which study results can be extrapolated beyond Chicago, the PHDCN data offer several advantages for addressing our research questions. First, the PHDCN study gathered in-depth information about the well-being and experiences of children and their families over time, including nativity, language use, and time in the United States. Second, the six years covered by the data we examined (1995 to 2001) encompass the implementation of welfare reform and other important macroeconomic changes, from the boom years of the late 1990s to the economic downturn that began in 2001.

The study's setting in Chicago also allows us access to a large sample of immigrants, particularly those from Mexico, who comprise the largest group of foreign-born in the United States. Chicago (and the state of Illinois) has historically been a gateway for immigrants. According to the 2007 American Community Survey, Chicago ranked tenth among metropolitan statistical areas in the size of its immigrant population (1.7 million), and had a foreign-born population well above the national average: 17.6 versus 12.6 percent (U.S. Bureau of the Census 2007).

Given our interest in welfare participation, we focused this study on PHDCN families with annual household incomes below 200 percent of the federal poverty level, adjusted for year and family size at the beginning of the study. We define this group as low-income families. To simplify the analysis and help with interpreting the results, we limited the sample to second-generation children (that is, U.S.-born children of immigrant parents), excluding a small number of foreign-born children (n = 88; mostly from the age six cohort). Thus our analysis sample consists entirely of citizen children who should have been eligible for assistance throughout the study (that is, before and after reform) regardless of their parents' eligibility. To further clarify the analysis, we excluded the small percentage, less than 5 percent, of second-generation children in the sample who were not Latino. Although children of native-born parents in this sample represent a wider range of racial-ethnic groups (that is, white, black, and Latino), our analyses control for this such that our primary comparison is between Latino children of foreign-born and native-born parents. Approximately 25 percent of children of native-born parents in our low-income sample were Latino.

We focused on the three PHDCN age cohorts for whom the best measures of health over time exist. Children in the infant cohort (n = 636) were born around the time of the first interview (Time 1; M_{age} = .57 years, SD = .34) and were approximately two years old (M_{age} = 2.51 years, SD = .63) at the time of the second interview (Time 2). Children in the age three cohort (n = 538, M_{age} = 3.15 years, SD = .32) were approximately age five (M_{age} = 5.28 years, SD = .56) at Time 2, and those in the age six cohort (n = 475; M_{age} = 6.16 years, SD = .33) were approximately age eight (M_{age} = 8.28 years, SD = .56) at Time 2.[2] Additional details concerning the data and our methodology are provided in appendix A.

Native and Immigrant Parents' Patterns of Welfare Use

Using survey data on whether native and immigrant families received income from public assistance (TANF) in the year before the Time 1 and Time 2 interviews, we identified six analysis groups: *native leavers* (native families who stopped receiving welfare by Time 2), *native stayers* (families who continued to receive assistance across both time points), *native nonrecipients* (those who reported no welfare receipt at either time point), *immigrant leavers, immigrant stayers,* and *immigrant nonrecipients*.[3] Immigrants were significantly more likely to be welfare leavers and nonrecipients—and less likely to be welfare stayers—than native parents (see table 7.1). The one exception to this is that a similar percentage of immigrant and native parents in the age three cohort were leavers. If we exclude the nonrecipients at Time 1, however, immigrants were more likely than natives to leave by Time 2.

In general, native and immigrant families in our sample differ in ways consistent with the literature (see appendix A). For example, low-income immigrant mothers had less education and were

TABLE 7.1 **Welfare Use of Parents**

	Native	Immigrant	Sig. Diff.
Infant cohort	(n = 352)	(n = 284)	
Leaver	16%	30%	I > N***
Stayer-beginner	57	11	I < N***
Nonrecipient	27	59	I > N***
Age three cohort	(n = 315)	(n = 223)	
Leaver	17	19	ns[a]
Stayer-beginner	56	18	I < N***
Nonrecipient	27	63	I > N***
Age six cohort	(n = 289)	(n = 186)	
Leaver	16	24	I > N*
Stayer-beginner	52	13	I < N***
Nonrecipient	32	63	I > N***

Source: Authors' compilation based on Project on Human Development in Chicago Neighborhoods (ICPSR, various years).
Note: [a]Among the subsample of families who were receiving public assistance at Time 1 (that is, excluding the nonrecipients), immigrants are significantly more likely to be in the leaver group than natives in all of the age cohorts.
†$p < .10$, *$p < .05$, **$p < .01$, ***$p < .001$.

slightly less likely to be employed at Time 1 than their native counterparts. At the same time, immigrant mothers were less likely to be single and more likely to have an employed spouse or partner in the household. For both native and foreign-born parents, employment and earnings were highest among welfare nonrecipients, followed by leavers and then stayers.

Linking Welfare Use to Child Health and Behavior

As part of the PHDCN home interviews, parents rated their children's overall physical health on a scale from 1 (poor) to 5 (excellent). This simple but commonly used measure has been shown to correspond to more detailed and objective assessments, including number of sick days, diagnosed chronic health conditions, and physician exams (Case, Lubotsky, and Paxson 2002). For the current analysis, we identified children in fair or poor health at each time point. A few studies of adult self-rated health suggest that Latinos may overreport fair and poor health compared to individuals of other ethnicities (Shetterly et al. 1996). Although it is possible that a similar bias may occur for parent ratings of child health, our focus on comparing Latino children of foreign-born versus native-born parents should reduce or eliminate this bias. Parental ratings on the Child Behavior Checklist (CBCL) are used to identify children with high levels (specifically, scores in the top quartile) of behavior problems compared to their same-age peers (Achenbach 1991).[4] The two subscales of the CBCL capture the frequency of children's internalizing (anxious, depressive, and overcontrolled) and externalizing (aggressive, hyperactive, noncompliant, and undercontrolled) problems.

Our basic approach for examining associations between welfare receipt and child well-being involved using the categories described to predict children's health and behavior at Time 2, controlling for their health and behavior at Time 1. As such, our analyses compared the experiences of children in immigrant leaver families not only to those of children in native leaver families but also to those of children in other immigrant families with different patterns of welfare use. Including Time-1 levels of child functioning in the analysis helps control for potential baseline differences among the six nativity welfare-use groups.[5]

Absent an experimental design in which families are randomly assigned to different welfare-use conditions, it is plausible that certain characteristics of parents and the home environment affect both the likelihood that parents will access resources and children's health and behavior. Failure to account for these characteristics could bias our estimate of the relationship between changes in welfare receipt and changes in child well-being. For example, parents with higher human and social capital may find it easier to leave welfare and be better equipped to promote children's development. In this case, a spurious positive correlation may exist between welfare-leaving and child outcomes. The direction of potential bias in the current study is not entirely clear, however, because it is also possible that more vulnerable immigrant parents (in terms of status in the United States and English language skills) were more likely to leave welfare and might also experience difficulties in securing the supports necessary to care for their children. Selection (or omitted variables) bias is one of the key challenges to estimating causal relations in developmental

TABLE 7.2 Linear Probability Models, Child Health

Controlling for Time 1 Levels, Child Is . . .	Model 1 Infant	Model 2 Age Three	Model 3 Age Six
In fair or poor health at Time 2	NS > NL, NN IL > NL, NS, NN IL > IN	IL > NL, NS, NN IL > IS, IN	
Internalizing problems at Time 2		NS, NN > NL	
Externalizing problems at Time 2			NN > NL

Source: Authors' compilation based on Project on Human Development in Chicago Neighborhoods (ICPSR, various years).
Note: NL = native leavers; NS = native stayers; NN = native nonrecipients; IL = immigrant leavers; IS = immigrant stayers; IN = immigrant nonrecipients.

studies (Duncan, Magnuson, and Ludwig 2004). In addition to including Time-1 measures of development to help address some of these issues, the analyses also control for an extensive set of child and family variables measured at Time 1, including demographic characteristics, multiple qualities of the home environment (positive parenting affect, cognitive stimulation, and physical safety), and indicators of parents' physical and mental health.

Our main results are summarized in table 7.2 and presented in detail in appendix B. We found that young children of immigrant welfare-leavers fared significantly worse in terms of their health than either native leavers or immigrant stayers. Health declines after parents left welfare were largest for immigrant preschool-age children, though we found similar, albeit smaller, effects for infants. Notably, we failed to find a link between changes in welfare status and the health trajectories of school-age children.[6] We also found no significant differences in children's behavior trajectories among immigrant families with different patterns of welfare use, nor between immigrant and native welfare-leaving families. Interestingly, however, native preschoolers whose parents stayed on or remained off welfare (that is, had no change in their welfare status) were less likely to have internalizing behavior problems than those whose parents left welfare over the study period. To check the robustness of our estimates, we performed a series of sensitivity analyses using alternative model and sample specifications (see appendix A). Notably, none of the alternative models produced different findings.

The Role of Postwelfare Economic Conditions

Our results raise questions about the potential mechanisms underlying differences in how native and immigrant children have fared since welfare reform. To some extent, these mechanisms are likely to be related to the reasons behind parents' welfare behavior. The current data, however, do not allow us to disentangle parents' reasons for leaving welfare from the behaviors that may accompany leaving. For example, increased parental employment (and the additional earnings it confers) may lead to leaving welfare or may be in response to having left welfare for other reasons, such as sanctions or changes in actual or perceived eligibility. In either case, the change in employment is likely to influence how the family and child fare once they no longer receive cash assistance.

With the PHDCN data, we were able to examine several (primarily economic) factors that might help explain the associations we observed between welfare use and child well-being, including household income, household income to poverty ratio, mothers' and partners' employment hours, material hardship, and overcrowded living conditions. Given that we found more negative health outcomes among children of immigrants leaving welfare than among any of their counterparts, we might expect that immigrants fared worse afterward, particularly if they left the system because of fear or confusion despite continued need. This scenario is consistent with the chilling effect hypothesis described earlier. To evaluate this possibility, we used the welfare-use-nativity indicators to predict families' economic circumstances at Time 2, controlling for their circumstances at Time 1.

Somewhat contrary to our expectations, we found that immigrant families leaving welfare did not appear to be financially worse off than their native counterparts. Across the three child-age groups, immigrant leavers did not report less income or more material hardship at Time 2 than other families (results shown in appendix B). Indeed, in the age three cohort, immigrant families had higher income-to-poverty ratios and reported less material hardship than native families. Immigrant mothers in the infant and age three groups did report less of an increase in their employment over the study period than native mothers; this, however, is offset by the fact that immigrant fathers tended to have a greater increase in their employment hours than native fathers. The most consistent result of these analyses is that native families remaining on welfare were economically worse off (less employment, earnings, and income) than natives leaving welfare. Because the data do not support the hypothesis that employment and income explain health differences, we need to consider alternate explanations, a point we expand on in the discussion that follows.

DISCUSSION

Latino immigrants, particularly those from Mexico, often arrive in the United States with little financial and human capital. At the same time, they tend to be strongly attached to the labor force and exhibit family forms and cultural values that may promote children's well-being. It has been suggested that public assistance serves as a potentially important form of investment for immigrant parents in building their children's human capital (Hofferth 1999). At the time the data used in this study were collected, however, the federal government was implementing new policies that restricted immigrants' access to federal health and welfare programs. In addition to these policy changes, it is possible to argue that the policy environment has become increasingly hostile toward immigrants in general over the past decade, with stricter enforcement of immigration laws across the country since the events of September 11, 2001.

Since PRWORA's passage in 1996, some benefits have been restored federally (for example, food stamps to legal immigrant children and some legal adults, Medicaid-SCHIP to legal children), and others have been restored in certain states using state-level funding. Illinois, the state in which the current study was conducted, continued to provide TANF, Medicaid, and SSI to legal immigrants who arrived before August 1996. Postenactment immigrants (those arriving after 1996) are largely ineligible for public benefits in Illinois, as elsewhere. However, Illinois does provide Medicaid to legal postenactment immigrants during the five-year federal bar on TANF and has recently extended this coverage to unauthorized immigrants as well, though this was not in place at the time the PHDCN data were collected (Capps and Fortuny 2006). Illinois also operates a state-funded food program open to most immigrants who arrived before August 1996 (and a limited number who arrived after that date), and a SCHIP program (KidCare, which began in 1998) for which immigrant children are eligible. Finally, unlike some other states, Illinois does not require that the income of an immigrant's sponsor be considered in the calculation of benefits. All in all, Illinois has been characterized as one of the nine states that made their safety nets the most available to immigrants (Zimmerman and Tumlin 1999). This relative generosity makes the current set of findings more of a concern, given that many groups of children in immigrant families may be at greater risk than those in our sample.

Our findings provide tentative evidence that the current policy approach of restricting immigrants' access to public assistance may be detrimental to the healthy development of young citizen children in these families. Within a sample of low-income families who lived in Chicago in the middle to late 1990s, we found that Latino immigrant preschoolers and, to a lesser extent, Latino infants in immigrant families leaving welfare suffered substantial and significant declines in their physical health over time relative to their native Latino counterparts. We found no such differences in children's levels of behavior problems. We also found no evidence that these health differentials were related to differences in native and immigrant leavers' postwelfare economic circumstances; in fact, where small differences did exist, they favored immigrant families.

Consistent with previous research, low-income immigrant families in our sample were less likely to be receiving assistance at Time 1 and were more likely to have left welfare by Time 2, despite their children's presumed continued eligibility, insofar as all of these children were U.S. citizens by birth. As mentioned, higher rates of welfare exits may reflect the tendency for immigrants to respond more quickly to the labor market (that is, to secure jobs in a boom economy) than their native counterparts; alternatively, immigrants may have left welfare more quickly because of fear and confusion around the new policies targeting noncitizens. With the current data, we are unable to test directly why families left welfare, or whether immigrants left for different reasons than natives. Our goal instead was to examine whether leaving welfare was associated differently with changes in children's health and well-being in the two populations. This said, our finding that immigrant leavers were not significantly worse or better off financially than native leavers (or immigrant stayers) suggests that neither of the two noted hypotheses appear to be driving our results.

One possibility is that immigrant families—many of whom may have left welfare because of misinformation about eligibility or fear of the consequences of program participation—were able to find employment and sustain their income in the economy of the late 1990s, but also faced barriers (whether real or perceived) to using other relevant programs after leaving welfare. These barriers might include individual beliefs and knowledge about services, language barriers that impede access, and misinformation on the part of agency staff (Maloy et al. 2000; Holcomb et al. 2003). Moreover, welfare participation could be one way families learn about, and access, other related programs, such that leaving the system disconnects them from a wider range of services. It could also be that this subsample contained an overrepresentation of undocumented parents or family members, in which case, fears of federal immigration enforcement agencies or of jeopardizing citizenship bids could be a factor. Finally, other research clearly indicates a lack of linguistically and culturally competent health-care providers and a lack of outreach efforts to enroll eligible children and families in public health programs (Flores et al. 2002). If the latter were more likely the case, then our findings are not specific to welfare reform per se. However, there are many reasons to believe that the long-recognized barriers to immigrants' participation in public programs may be exacerbated in the postwelfare-reform climate, which engendered misinformation, reluctance, and fear among some immigrants regarding their use of such programs.

We find associations between leaving welfare and poorer health for infants and preschool-age children but not for the school-age children in the sample. The importance of investments in early childhood for later development has been well documented (Case, Fertig, and Paxson 2005; Duncan and Brooks-Gunn 1997); it is thus worrisome to see so substantial an impact on this particular group of children. It is possible that school-age children are buffered from any negative impact by virtue of having to meet the health criteria required for school entry (for example, a physical and immunizations) and having some monitoring of their health within school settings. In addition, older children in immigrant families have been shown to play a substantial role in accessing resources for themselves and their families. Often more skilled in English than their parents, older children act as interpreters and translators to help their families navigate health and educational systems in the community (Orellana et al. 2003). Preschool-age children of immigrant parents are presumably less able to serve in this role because they are less likely than children of natives to be in early-education settings, including center-based care, which may include a health component. We note that having a school-age older sibling in the household did not appear to buffer preschool children in leaver families against a health decline, given that this variable was controlled in our analysis.

Limitations

The findings from this study, though consistent with others that have suggested a drop-off in benefit receipt among eligible families due to a chilling effect, cannot be generalized beyond Chicago during the late 1990s. Furthermore, our data speak primarily to the experience of Mexican-origin immigrants, and the results reported here may not extend to other immigrant populations. Our analyses are limited by the fact that the data contain only gross measures of welfare receipt and, most regrettably, none of Medicaid, SCHIP, or employer-sponsored health insurance. Moreover, despite our efforts to control for factors that might lead parents to avoid programs and fail to promote their children's health, selection bias in this nonexperimental framework remains a threat to our interpretation of these results.

Finally, the cell sizes for the key groups of interest are small and thus these results must be characterized as speculative. In addition, the small sample sizes may have limited the power to detect significant effects. For example, several of the point estimates in the regression tables are large in size but statistically insignificant with large standard errors. Researchers need to replicate these findings with other datasets and to examine the processes involved in welfare-leaving and in immigrant perceptions of welfare reform and program use more broadly. Especially in the wake of welfare reform, it is important to understand immigrant families' service needs and how they learn about and access such services. At issue is not only eligibility but also whether families are informed about and have real access to services in their communities.

CONCLUSIONS

Newly arrived American families face many challenges, often navigating linguistic and cultural differences, the hazards of the low-wage labor market, and significant financial hardship. Our results provide tentative evidence that young children of immigrants may pay a cost in a policy environment where some parents are barred from receiving assistance. Legal permanent immigrants who have arrived since 1996 cannot obtain federal assistance for at least their first five years in the United States. This raises concerns about putting families in a vulnerable position during children's formative years and about the spillover effects of poor health in early life on subsequent steps in healthy development, such as school readiness (Currie 2005).

Adding to this concern is that the immigrant families who participated in the current study are likely to be relatively advantaged compared to more recently arrived groups. In fact, because of their arrival in the United States before 1996 (and the U.S. citizenship status of their children), their eligibility for assistance would not have been affected by the reforms—raising important questions about the potentially far-reaching (and unintended) consequences of the reform policies. Our results underscore the need for further research focused on understanding immigrant families' interactions with public-benefit programs and services.

Also notable is that this sample of immigrant families lived in a state that, as noted, is considered relatively generous in terms of its safety net for immigrants (Zimmermann and Tumlin 1999). We might therefore expect the negative associations between leaving welfare and child well-being to be even more dramatic for recent immigrants and those who live in less generous states. As the number of postenactment immigrants quickly approaches the number of preenactment immigrants, it is critical that more be known about how children in these families are faring in the current policy environment.

APPENDIX A: STUDY METHODOLOGY

The following material provides a detailed description of the data and sample, the measures, and our empirical strategy. Detailed tables with the results from the multivariate regressions are included at the end of this section.

Data and Sample

With the intention of yielding a representative-probability sample of Chicago residents, PHDCN screened approximately 35,000 households in eighty neighborhood clusters and identified 8,347 participants in seven age cohorts (at birth, age three, six, nine, twelve, fifteen, and eighteen). During the first wave of data collection, 1995 through 1997, 75 percent of eligible participants were interviewed; a second wave of data was collected approximately two years later, with a response rate of 86 percent. At each assessment, extensive data regarding child and family functioning were gathered through face-to-face interviews and direct assessments with children and their caregivers (the respondents were primarily mothers). The complete protocol was translated into Spanish; in the full sample, approximately 25 percent of the interviews were conducted in Spanish.

Parents in PHDCN reported their birthplace, those of their children, their parents, their partner, and their partner's parents. Mothers also reported whether they were citizens. Data on the fathers' or partners' citizenship status is not available. For this study, we adopted the common convention of identifying children as immigrant if they, or at least one of their parents, were foreign-born; all others were categorized as native. Our analysis excluded the small number of foreign-born children (n = 88; mostly from the age six cohort) and children with a parent from refugee-sending countries (n = 2) to achieve a homogeneous sample of citizen children who remained eligible for assistance throughout the study period. We further excluded non-Latino children of immigrants from the analysis, because they constituted fewer than 5 percent of the low-income children of immigrant sample in PHDCN. Similar to others, we categorized parents who were born in U.S. territories off the mainland, such as Puerto Rico (N = 40) as native because of their status as U.S. citizens and full eligibility for programs (see, for example, Van Hook 2003).

Measures

An extensive set of variables capturing child, parent, and household characteristics at Time 1 were included as covariates in the analyses. These include child's gender; dummy indicators of child's race-ethnicity (black, Latino/a [omitted group], white, or other); primary caregiver's age and years of completed education (as continuous variables); an indicator for whether the primary caregiver is someone other than the mother; indicators of family structure (married, cohabiting, or single [omitted group]); number of household members; presence of a school-age sibling (in the models for the age six cohort, variable identifies presence of a preschool-age sibling); whether the mother is employed; whether there is an employed partner-spouse in the household; annual household income; whether the family owns their home; and the length of follow-up between the Time-1 and Time-2 surveys (in years).

Along with these basic demographic controls, our analyses controlled for several aspects of quality of the home environment at Time 1. The PHDCN Homelife Interview—based on the widely used Home Inventory for Measurement of the Environment (HOME)—consists of parent survey items and interviewer observation and is intended for use with a broad age range and a racially, ethnically, and economically diverse sample. Extensive psychometric work has identified three internally consistent, cohesive scales—parental warmth (nine items) and lack of hostility (four items), observations of the safety of the internal (eight items) and external environment (four items), and cognitive stimulation (eleven items) (Leventhal et al. 2004).

The measure of parental warmth and lack of hostility was based on interviewer observations of such behaviors as encouragement and praise of child and physical affection. The measure of cognitive stimulation was based on survey items about the availability of developmentally appropriate materials in the home, such as puzzles and books, and activities done with the child based on the age of the child, such as reading and visiting museums. The measure of the physical environment was based on interviewer observations of the exterior (such as noise and activity around dwelling, physical conditions of housing) and interior environment (such as crowdedness, cleanliness). All items were coded dichotomously; the score for each scale ranges from 0 to 100, with higher scores being more favorable. A slightly reduced set of Time-1 variables were available for the infant cohort as many children were born after the Time-1 survey; the only scale score available for this group was the interviewer observation of the physical environment.

Finally, we included a control variable for whether any parent in the household has a problematic physical health condition (1 = yes, 0 = no) at Time 1 and an index of mothers' depressive symptoms, which was available only at Time 2. The measure of physical health conditions was based on responses to the dichotomous variable asking whether the child's mother or father had diabetes, high blood pressure, heart problem, cancer, stroke, or asthma. The latter measure is the sum of seven dummy variables measuring depressive symptoms (such as feels sad, lonely), and thus ranges from 0 to 7 (see table 7A.1 for more detail).

TABLE 7A.1 Baseline Descriptives

	Native			Immigrant		
	Leaver (n = 156)	Stayer (n = 526)	Nonrecipient (n = 275)	Leaver (n = 173)	Stayer (n = 95)	Nonrecipient (n = 424)
Child is male (percentage)	50	49	54	50	54	48
Child race-ethnicity (percentage)						
Latino	41	16	33	100	100	100
Black	51	71	48			
White	4	10	17			
Other	4	4	2			
Mother not primary caregiver (percentage)	4	4	7	1	1	2
Mother's age	27.18	28.18	31.12	28.90	28.69	30.03
	(7.10)	(7.97)	(9.61)	(6.91)	(7.15)	(6.33)
Mother's completed years of school	12.99	12.76	13.82	9.29	8.82	9.29
	(2.38)	(2.05)	(2.58)	(4.33)	(4.13)	(3.98)
Mother married (percentage)	13	10	42	58	54	82
Mother cohabiting (percentage)	21	18	12	28	22	12
Household size	5.29	5.94	5.35	5.64	6.07	5.57
	(2.16)	(2.37)	(2.19)	(2.01)	(1.91)	(1.82)
Mother employed (percentage)	38	23	57	28	19	42
Employed partner in household (percentage)	27	17	44	81	65	87
Time-1 household income ($1998)	$14,770	$11,459	$22,788	$14,318	$13,973	$20,604
Owns home (percentage)	6	7	26	13	8	38
Home quality, parental warmth	0.84	0.78	0.85	0.83	0.82	0.86
	(.18)	(.19)	(.16)	(.20)	(.20)	(.17)
Home quality, cognitive stimulation	0.76	0.73	0.81	0.61	0.56	0.62
	(.18)	(.18)	(.13)	(.23)	(.23)	(.21)
Home quality, physical environment	0.56	0.55	0.66	0.58	0.57	0.67
	(.22)	(.21)	(.20)	(.20)	(.17)	(.19)
Parent health condition (percentage)	35	37	36	18	19	14
Maternal depressive symptoms (0 to 7)	1.08	1.37	.93	.79	1.10	.66
	(2.23)	(2.30)	(1.97)	(1.82)	(2.15)	(1.67)

Source: Authors' compilation based on Project on Human Development in Chicago Neighborhoods (ICPSR, various years).
Note: Robust standard errors in parentheses.

Children's Physical Health

As part of the Time-1 and Time-2 assessments, mothers were asked to rate their child's general health (1 = poor, 2 = fair, 3 = good, 4 = very good, 5 = excellent). For the analysis, a dichotomous variable was created to identify children who were in fair or poor health at each time point. Virtually no parents, at either time point, however, rated their child's health as poor. Adult ratings of their own health predict both demand for medical care services and medical outcomes (see Idler and Benyamini 1997). Parental ratings of child health have been less examined; however, this measure has been used in several national studies of child well-being, including the National Longitudinal Study of Youth, the Panel Study of Income Dynamics, the National Health Interview Survey, and the National Health and Nutrition Examination Survey. Moreover, studies with multiple health measures reveal similar results with parent ratings of general health as with more detailed assessments of child health, such as bed days, hospitalization, chronic conditions, and physician examinations (Case et al. 2002).

Because Time-1 health ratings are not available for the infant cohort (many were born shortly after the first interview), we created an index (from 0 to 4) of the presence of four prenatal and perinatal health risks—no prenatal care in the first trimester of pregnancy; drug, alcohol, or tobacco use during pregnancy; premature birth; and newborn hospitalization for more than four days. From this index, we created a dummy variable to identify infants who have experienced two or more risks (1= yes, 0 = no). This indicator of early health is used as a control in predicting Time-2 health ratings for the infant cohort.

As part of the Time 1 and Time 2 surveys, parents completed the Child Behavior Checklist (Achenbach 1991), one of the most widely used standardized assessments of children's behavioral and emotional adjustment. Presented with a list of behaviors and characteristics, parents rate how well each described their child in the past six months, using a Likert-type scale (0 = not true, 1 = somewhat true, or 2 = very true). Two age-appropriate versions of the CBCL were used in this study: one designed for two- to three-year-olds (used at Time 1 for cohort 3 and at Time 2 for cohort 0),

TABLE 7A.2 Descriptives for Child Health and Behavior

	Native			Immigrant		
	Leaver	Stayer	Nonrecipient	Leaver	Stayer	Nonrecipient
Infant cohort	(n = 57)	(n = 201)	(n = 95)	(n = 86)	(n = 31)	(n = 167)
Time 1						
Two or more prenatal-perinatal risks	16	24	11	7	0	13
Time 2						
General health fair or poor	0	4	2	20	16	8
High internalizing problems	30	35	31	21	35	17
High externalizing problems	40	40	33	32	32	31
Age three cohort	(n = 53)	(n = 174)	(n = 86)	(n = 43)	(n = 40)	(n = 140)
Time 1						
General health is fair or poor	17	6	6	19	20	09
High internalizing problems	32	39	27	35	31	26
High externalizing problems	36	30	32	35	28	22
Time 2						
General health fair or poor	8	6	2	40	18	10
High internalizing problems	36	24	25	46	41	30
High externalizing problems	32	39	32	29	33	21
Age six cohort	(n = 46)	(n = 151)	(n = 94)	(n = 44)	(n = 24)	(n = 117)
Time 1						
General health fair or poor	2	5	4	16	4	9
High internalizing problems	30	33	19	45	33	29
High externalizing problems	39	42	20	32	17	18
Time 2						
General health fair or poor	2	6	2	7	17	9
High internalizing problems	24	36	33	30	25	37
High externalizing problems	29	42	39	23	25	20

Source: Authors' compilation based on Project on Human Development in Chicago Neighborhoods (ICPSR, various years).
Note: Numbers in percentages.

and a second, designed for children ages four to eighteen (used at Time 1 for cohort 6 and at Time 2 for cohorts 3 and 6). Time 1 measures included the complete set of items; whereas a reduced form of the CBCL was used at Time 2. Items on the checklist compose two summary scales capturing internalizing (anxious, depressive, and overcontrolled) and externalizing behaviors (aggressive, hyperactive, noncompliant, and undercontrolled). Scores for each scale were summed and dichotomous variables were created to identify children with high levels of internalizing and externalizing problems compared to their same age peers (scores in the top quartile; see table 7A.2 for more detail).

Empirical Strategy

Our primary models are estimated as linear probability models and regress children's health at Time 2 on the corresponding measure at Time 1, the set of five mutually exclusive variables capturing patterns of welfare use by native and immigrant parents during this same period (native leavers are the reference group), as well as the baseline demographic, economic, and family characteristics control variables described above. The model takes the following form:

$$h_{t+1} = \alpha + \beta'_t X_t + \lambda h_t + \delta\ NS + \phi\ NNR + \eta\ IL + \sigma\ IS + \rho\ INR + u$$

where h_{t+1} is a dichotomous variable indicating the child's health at follow-up, X_t is a vector of controls taken at baseline, h_t is the health measure taken at baseline, NS is an indicator variable that the child is in a native stayer family, NNR is an indicator variable that the child is in a native nonrecipient family, IL is an indicator variable that the child is in an immigrant leaver family, IS is an indicator variable that the child is in an immigrant stayer family, and INR is an indicator variable that the child is in an immigrant nonrecipient family.

Separate models are estimated for each age group (infant cohort, age three cohort, and age six cohort) rather than as one model with age-interaction terms, given the lack of comparable Time-1 health measures for the infant group. A Chow test of the equivalency of coefficients across age groups supported the decision to run separate models. The PHDCN sampling procedure was such that more than one child per household could be selected to participate. Though the incidence of siblings in any one age cohort is low, we accounted for multiple child observations per family by calculating robust standard errors using the cluster option in STATA.

To assess whether postwelfare economic conditions help explain any associations between welfare use and child outcomes, we regressed family economic outcomes at Time 2 on our welfare-use indicators, controlling for the baseline measure of each outcome and the same set of covariates included in the child-health models. The economic variables examined include total household income, household income-to-poverty ratio (based on federal threshold for year and family size), parental earnings, mothers' and partners' employment hours, material hardship, and overcrowded living conditions (less than 100 square feet of living space per person). The dichotomous measure of material hardship indicates whether the family experienced any of the following events in the six months before the Time-2 survey, according to mothers' reports: lack of money to buy food, meal sizes cut for financial reasons, utilities shut off for nonpayment, inability to pay for housing, eviction, or household member unable to seek needed medical attention.

APPENDIX B: RESULTS TABLES

Tables 7B.1, 7B.2, and 7B.3 present the regression-adjusted associations between the indicators of welfare use by native and immigrant parents and Time-2 health and behavior for children in the infant, age three, and age six cohorts, respectively. Each of the tables presents results for each of the three outcomes (general health and the two measures of behavior problems). The notes to the tables list the control variables included in the models.

TABLE 7B.1 Linear Probability Models, Child Health and Behavior, Infant Cohort

	Model 1	Model 2	Model 3
	Health Fair or Poor	Internalizing Problems	Externalizing Problems
Native leaver (omitted)			
Native stayer	0.04*	0.06	0.04
	(0.02)	(0.08)	(0.09)
Native nonrecipient	−0.03	0.05	−0.05
	(0.02)	(0.09)	(0.09)
Immigrant leaver	0.16**	−0.06	−0.13
	(0.05)	(0.10)	(0.11)
Immigrant stayer	0.12	0.12	−0.12
	(0.08)	(0.12)	(0.13)
Immigrant nonrecipient	0.05	−0.09	−0.10
	(0.04)	(0.09)	(0.11)
Constant	−0.03	0.54**	0.46 *
	(0.09)	(0.17)	(0.20)
Observations	572	524	524
R^2	0.09	0.06	0.03

Source: Authors' compilation based on Project on Human Development in Chicago Neighborhoods. (ICPSR, various years).

Notes: Robust standard errors in parentheses.
Model 1 controls for the presence of two or more prenatal-perinatal risks; child gender and race (non-Hispanic black, non-Hispanic white, Hispanic [omitted]); primary caregiver is not the mother; mother's age, education, and marital status (married, cohabiting, single [omitted]); household size; presence of school-age sibling; Time-1 income; family owns home; mother working at Time 1; presence of employed partner at Time 1; quality of the home physical environment; parent has health condition; maternal depressive symptoms at Time 2; and, length of follow-up period. Post-hoc tests indicate that immigrant leavers are more likely to be in poor health than immigrant nonrecipients ($p < .05$), native stayers ($p < .05$), and native nonrecipients ($p < .001$). Native stayers are more likely to be in poor health than native nonrecipients ($p < .01$).

TABLE 7B.2 **Linear Probability Models, Child Health and Behavior, Age Three Cohort**

	Model 1 Health Fair or Poor	Model 2 Internalizing Problems	Model 3 Externalizing Problems
Native leaver (omitted)			
Native stayer	0.00	−0.22**	0.03
	(0.05)	(0.08)	(0.09)
Native nonrecipient	−0.04	−0.23**	−0.06
	(0.05)	(0.09)	(0.10)
Immigrant leaver	0.26**	0.09	−0.08
	(0.09)	(0.11)	(0.12)
Immigrant stayer	−0.01	0.05	−0.03
	(0.07)	(0.11)	(0.13)
Immigrant nonrecipient	−0.02	−0.10	−0.12
	(0.06)	(0.10)	(0.11)
Constant	0.12	0.24	0.25
	(0.17)	(0.26)	(0.26)
Observations	451	404	404
R^2	0.28	0.20	0.18

Source: Authors' compilation based on Project on Human Development in Chicago Neighborhoods. (ICPSR, various years).
Notes: Robust standard errors in parentheses.
Model 1 controls for fair or poor health at Time 1; child gender and race (non-Hispanic black, non-Hispanic white, Hispanic [omitted]); primary caregiver is not the mother; mother's age, education, and marital status (married, cohabiting, single [omitted]); household size; presence of school-age sibling; Time-1 income; family owns home; mother working at Time 1; presence of employed partner at Time 1; quality of the home environment (parental warmth, cognitive stimulation, physical environment); parent has health condition; maternal depressive symptoms at Time 2; and, length of follow-up period. Post-hoc tests indicate that immigrant leavers are more likely to be in fair or poor health at Time 2 than immigrant stayers ($p < .01$), immigrant nonrecipients ($p < .001$), native stayers ($p < .01$), and native nonrecipients ($p < .001$).

TABLE 7B.3 **Linear Probability Models, Child Health and Behavior Age Six Cohort**

	Model 1	Model 2	Model 3
	Health Fair or Poor	Internalizing Problems	Externalizing Problems
Native leaver (omitted)			
Native stayer	0.02	0.02	0.06
	(0.04)	(0.09)	(0.08)
Native nonrecipient	−0.04	0.11	0.20*
	(0.03)	(0.09)	(0.09)
Immigrant leaver	−0.01	−0.05	0.04
	(0.04)	(0.12)	(0.11)
Immigrant stayer	0.13†	−0.14	0.05
	(0.08)	(0.13)	(0.11)
Immigrant nonrecipient	0.02	0.08	0.10
	(0.05)	(0.12)	(0.10)
Constant	0.24	0.65*	0.00
	(0.15)	(0.29)	(0.27)
Observations	406	364	364
R^2	0.14	0.18	0.32

Source: Authors' compilation based on Project on Human Development in Chicago Neighborhoods. (ICPSR, various years).
Notes: Robust standard errors in parentheses.
model 1 controls for fair or poor health at Time 1; child gender and race (non-Hispanic black, non-Hispanic white, Hispanic [omitted]); primary caregiver is not the mother; mother's age, education, and marital status (married, cohabiting, single [omitted]); household size; presence of preschool-age sibling; Time 1 income; family owns home; mother working at Time 1; presence of employed partner at Time 1; quality of the home environment (parental warmth, cognitive stimulation, physical environment); parent has health condition; maternal depressive symptoms at Time 2; and, length of follow-up period. Post-hoc tests indicate that immigrant stayers are more likely to be in poor or fair health at Time 2 than native nonrecipients ($p < .05$) and immigrant leavers ($p < .10$).
†$p < .10$, *$p < .05$, **$p < .0$.

TABLE 7B.4 OLS Regression Linear Probability Models, Time 2 Economic Outcomes, Infant Cohort

	Household Income	Income-to-Poverty Ratio	Combined Parental Earnings	Mother's Weekly Employment Hours	Partner's Weekly Employment Hours	Material Hardship	Over-Crowded Living Conditions
Native leaver (omitted)							
Native stayer	-8,328.49**	-0.45**	-9,224.70**	-10.61**	-0.40	0.00	-0.09
	(2390.42)	(0.13)	(2281.82)	(2.85)	(2.93)	(0.09)	(0.07)
Native nonrecipient	2689.86	0.17	2206.49	-2.07	4.13	-0.24*	-0.02
	(2655.45)	(0.15)	(3576.81)	(3.15)	(3.50)	(0.09)	(0.07)
Immigrant leaver	1594.75	0.07	-1043.33	-8.60*	6.98†	-0.16	0.03
	(2845.12)	(0.17)	(3668.09)	(3.99)	(3.92)	(0.11)	(0.08)
Immigrant stayer	-2213.03	-0.17	-7,734.49*	-18.39**	1.84	0.10	-0.08
	(3231.76)	(0.17)	(3695.71)	(4.00)	(4.59)	(0.13)	(0.11)
Immigrant nonrecipient	120.99	0.01	-2524.16	-13.69**	7.60*	-0.23*	0.04
	(2693.42)	(0.15)	(3543.34)	(3.60)	(3.74)	(0.10)	(0.07)
Constant	-1310.91	-0.13	-4090.60	3.18	11.41	0.37	0.53**
	(5525.90)	(0.28)	(6719.20)	(7.05)	(6.94)	(0.20)	(0.15)
Observations	572	571	572	563	547	538	513
R^2	0.28	0.31	0.31	0.27	0.45	0.09	0.13

Source: Authors' compilation based on Project on Human Development in Chicago Neighborhoods. (ICPSR, various years).

Notes: Robust standard errors in parentheses. Income is adjusted to 1998 dollars. Models control for the baseline measure of the respective outcome variable (except for material hardship and crowdedness, which lack a Time-1 measure); presence of two or more pre-perinatal risks; child gender and race (non-Hispanic black, non-Hispanic white, Hispanic [omitted]); primary caregiver is not the mother; mother's age, education, and marital status (married, cohabiting, single [omitted]); household size; presence of school-age sibling; Time-1 income (except the model predicting income-to-poverty ratio); family owns home; mother working at Time 1; presence of employed partner at Time 1; quality of the home environment (parental warmth, cognitive stimulation, physical environment); parent has health condition; and length of follow-up period.

†$p < .10$, *$p < .05$, **$p < .01$.

Table 7B.5 OLS Regression Linear Probability Models, Time 2 Economic Outcomes, Age Three Cohort

	Household Income	Income-to-Poverty Ratio	Combined Parental Earnings	Mother's Weekly Employment Hours	Partner's Weekly Employment Hours	Material Hardship	Over-Crowded Living Conditions
Native leaver (omitted)							
Native stayer	−6,273.39**	−0.32**	−4153.53	−3.63	−0.41	−0.08	−0.08
	(2276.14)	(0.12)	(2779.93)	(3.40)	(3.87)	(0.09)	(0.07)
Native nonrecipient	4999.58	0.34*	4243.56	1.24	−1.63	−0.33**	0.00
	(2685.40)	(0.14)	(3571.87)	(3.88)	(4.41)	(0.10)	(0.08)
Immigrant leaver	3860.59	0.29†	1847.51	−9.41*	9.93†	−0.29*	−0.02
	(3002.11)	(0.16)	(3303.60)	(4.77)	(5.35)	(0.13)	(0.09)
Immigrant stayer	4755.15	0.34†	−2690.35	−12.33**	3.88	−0.23†	−0.13
	(3009.61)	(0.18)	(3089.61)	(4.61)	(5.75)	(0.13)	(0.10)
Immigrant nonrecipient	3886.07	0.28†	3265.61	−8.02†	6.96	−0.38**	−0.01
	(2765.60)	(0.15)	(3077.52)	(4.40)	(5.22)	(0.11)	(0.08)
Constant	3903.86	0.46	10150.69	16.80	18.69	0.24	0.69
	(7192.64)	(0.36)	(7212.27)	(9.81)	(11.15)	(0.29)	(0.22)
Observations	452	450	452	447	432	432	419
R^2	0.42	0.42	0.46	0.25	0.41	0.1	0.15

Source: Authors' compilation based on Project on Human Development in Chicago Neighborhoods. (ICPSR, various years).
Note: Robust standard errors in parentheses. Income is adjusted to 1998 dollars. Models control for baseline measure of the respective outcome variable (except for material hardship and crowdedness, which lack a Time-1 measure); child fair or poor health at Time 1; child gender and race (non-Hispanic black, non-Hispanic white, Hispanic [omitted]); primary caregiver is not the mother; mother's age, education, and marital status (married, cohabiting, single [omitted]); household size; has school-age sibling; Time-1 income (except the model predicting income-to-poverty ratio); family owns home; mother working at Time 1; presence of employed partner at Time 1; quality of the home environment (parental warmth, cognitive stimulation, physical environment); parent has health condition; and length of follow-up period.
†$p < .10$, *$p < .05$, **$p < .01$.

Table 7B.6 OLS Regression Linear Probability Models, Time 2 Economic Outcomes, Age Six Cohort

	Household Income	Income-to-Poverty Ratio	Combined Parental Earnings	Mother's Weekly Employment Hours	Partner's Weekly Employment Hours	Material Hardship	Over-Crowded Living Conditions
Native leaver (omitted)							
Native stayer	-4,745.79	-0.22	-1,463.57	-4.05	-1.92	0.05	-0.14
	(2,526.09)	(0.12)	(2,396.04)	(4.09)	(3.66)	(0.10)	(0.08)
Native nonrecipient	2,226.37	0.16	5,747.72	3.19	2.26	-0.04	0.04
	(2,816.01)	(0.15)	(3,379.33)	(4.32)	(3.97)	(0.11)	(0.08)
Immigrant leaver	897.83	0.01	-3,681.87	-4.26	3.09	-0.04	-0.01
	(3,224.98)	(0.16)	(3,605.59)	(5.07)	(5.03)	(0.13)	(0.10)
Immigrant stayer	-1,908.77	-0.09	-7,054.28	-0.85	-3.70	0.12	-0.06
	(3,682.58)	(0.18)	(3,698.30)	(5.81)	(6.39)	(0.16)	(0.13)
Immigrant nonrecipient	1,482.99	0.02	-4,250.02	-1.95	1.86	-0.05	0.05
	(2,952.98)	(0.15)	(3,491.35)	(4.34)	(4.51)	(0.12)	(0.09)
Constant	-5,455.06	-0.28	7,651.46	22.53*	17.33	0.21	0.69**
	(7,478.51)	(0.39)	(8,199.75)	(11.27)	(11.30)	(0.35)	(0.24)
Observations	407	406	407	400	383	387	374
R^2	0.35	0.4	0.37	0.31	0.45	0.11	0.18

Source: Authors' compilation based on Project on Human Development in Chicago Neighborhoods. (ICPSR, various years).
Note: Robust standard errors in parentheses. Income is adjusted to 1998 dollars. Models control for the baseline measure of the respective outcome variable (except for material hardship and crowdedness, which lack a Time-1 measure); child fair or poor health at Time 1; child gender and race (non-Hispanic black, non-Hispanic white, Hispanic [omitted]); primary caregiver is not the mother; mother's age, education, and marital status (married, cohabiting, single [omitted]); household size; has preschool-age sibling; Time-1 income (except the model predicting income-to-poverty ratio); family owns home; mother working at Time 1; presence of employed partner at Time 1; quality of the home environment (parental warmth, cognitive stimulation, physical environment); parent has health condition; and length of follow-up period.

NOTES

1. Source: Unpublished analysis by the Urban Institute of March 2005 U.S. Current Population Survey, Annual Social and Economic Supplement.
2. Examining changes in health for older children (ages nine to fifteen) was less straightforward (and is not presented here) because of measurement differences across the two interviews (youths provided self-reports of health at Time 1 and parental reports were collected at Time 2).
3. A small number (less than 5 percent of the sample) of welfare beginners who did not receive welfare at Time 1 but did by Time 2 are combined with the stayers, as both represent families not deterred from using assistance following welfare reform. Analyses with beginners as a separate group did not alter any of the results.
4. Spanish-speaking parents in the PHDCN completed the Spanish-language version of the CBCL, which has demonstrated good reliability and validity in other samples (Rubio-Stipec et al. 1990).
5. Models for the infant group differed slightly from those for older children because many were born shortly after the Time 1 interview and thus lacked comparable Time 1 measures. Infant models controlled instead for the presence of multiple pre- and perinatal health risks (such as late prenatal care, substance use by mother during pregnancy, premature birth, or hospitalization as a newborn).
6. Although the results presented here for school-age children are limited to the age six cohort, similar analyses for older age cohorts (nine to fifteen) in the PHDCN sample similarly indicate no relationship between welfare use and child health in native and immigrant families.

REFERENCES

Achenbach, T. M. 1991. *Manual for the Child Behavior Checklist/4–18 and 1991 Profile*. Burlington: University of Vermont, Department of Psychiatry.

Blank, Rebecca M. 2002. "Evaluating Welfare Reform in the United States." *Journal of Economic Literature* 40(4): 1105–166.

Borjas, George J. 1998. "Immigration and Welfare: A Review of the Evidence." In *The Debate in the United States over Immigration*, edited by Peter J. Duignan and Lewis H. Gann. Stanford, Calif.: Hoover Institution Press.

Camarota, Steven A. 2001. *Immigrants in the United States—2000: A Snapshot of America's Foreign-Born Population.* Washington, D.C.: Center for Immigration Studies.

Capps, Randolph. 2001. *Hardship Among Children of Immigrants: Findings from the 1999 National Survey of America's Families.* Series B, no. B-29. Washington, D.C.: The Urban Institute.

Capps, Randolph, Michael E. Fix, Jason Ost, Jane Reardon-Anderson, and Jeffrey Passel. 2004. *The Health and Well-Being of Young Children of Immigrants.* Washington, D.C.: The Urban Institute.

Capps, Randolph, Michael E. Fix, Jeffrey Passel, Jason Ost, and Daniel Perez-Lopez. 2003. *A Profile of the Low-Wage Immigrant Workforce.* Washington, D.C.: The Urban Institute.

Capps, Randolph, and Katrina Fortuny. 2006. *Immigration and Child and Family Policy.* Washington, D.C.: The Urban Institute.

Case, Anne, Angela Fertig, and Christina Paxson. 2005. "The Lasting Impact of Childhood Health and Circumstance." *Journal of Health Economics* 24(2): 365–389.

Case, Anne, Darren Lubotsky, and Christina Paxson. 2002. "Economic Status and Health in Childhood: The Origins of the Gradient." *The American Economic Review* 92(5): 1308–334.

Crosnoe, Robert. 2006. "Health and the Education of Children from Race/Ethnic Minority and Immigrant Families." *Journal of Health and Social Behavior* 47(1): 77–93.

Currie, Janet M. 2005. "Health Disparities and Gaps in School Readiness." *The Future of Children* 15(1): 117–38.

Danziger, Sheldon, Colleen M. Heflin, Mary Corcoran, Elizabeth Oltmans, and H. C. Wang. 2002. "Does It Pay to Move from Welfare to Work?" *Journal of Policy Analysis and Management* 21(4): 671–92.

Duncan, Greg J., and Jeanne Brooks-Gunn. 1997. *Consequences of Growing Up Poor.* New York: Russell Sage Foundation.

Duncan, Greg J., Katherine Magnuson, and Jens Ludwig. 2004. "The Endogeneity Problem in Developmental Studies." *Research in Human Development* 1: 59–80.

Duncan, Greg J., W. J. Yeung, Jeanne Brooks-Gunn, and J. Smith. 1998. "How Much Does Childhood Poverty Reduce the Life Chances of Children?" *American Sociological Review* 63(3): 406–24.

Fix, Michael E., and Ron Haskins. 2002. "Welfare Benefits for Noncitizens: Welfare Reform and Beyond." CCF policy brief no. 15. Washington, D.C.: The Brookings Institution. Available at: http://www.brookings.edu/papers/2002/02immigration_fix.aspx (accessed January 1, 2003).

Fix, Michael E., and Jeffrey S. Passel. 1999. *Trends in Noncitizens' and*

Citizens' Use of Public Benefits Following Welfare Reform: 1994–97. Washington, D.C.: The Urban Institute.

Flores, Glenn, Elena Fuentes-Afflick, Oxiris Barbot, Olivia D. Carter, Luz Claudio, Marielena Lara, Jennie A. McLaurin, Lee Pachter, Francisco J. Ramos-Gomez, Fernando Mendoza, R. Burciaga Valdez, Antonia M. Villaruel, Ruth E. Zambrana, Robert Greenberg, and Michael Weitzman. 2002. "The Health of Latino Children: Urgent Priorities, Unanswered Questions, and a Research Agenda." *Journal of the American Medical Association* 288(1): 82–90.

Fuligni, Andrew J. 1998. "The Adjustment of Children from Immigrant Families." *Current Directions in Psychological Science* 7(34): 99-103.

Haider, Steven J., Robert F. Schoeni, Yuhua Bao, and Caroline Danielson. 2004. "Immigrants, Welfare Reform, and the Economy." *Journal of Policy Analysis and Management* 23(4): 745–64.

Hernandez, Donald J. 2004. "Demographic Change and the Life Circumstances of Immigrant Families." *The Future of Children* 14(2): 17–47.

Hofferth, Sandra L. 1999. "Receipt of Public Assistance by Mexican American and Cuban American Children in Native and Immigrant Families." In *Children of Immigrants: Health, Adjustment and Public Assistance*, edited by Donald J. Hernandez. Washington, D.C.: National Academies Press.

Holcomb, Pamela A., Karen C. Tumlin, Robin Koralek, Randolph Capps, and Anita Zuberi. 2003. *The Application Process for TANF, Food Stamps, Medicaid and SCHIP: Issues for Agencies and Applicants, Including Immigrants and Limited English Speakers.* Washington: The Urban Institute / U.S. Department of Health and Human Services.

Idler, Ellen L., and Yael Benyamini. 1997. "Self-Rated Health and Mortality: A Review of Twenty-Seven Community Studies." *Journal of Health and Social Behavior* 38(1): 21–37.

Inter-University Consortium for Political and Social Research. (ICPSR). Various years. Project on Human Development in Chicago Neighborhoods [dataset, by special permission]. Ann Arbor: University of Michigan. Information about the project available at: http://www.icpsr.umich.edu/PHDCN.

Kaestner, Robert, and Neeraj Kaushal. 2005. "Immigrant and Native Responses to Welfare Reform." *Journal of Population Economics* 18(1): 69–92.

Kaushal, Neeraj, and Robert Kaestner. 2005. "Welfare Reform and Health Insurance of Immigrants." *Health Services Research* 40(3): 697–722.

Ku, Leighton, and Shannon Blaney. 2000. *Health Coverage for Legal Immigrant Children: New Census Data Highlight Importance of Restoring Medicaid and SCHIP Coverage.* Washington, D.C.: Center on Budget and Policy Priorities.

Ku, Leighton, and Sheetal Matani. 2001. "Left Out: Immigrants' Access to Health Care and Insurance." *Health Affairs* 20(1):247–56.

Leventhal, Tama, Mary Beth Selner-O'Hagan, Jeanne Brooks-Gunn, Jeffrey B. Bingenheimer, and Felton Earls. 2004. "The Homelife Interview from the Project on Human Development in Chicago Neighborhoods: Assessment of Parenting and Home Environment for 3- to 15-Year-Olds." *Parenting: Science and Practice* 4(2–3): 211–42.

Lofstrom, Magnus, and Frank D. Bean. 2002. "Assessing Immigrant Policy Options: Labor Market Conditions and Post-Reform Declines in Welfare Receipt among Immigrants." *Demography* 39(4): 617–37.

Lurie, Irene. 2008. "Welfare Reform and the Decline in the Health-Insurance Coverage of Children of Non-Permanent Residents." *Journal of Health Economics* 27(3): 786–93.

Maloy, Kathleen, Julie Darnell, Lea Nolan, Kyle Anne Kenney, and Soeurette Cyprien. 2000. *Effect of the 1996 Welfare and Immigration Reform Laws on Immigrants' Ability and Willingness to Access Medicaid and Health Care Services: Findings from Four Metropolitan Sites.* Washington, D.C.: George Washington University, Center for Health Services Research and Policy.

Marmot, Michael G., and Michael E. Wadsworth, eds. 1997. "Fetal and Early Childhood Environment: Long-Term Health Implications." *British Medical Bulletin* 53(1): 1–222.

Mendoza, Fernando S., and L. Beth Dixon. 1999. "The Health and Nutritional Status of Immigrant Hispanic Children: Analyses of the Hispanic Health and Nutrition Examination Survey." In *Children of Immigrants: Health, Adjustment, and Public Assistance*, edited by Donald J. Hernandez. Washington, D.C.: National Academies Press.

Nord, Christine Winquist, and James A. Griffin. 1999. "Educational Profile of 3- to 8-Year Old Children of Immigrants." In *Children of Immigrants: Health, Adjustment, and Public Assistance*, edited by Donald J. Hernandez. Washington, D.C.: National Academies Press.

Orellana, Marjorie Faulstich. 2003. "Responsibilities of Children in Latino Immigrant Homes." *New Directions for Youth Development: Understanding the Social Worlds of Immigrant Youth* 100(winter): 25–39.

Orellana, Margorie Faulstich, Jennifer Reynolds, Lisa Dorner, and Lucila Pulido. 2003. "Accessing Assets, Immigrant Youth as Family Interpreters." *Social Problems* 50(5): 505–24.

Page, Benjamin I., and James R. Simmons. 2000. *What Government Can Do: Dealing with Poverty and Inequality.* Chicago: University of Chicago Press.

Reardon-Anderson, Jane, Randolph Capps, and Michael E. Fix. 2002. *The Health and Well-Being of Children in Immigrant Families.* Series B, no. B-52. Washington, D.C.: The Urban Institute.

Rubio-Stipec, Maritza, Hector Bird, Glorisa Canino, and Madelyn Gould. 1990. "The Internal Consistency and Concurrent Validity of a Spanish Translation of the Child Behavior Checklist." *Journal of Abnormal Child Psychology* 18(4): 393–406.

Shetterly, Susan M., Judith Baxter, Lynn D. Mason, and Richard F. Hamman. 1996. "Self-Rated Health among Hispanic vs. Non-Hispanic White Adults: The San Luis Valley Health and Aging Study." *American Journal of Public Health* 86(12): 1798–801.

Shields, Margie K., and Richard E. Behrman. 2004. "Children of Immigrant Families: Analysis and Recommendations." *The Future of Children* 14(2): 4–16.

Takanishi, Ruby. 2004. *Leveling the Playing Field: Supporting Immigrant Children from Birth to Eight*. New York: Foundation for Child Development.

U.S. Bureau of the Census. 2007. *American Community Survey 2005–2007* [dataset]. Data available at http://factfinder.census.gov/ (accessed January 1, 2008).

Valenzuela, Angela. 1999. *Subtractive Schooling: U.S. Mexican Youth and the Politics of Caring*. Albany: State University of New York Press.

Van Hook, Jennifer. 2003. "Welfare Reform Chilling Effects on Noncitizens: Changes in Noncitizen Recipiency or Shifts in Citizenship Status?" *Social Science Quarterly* 84(3): 613–31.

Van Hook, Jennifer, and Kelly S. Balistreri. 2006. "Ineligible Parents, Eligible Children: Food Stamps Receipt, Allotments, and Food Insecurity among Children of Immigrants." *Social Science Research* 35(1): 228–51.

Ventura, Stephanie J., Joyce A. Martin, Sally C. Curtin, Thomas J. Mathews, and Melissa M. Park. 2000. "Births: Final Data for 1998." *National Vital Statistics Report* 48(3). Hyattsville, Md: National Center for Health Statistics.

Zimmerman, Wendy, and Karen Tumlin. 1999. "Patchwork Policies: State Assistance for Immigrants under Welfare Reform." *Assessing the New Federalism* occasional paper 24. Washington, D.C.: The Urban Institute.

Index

Boldface numbers refer to figures and tables.

Agriculture, Research Extension and Education Reform Act of 1998, 14
Agriculture, U.S. Department of, Food and Nutrition Service (FNS), 177, 182
Aid to Families with Dependent Children (AFDC): models of recipiency and exit from, **115**; perspectives on welfare receipt, empirical data regarding, 98–106, 111–16; receipt and exit, timing of, **105**; recipiency, early 1990s, **101**; TANF as replacement for, 7
Aliessa v. Novello, 75
Annie E. Casey Foundation, 2
armed forces personnel, veterans, and their spouses, 10, 40
asylees: described, 10, 64*n*3, 124; eligibility under welfare reform, 40

Balanced Budget Act of 1997, 14, 42
Balistreri, Kelly, 109
Bean, Frank, 24–25, 30
Besharov, Doug, 47
Blackmun, Harry, 73
Borjas, George: chilling effect of Proposition 187 in California, 31*n*8; food insecurity in states with state-funded assistance for noncitizens *vs.* those without assistance, 183; magnet hypothesis, 16–17, 46, 97, 100, 102–3; negative-acculturation hypothesis, 103–4; relative education levels of immigrants, 62
Brown, Susan K., 30
Burtless, Gary, 93–94
Bush, George W., 14, 42
Butler, Amy, 107

California: benefits to postenactment immigrants, budget crisis threatening, 13; Proposition 187, 31*n*8, 126, 147*n*4

Capps, Randy, 20, 25–27, 62, 161
Chicanos Por La Causa, Inc. v. Napolitano, 77
children: arguments for extending public benefits to noncitizen, 51–52; food insecurity for, 183–84; health and behavior of, welfare transitions and (*see* childrens' health and behavior); health insurance coverage of (*see* health insurance coverage of low-income children); of immigrants, disadvantageous conditions experienced by, 193–94; poverty rates among foreign born and native born, 60–61, **61**; problems faced by immigrant, 62–63; welfare reform's impact on, 27–28, 194–96 (*see also* childrens' health and behavior)
childrens' health and behavior: age and the impact of welfare transitions following PRWORA on, 197–98; analysis groups based on welfare use, **201**; empirical study of the impact of welfare transitions following PRWORA on, 198–201; impact of welfare transitions following PRWORA on, 195–96, 205–8, 209–10; limitations of the study, 208–9; methodology of the study, 210–17; postwelfare economic conditions and, 204–5; regression-adjusted associations reported in results tables, **218–23**; significance of, 196–97; welfare use and, linking of, 201–4
Children's Health Insurance Program Reauthorization Act of 2009, 14–15, 154, 185
chilling effects: of California's Proposition 187, 31*n*8; of PRWORA, 18–19, 126, 157–58, 194–95
Chiswick, Barry, 106

citizens: health insurance coverage for low-income children of (*see* health insurance coverage of low-income children); native-born, 125; naturalized (*see* naturalized citizens)

Citizenship and Immigration Services, U.S. *See* Immigration and Naturalization Service

Clinton, Bill, 1, 42, 71

Congressional Budget Office (CBO), 46–48

Congressional Research Service, 43, 46–47

Cortes, Kalina, 108

courts and constitutional issues: food stamps and SSI, noncitizen eligibility restrictions upheld, 82*n*2; limited judicial action, implication of, 81; PRWORA: the equal protection clause and discrimination against lawful permanent residents, 22–23, 69–76; state and local activity addressing immigration, exclusion of undocumented immigrants and, 70–71, 76–80; state restrictions on benefits to noncitizens, decision regarding, 44

Crosby, Danielle, 28

Cuban-Haitian entrants, 10

cultural theories of welfare, 96

De Canas v. Bica, 79–80

Deficit Reduction Act of 2005, 15–16, 31*n*7, 155, 185

Doe v. Commissioner of Transitional Assistance, 75

Earned Income Tax Credit, 41

economic choice theory, 96

education, low levels among immigrants, 62

Ehrenreich, Barbara, 107

Ehrlich v. Perez, 75

eligibility restrictions: arguments opposing, 50–52; arguments supporting, 43–50, 63; comprehensive effort to limit access to federal means-tested entitlements through, welfare reform as, 6; immigrant eligibility categories, 9–11; for Medicaid and the Food Stamp Program, 154–57; naturalized citizens and noncitizens, distinction between, 8; overview of, 8–12, 39–41, 99, 194; post-PRWORA legislation affecting legal immigrants, 14–15, 154, **156**; qualified and unqualified aliens, distinction between, 8–9, 39–40; qualified preenactment and qualified postenactment immigrants, distinction between, 11–12, 40; state choices, 12–13

emergency benefits, 40

families: low-income defined, 147*n*1; mixed-status, 19

family incomes of immigrants, 1994-2004, 127; families with low-income children, **128**; native and legal permanent resident families, 127–28; naturalized citizen families, 129–30; refugee families, 128–29

Farm Security and Rural Investment Act of 2002, 14, 154, 178, 182–83

federal benefit rate (FBR), 7

federalism: PRWORA's invitation to states to discriminate, 69–72; state and local actions addressing immigrants, 76–80; state restrictions on welfare benefits to noncitizens, constitutional issue regarding, 44; welfare reform and, 22–23

Finegold, Kenneth, 5

Fix, Michael, 19–20, 25–27, 62, 161

Flores, Glenn, 160

FNS. *See* Agriculture, U.S. Department of, Food and Nutrition Service

Food Stamp Program (FSP): analysis of trends in individual-level participation, 176–78; consequences of losing benefits, 183–84; eligibility and participation, changes in, **179–80**; eligibility criteria for, 40, 154–57; eligibility criteria *vs.* other factors in post-PRWORA decline in participation, 180–83; overview of, 7–8; participation in after welfare reform, 27, 52–53, 131–36, 178–80; post-PRWORA legislation restoring some benefits, 14, 42, 154, 178, 182–83; social and community factors that might affect participation in, 157–59

Foundation for Child Development, 2

FSP. *See* Food Stamp Program

Galster, George, 103

Graham v. Richardson, 44, 73–75, 79–80

Hao, Lingxin, 103

Haskins, Ron, 22, 24, 28, 127

Head Start, 41

health insurance coverage: analysis of trends in, 160–62; changes in coverage of low-income adults, **166**; changes in coverage of low-income elderly, **170**; consequences of losing, 175–76; of the elderly, 168–71; language access, assistance with, 174–75; low-income parents uninsured or covered by Medicaid, **165**; of nonelderly adults, 165–68; sponsors, role of, 171–74

health insurance coverage of low-income

children, 136; changes in, **164**; employer and other private coverage, 138–40; Medicaid and SCHIP, 136–38; outreach effort to improve rate of, 160; trends in, 162–65; the uninsured, 140–41
Henderson, Everett, 20, 25–27, 161
Hilton, Lynette, 100, 103–4
Homeland Security, U.S. Department of, 31n6

ICE. *See* Immigration and Customs Enforcement, U.S. Bureau of
Illegal Immigration Reform and Immigrant Responsibility Act of 1996 (IIRIRA), 2, 13–14, 43, 153, 171
Immigration Reform and Control Act of 1986, 130
immigrants: economic integration, welfare use and, 93–95, 106–9; eligibility restrictions under welfare reform (*see* eligibility restrictions); public assistance for, possibilities for improving, 185–86; unauthorized, impact of welfare reform on, 15–16; welfare use after welfare reform (*see* immigrants' use of welfare after welfare reform); welfare use before welfare reform (*see* immigrant welfare receipt)
immigrants' use of welfare after welfare reform: economic context for, 127–30; eligibility restrictions affecting (*see* eligibility restrictions); health insurance coverage including Medicaid and SCHIP (*see* health insurance coverage; health insurance coverage of low-income children); interplay of social factors determining, 154–60, 184–85; lawful/legal permanent residents, 130–33; lawful/legal permanent residents and native-born citizen families with children, use of public assistance programs by, **131**; literature on, 16–20, 126–27; low-income naturalized and native-born citizen families with children, use of public assistance programs by, **135**; low-income refugee and native-born citizen families with children, use of public assistance programs by, **134**; methodology for analyzing, 143–47; naturalized citizens, 134–36; overview of research and conclusions regarding, 25–27; participation in programs following PRWORA, 52–57; participation of low-income citizen and noncitizen families with children following PRWORA, **53**; participation of low-income citizen and refugee families with children following PRWORA, **57**; possibilities for improving, 185–86; program access and outreach efforts affecting, 159–60; refugees, 133–34; social and community factors affecting, 157–59; TANF, 52–53; trends in, 123–26, 141–43
immigrant welfare receipt: after welfare reform (*see* immigrants' use of welfare after welfare reform); empirical research focused on prereform period, 98–106, 111–16; magnet hypothesis, 16–17, 23–25, 97; magnet hypothesis, evidence for, 99–103; negative-acculturation hypothesis, 18, 24, 97–98; negative-acculturation hypothesis, evidence for, 103–6; opposing views of, 93–95, 109–11; theories relevant to, 95–98; welfare as settlement assistance, perspective and evidence for, 106–9
immigration: generous rules for and poorly defined integration policies, impacts of mismatch between, 4; politics of (*see* politics of immigration)
Immigration and Customs Enforcement, U.S. Bureau of (ICE), 77–78
Immigration and Naturalization Service (INS), 44–45

Justice, U.S. Department of, 31n6

Kaestner, Robert, 19
Kaiser Commission on Medicaid and the Uninsured, 19
Kalil, Ariel, 28
Kaplan v. Chertoff Civil Action No. 06-5305, 31n6
Kaushal, Neeraj, 17, 19
Kawano, Yukio, 103
Ku, Leighton, 20, 26–27, 148n14

LA-FANS. *See* Los Angeles Family Neighborhood Study
lawful/legal permanent residents (LPRs): described, 9, 124; discrimination against in PRWORA, constitutionality of, 69–76; family incomes of, 127–28; health insurance coverage for low-income children of (*see* health insurance coverage of low-income children); welfare receipt after PRWORA, 130–33. *See also* immigrants
Leach, Mark, 108
Los Angeles Family Neighborhood Study (LA-FANS), 108, 116n1
LPRs. *See* lawful/legal permanent residents

magnet hypothesis, 16–17, 23–25, 97, 99–103
Martin, Sam, 46
material deprivation perspective, 95–96
Mathematica Policy Research, Inc., 177
Mathews v. Diaz, 73–74
Matsui, Robert, 65n14
Medicaid: income eligibility limit for, 187n5; overview of, 8; participation in following welfare reform, 53–54, 132–38; post-PRWORA legislation restoring some benefits, 14, 42; PRWORA's invitation to states to discriminate against noncitizens, 69–72; social and community factors that might affect participation in, 157–59; welfare reform eligibility restrictions regarding, 40. *See also* health insurance coverage
Medicare, 65n8, 168–71
methodology: choices regarding, significance of, 20–21; for empirical study of immigrant welfare receipt, 111–16; for empirical study of impact of welfare transitions on childrens' health and behavior, 210–17; for measuring changes in benefits use, 143–47
Metzger, Kurt, 103
Migration Policy Institute, 2
military personnel. *See* armed forces personnel, veterans, and their spouses
Motomura, Hiroshi, 30, 82n4

National Assessment of Educational Progress, 62
National Health Law Program, 19
National Immigration Law Center, 19
native-born citizens, 125
naturalized citizens: description, 9, 125; family incomes of, 129–30; welfare receipt after PRWORA, 134–36
negative-acculturation theory, 18, 24, 97–98, 103–6
No Child Left Behind Act of 2001 41

Obama, Barack, 14

Passel, Jeffrey, 19
Personal Responsibility and Work Opportunity Reconciliation Act of 1996 (PRWORA): constitutional issues raised by (*see* courts and constitutional issues); goals of, 1–2, 5–6, 153; immigrant eligibility restrictions (*see* eligibility restrictions); legislative history of, 22, 43–49; political wisdom of, 41–42; principal findings regarding impact on immigrants, 21–28; results of, 13–14, 28–30 (*see also* childrens' health and behavior; immigrants' use of welfare after welfare reform); signing of, 1; subsequent welfare legislation, 14–15, 42, 154, **156**; termination of benefits for the elderly and disabled, unfairness of, 41; two themes of, 40–41; unauthorized immigrants and, 15–16. *See also* welfare reform
Pew Hispanic Center, 144, 146
PHDCN. *See* Project on Human Development in Chicago Neighborhoods
Plyer v. Doe, 80
politics of immigration: arguments opposing eligibility restrictions, 50–52; arguments supporting eligibility restrictions, 43–50; exclusion *vs.* integration contest, 70–71, 76–81; federal government *vs.* the states, shifting ground for the struggle over, 23
postenactment immigrants, 10
poverty: impact of welfare reform on, 59–61; level, 30–31n3, 31n5; rates among foreign born and native born, **59**; rates among foreign born and native born children, **61**
preenactment immigrants, 9
Project on Human Development in Chicago Neighborhoods (PHDCN), 28, 198–200, 210–11
PRWORA. *See* Personal Responsibility and Work Opportunity Reconciliation Act of 1996
public benefits. *See* welfare

qualified aliens, 9

Reardon-Anderson, Jane, 62
Refugee Resettlement, Office of, 129
Refugee Resettlement Program, 17
refugees: countries sending, 116–17n2; described, 10, 64n3, 124; eligibility under welfare reform, 40; family incomes of, 128–29; health insurance coverage for low-income children of (*see* health insurance coverage of low-income children); welfare receipt after PRWORA, 56, 133–34; welfare used as settlement assistance by, 108
Russell Sage Foundation, 2

SCHIPs. *See* State Children's Health Insurance Programs
Shays, Christopher, 47–48

Shipler, David, 107
Smith, Lamar, 171
SNAP. *See* Supplemental Nutrition Assistance Program
Social Security, 64–65*n*8
Soskin v. Reinertson, 75–76
sponsors: health insurance coverage, role in, 171–74; INS procedure knocked down by the courts, 44–45; requirement for in IIRIRA, 43, **156,** 171
SSI. *See* Supplemental Security Income
State Children's Health Insurance Programs (SCHIPs): overview of, 8, 65*n*11; receipt of after PRWORA, 132–38. *See also* health insurance coverage; Medicaid
State v. Binder, 45
Supplemental Nutrition Assistance Program (SNAP), 8, 154. *See also* Food Stamp Program
Supplemental Security Income (SSI): alien eligibility restrictions included in, 45; fraud revealed in congressional hearings on, 46; noncitizens receiving, **49, 55**; noncitizens receiving, rapid increase in, 48–49; overview of, 7; post-PRWORA legislation restoring some benefits, 14, 42, 56; receipt of after PRWORA, 54–56, 131–36; welfare reform eligibility restrictions regarding, 40

Temporary Assistance for Needy Families (TANF): overview of, 7; participation in following welfare reform, 52–53, 130–31, 133–36; PRWORA's invitation to states to discriminate in providing benefits under, 69–72; welfare reform eligibility requirements regarding, 40
temporary legal migrants, 124
Tiaja, Raj, 108
Toll v. Moreno, 73
Trejo, Stephen, 17, 97

unauthorized immigrants, 10, 15–16, 125
unqualified aliens, 10–11
Urban Institute, 126, 144, 146

Van Hook, Jennifer, 24–25, 30
Villas at Parkside Partners v. City of Farmers Branch, 80

Waite, Ruth, 103
Ways and Means Committee, hearings on SSI fraud, 46
Weil, Alan, 5
welfare: childrens' health and behavior and, 201–4 (*see also* childrens' health and behavior); dependency, 18, 59 (*see also* negative-acculturation theory); economic integration of immigrants and receipt of, 93–95, 110–11 (*see also* immigrant welfare receipt); immigrants' use of after welfare reform (*see* immigrants' use of welfare after welfare reform); immigrants' use of before welfare reform (*see* immigrant welfare receipt); possibilities for helping noncitizens through, 185–86; as settlement assistance for immigrants, 106–9; theories explaining receipt of, 95–96; types of factors affecting immigrants' use of, **155**
welfare reform: arguments favoring noncitizen prohibitions, 45–50, 63; arguments opposing noncitizen prohibitions, 50–52; chilling effects of, 18–19, 126, 157–58, 194–95; immigrant assimilation and, 111 (*see also* immigrant welfare receipt); immigrants' use of public assistance after (*see* immigrants' use of welfare after welfare reform); impact on the conditions of noncitizens, 59–61; legislation following PRWORA, 14–15, 42, 154, **156**; work incentives and, 58–59. *See also* Personal Responsibility and Work Opportunity Reconciliation Act of 1996
Wishnie, Michael J., 15, 22–23, 82*n*5
Workforce Investment Act, 41
work history requirement, 9–10

Yzaguirre, Raul, 65*n*14

Zavodny, Madeline, 16–17